350

PEOPLE
POTHOLES
and
CITY
POLITICS

PEOPLE
POTHOLES
and
CITY
POLITICS

Karen Herland

A Québec Public Research Interest Group Project

Montréal/New York

BLACK ROSE BOOKS No. V187
Hardcover ISBN: 1-895431-53-0
Paperback ISBN: 1-895431-52-2
Library of Congress Catalog No. 92-74578

Canadian Cataloguing in Publication Data

Herland, Karen
People, potholes and city politics

Includes index.
ISBN: 1-895431-53-0 (bound) —
ISBN: 1-895431-52-2 (pbk.)

1. Montréal (Québec) — Politics and government. 2. Montreal Citizens'
Movement. I. Title.

JS1761.2.H47   1992   352.0714'28   C92-090362-2

Cover Design: Zab Design

Mailing Address

BLACK ROSE BOOKS
C.P. 1258
Succ. Place du Parc
Montréal, Québec
H2W 2R3 Canada

BLACK ROSE BOOKS
340 Nagel Drive
Cheektowaga, New York
14225 USA

A publication of the Institute of Policy Alternatives of Montréal (IPAM)

Table of Contents

SECTION III - BEYOND THE CITY

SECTION IV — MONTRÉAL IN PIECES

SECTION V — NOW WHAT?

APPENDICES

INTRODUCTION

Politics, in one form or another, surround us all the time. The media brings the latest legislation and endless accounts of the constitution or whatever else they decide is "news" into our homes every day. We watch our predominantly white male "leaders" pontificate, bargain, plead and denounce with and against each other constantly. For the most part, we expect the media to explain what it all means, and whatever their biases, we passively accept them. We may even get passionate about a particular issue, or infuriated over a specific decision. But, by the end of it all legislation is proposed and tabled, polices and ideas are raised, watered-down, and often discarded...and very little of it changes our daily routines.

Each day we have to figure out the best way to get to work (or how to get work if we're looking for it), where our children can play, where to dump our accumulated bottles and newspapers and what's happening to that boarded up building on the corner. These are the issues that are dealt with at City Hall. As well, they decide how to set business taxes, how to organize recreational facilities, whether development is going to take the place of low-cost housing and if parks or parking lots are going to occupy empty lots. These are issues that effect our daily lives, but we often have no idea how to make our opinions known, or even who to express them to.

Although election campaigns seem to turn on issues like commercial zoning and potholes, the political impact of these decisions can't be ignored. Real participation in a system that addresses our daily needs is the first step to accessing our own power and place within structures that can seem daunting. When faced with a bureaucracy of 13,000 employees, 51 elected representatives — including the Mayor, a maze of services, committees and corporations, the answers aren't always obvious. Stir things up with four different political parties, district advisory councils, consultations, Access-Montréal offices and many people would rather just give it up and allow their decisions to be made by someone else.

Municipal government is an obvious place to make your voice heard. It is here that the character and shape of your environment is determined. Sound municipal government extends beyond traffic planning to include a sense of yourself, and the quality of your life. Montréalers were promised that for a short time when the Montréal Citizens' Movement (MCM) emerged in the seventies. But the promise was merely a whisper by the time the party took control of City Council in 1986. Midway through their second term in office, they have strayed

1

far from their original ideals and find themselves facing internal and external criticism and a mounting sense of betrayal.

This book is intended for those of you who don't know where to begin, or who understand one aspect of the city, but want to know more about the big picture and how everything fits together. The Québec Public Interest Group (QPIRG) was founded on the premise that knowledge is power. Not all knowledge is shared equally, but knowing what's going on and how it works means that you're halfway toward changing it. QPIRG hired me to work on this project in the summer of 1990. It was the first time I'd ever heard the term "political landscaping," but it made sense — find out the lay of the land as it applies to municipal government and decision-making. At the time, I didn't know much about the city, but I knew enough about research, and I didn't think it would be hard to put the existing information into one accessible package.

So I started at Access-Montréal. I asked for a guide on how city government works. No such thing. So I asked how the people who work at Access-Montréal learn who does what. It takes them four months of meetings with bureaucrats. So I asked if there was anywhere I could go to find out how all the services in City Hall work. "Not even the Mayor knows that." Not terribly encouraging, but over the next ten months I got answers to enough questions to be able to lay the groundwork.

It was a year after I handed in my report that I received a call that it was to be published. By then I was working as a city reporter at the *Montreal Mirror* so it was fairly easy to update the book. Even so, city politics change quickly: offices are closed and reconstituted, City Councillors have been leaping parties on a regular basis and in the two months I had to update the material, the city released 600 pages of its master urban plan — the government's wide-ranging blueprint for future development and our role in it. To the best of my knowledge, this book is accurate up to the summer of 1992 — white Montréal's 350th birthday. Things change constantly so apologies in advance for phone numbers that don't work or services that no longer exist. By-elections, budgets and changes in priorities are more than likely going to mean changes between the time this book is in my hands and yours. Yet the information here can help you to track down subsequent changes, or to better understand the context in which these changes occur.

Over the course of my research, I found the municipal library on Sherbrooke Street facing Lafontaine Park, the archives in City Hall's basement, and the city government telephone book, invaluable. Later, I discovered the support Office for City Councillors and Committees to be helpful as well.

This book is simply a one-stop directory to the basics, much of it culled from municipal documents and headlines over the last two years. It would be impractical to provide more specifics. Researching each and every issue touched on here would take years of full-time work, and even then, the crucial piece you needed might be missing. This book is also not intended as the last word on municipal politics in either a historic or theoretical sense. The information here applies to Montréal, as recently as is possible. How you use this information is also up to you. You can as easily find information on how to get involved in government bodies and programs as find ammunition to challenge the system.

Naturally, the more you deal with City Hall, the more familiar it will become. You may not find it necessary to read this book from cover to cover. With this in mind, there is some repetition of key facts. Some information on how it's organized will help you find what you're looking for.

The book begins with a general overview of Montréal as a city. The section then outlines the politics at work at City Hall. The last six years have seen a virtual takeover by the MCM amidst promises for access and power to all residents. The reality of the situation falls short of the ideal. Through news clippings, the MCM party program and some references to performance, this section explores the way politics are played out on a municipal level.

The second section provides you with the nuts and bolts of Montréal's government and bureaucracy. The provincial government is ultimately responsible for dictating what any city can and can't do. The roles and responsibilities of both Montréal's elected officials and civil service are outlined along with phone numbers and some hints on how to find useful information. In short, this section is a simple guide to who controls what and just how much you can expect from any level of government. The role of the city-backed paramunicipal corporations is also examined.

Unfortunately, not only can the buck get passed within City Hall, it can also be sent beyond Montréal to the Montréal Urban Community (MUC). Where jurisdictions begin and end, as well as information about services that are not specifically Montréal's (like public transportation and the police force) can be found in Section III.

Once you know a bit about how the city works, you can start thinking about applying this information. Section IV guides you through all nine districts as defined by the city for planning purposes. Each part provides a thumb-nail sketch of the demographics, standard of living, resources, and problems to be found in the neighbourhoods. Although based on 1986 statistics, this data can be helpful when organizing. Information on some community advocacy groups active in each area is also provided. Knowing who you're trying to reach and what local concerns are go a long way toward getting people organized.

The last section has some general tips on how to go about getting on the agenda at City Hall, or how to react once an issue is on the agenda and you have something to say about it. Throughout the book you'll find information on the city's policies and progress on a variety of issues. Although this information is in no way complete, it can help get you started.

Finally, the appendices provide some concrete information on the current Councillors. Everything from alliances, Committee memberships, financial holdings, addresses and election results are included so that you can track down a Councillor who may be interested in helping you, or get to know more about your own representative. Contact information is also provided for MUC Councillors. As well, a guide to all of the acronyms inevitable in a book about bureaucracy is included.

Four digit numbers used throughout the book refer to City Hall phone numbers and all are preceded by 872-. A note on the footnoting system: since most of the information in this book comes from public documents (nearly all of the statistical information comes from various documents produced by the city), it didn't seem necessary to provide their sources. Specific quotes and analysis provided by journalists or authors are footnoted. However, all documents referred to for any section are listed at the end of each chapter.

You will also notice that equal time for the MCM government itself is glaringly absent. Politicians can easily reach their constituents using a fleet of public relations experts to control how that information gets out and with a generally louder voice. This book intends to ensure that power can move in the opposite direction, as well.

I would like to take this opportunity to thank those at QPIRG who helped to get this project into your hands. I would also like to thank Lisa Vinebohm for her painstaking editing, Mary Lamey for her help, and everyone else who listened to me spouting budget line items over the last two years. Finally, a thank you to all of the municipal reporters who have taken the time to write about the things that make a difference in all our lives.

This book is dedicated to them and anyone else who wants to use power instead of being used by it. Here are the tools, what you build is up to you.

Section I

Montréal in Context

Map of municipal electoral districts

1. Cartierville
2. L'Acadie
3. Ahuntsic
4. Saint-Sulpice
5. Fleury
6. Sault-au-Récollet
7. Saint-Michel
8. Jean-Rivard
9. François-Perrault
10. Villeray
11. Octave-Crémazie
12. Jarry
13. Park-Extension
14. Saint-Édouard
15. Père-Marquette
16. Louis-Hébert
17. Étienne-Desmarteau
18. Marie-Victorin
19. Bourbonnieère
20. Rosemont
21. De Lorimier
22. Plateau-Mont-Royal
23. Laurier
24. Mile-End
25. Jeanne-Mance
26. Peter McGill
27. Côte-des-Neiges
28. Darlington
29. Victoria
30. Snowdon
31. Notre-Dame-de-Grâce
32. Loyola
33. Décarie
34. Émard
35. Saint-Paul
36. Saint-Henri
37. Pointe-Saint-Charles
38. Saint-Jacques
39. Sainte-Marie
40. De Maisonneuve
42. Pierre-de-Coubertin
43. Louis-Riel
44. Longue-Pointe
45. Honoré-Beaugrand
46. Tétreaultville
47. Marc-Aurèle-Fortin
48. Rivière-des-Prairies
49. Pointe-aux-Trembles
50. Bout-de-l-île

Map courtesy of the Elections office, Office of the City Clerk, 1990

1.1 THE CITY

Before plunging into a detailed investigation of Montréal's government, bureaucracy and population, a few words in general might be useful. The City of Montréal exists as a patchwork primarily through the centre of the island. The pieces trace a history of annexations (many for financial reasons) that started in 1840 and continued right up to 1982, when Pointe-aux-Trembles, at the eastern tip of the island, was added. Over that time, the city's form of government has changed seven times and its importance in the economic and social context of North America has varied considerably.

Although Montréal's government is responsible for its own territory, several issues that effect all local governments (such as public transit, air and water pollution and public security), extend beyond the boundaries of the city proper to include the island as a whole. The 29 municipalities on the island are recognized as the Montréal Urban Community (MUC) and their interests are represented collectively through another government at that level.

The relationship of Montréal to the suburbs is far from one of dictatorial paternalism, even given the city's greater population and tax base. Montréal is by far the largest municipality within the MUC, it's population represents just over half of all people represented by the MUC. Montréal's size and urban character mean that many services such as museums, universities, resources are located on its territory, but used by adjoining municipalities. At the same time, the suburbs often have the advantage of lower business taxes, more green space and a higher standard of living.

A North American trend towards suburban over urban living has shifted the balance in various ways. More and more industries are passing by the urban core and establishing headquarters in the suburbs. According to a study produced by GIUM, a group of urban planning and design consultants, the City of Montréal is getting poorer while the Greater Montréal (the MUC and suburbs along the opposite north and south shores of the Saint Lawrence River) area is prospering. The gap between them is growing steadily. For instance, between 1971 and 1986 the population of Montréal dropped by 16%, while that of the suburbs rose by 25%.[1] Montréal's government argues that this trend has been slowing down since 1986, but this can only be revealed when 1991 census figures are analysed.

Even so, the population shift is certainly a concern of the current government. In the summer of 1992, the City unveiled a 600-page Master Urban Plan for it's territory, defining everything from future developments to traffic routes. One reporter wrote, "The main thrust of Montréal's plan is to make the city a better place to live, so it can woo back some of the residents it has lost to the suburbs over the years."[2]

As for standard of living, the average household income is now $37,671 in the suburbs, compared to $26,338 for the city itself. In terms of poverty, 25% of Montréal households vs. 12% of Greater Montréal earn under $10,000/yr. The percentage of single-parent households and unemployed is also higher in the city proper than in outlying areas. Finally, less than half of the households in the region rent their dwellings — that proportion is closer to three-quarters in the city itself.[3]

While it is true that 40% of Greater Montréal's employment is available in the City of Montréal, the city's economy has shifted over the last fifty years. At the beginning of the century, Montréal's employment was primarily industrial. The last decade has seen a shift to 80% of all Montréal jobs being service related.[4] The city has not always managed to keep up with the shift and southern pockets of the island have seen record-breaking unemployment (with the social problems that implies) as a result.

Similar trends can be seen in terms of development. Residential and industrial construction-permit values have nearly doubled in the Greater Montréal area between 1983-1990. Residential permits for the City of Montréal have dropped by nearly 40%. While industrial construction is up in the city, the total value of permits was only 16% of the total for Greater Montréal in 1990.

Currently, the city has one of the largest and most costly governments of any North American city. Montréal's 1,014,945 residents are represented by 50 Councillors and Mayor Jean Doré. This means each electoral district represents about 20,000 citizens, compared with only 17 aldermen in Toronto who each represent about 38,000. There are actually fewer electoral districts than there were a few years ago, but Montréal's ever-expanding bureaucracy has kept administration costs climbing steadily.

Any decisions about the kind and quality of power Montréal's government can have are made at the provincial level. The provincial government regulates the governments of the 300 or so municipalities in Québec. Most of them are generally managed through a provincial law on cities and towns, but both Montréal and Québec City have separate charters encompassing all regulations from how the government is run to what powers the government can exercise. Discussions have begun in Québec City to either reorganize or redefine the municipalities and their relationships. The Toronto model, a government with far fewer City Councillors for the city itself, and only a handful of recognized municipalities surrounding it, is being considered. These talks are still in the preliminary stages and their results won't be seen for years.[5]

History

The City of Montréal was constituted in 1840 when it received it's official charter. At the time, the city was only a small southern piece of the island, along the Saint Lawrence River. At the turn of the century, 23 suburbs were annexed, extending Montréal further north and expanding it's territory. Two further annexations on the eastern tip of the island in the later part of this century brought Montréal's total area to 175 km².

The depression hit Montréal hard, particularly because of its industrial-based economy. In the late thirties, the city borrowed more money than Toronto, Hamilton, Winnipeg, Ottawa, Calgary, Edmonton and Verdun combined to help provide relief to the city's unemployed. This led the city to declare bankruptcy in 1940, when it was put under the trusteeship of the province's Municipal Affairs Commission. During this period, the city also relied heavily on exercising its right to various municipal taxes, causing many to cite Montréal as the most heavily taxed city of the era.

The fifties were a time of rebuilding. By the late fifties, Jean Drapeau's autocratic rule through the Civic Party had begun, just in time to take advantage of a general period of economic recovery across the continent. Growth during the sixties extended to the various other autonomous municipalities scattered across the island. This led to the creation of the MUC.[6]

The Men that Run the Machine

The last decade has seen Montréal, like most urban centres, fall into decline. The federal Goods and Services Tax, and a recent decision by the province to end transfer payments to municipalities for public transportation and change school taxation formulas have meant that Montréal costs more to run. Add to that rising unemployment and a shift in Montréal's economy from an industrial to service base, and the financial burden on the city is even heavier. The financial burden shifted onto Montréal demanded a forceful response, a political strategy that could defend the city from the whims of other levels of government.

Although the MCM worked hard during its first mandate, (from 1986-1990), to try to keep business taxes down and encourage economic growth (particularly in high-tech, aviation and bio-medical fields), it's 1992 budget represented a complete turn-around. To compensate for the city's lost revenues, an enormous tax burden was placed on Montréal businesses, a move that alienated both left- and right-wing opposition Councillors, as well as many members of the MCM itself.

With all of these external factors begging the need for curbed municipal spending, Montréal is run by a bureaucracy worthy of awe for its sheer weight. One in every 76 Montréalers is employed by the municipal government. In the past five years, the cost of the civil service has jumped by 39%, although the city's population has been in decline.[7] Many of the city's top bureaucrats are amongst the highest paid in North America. The city's Secretary General (an office created by the MCM specifically to streamline spending), Pierre Le François earns $133,000 annually. This figure is close to the salary of the man responsible for the same task for the federal government in Ottawa.[8]

The city also backs a series of paramunicipal corporations. These bodies are autonomous only in as much as the city is kept an arm's length distance from their management. Financially, the city underwrites many of their investments, with the burden for unsound business decisions and bad debts eventually falling unto the taxpayer. In fact, each Montréaler currently owes $1,247 against the city government's total debt.[9]

The MCM seems to be concentrating on passing its master urban plan as its major accomplishment in time for the next municipal election in 1994. Although a full-scale development plan, with economic incentives may have long-term trickle down effects, the plan itself has no real deadlines for implementation. Meanwhile, Montréal's population is growing poorer and an economic booster shot may well prove to be too little, too late.

NOTES

1. GIUM, *Dossier Urbain: Arrondissement Rosemont/Petite-Patrie*, Prepared for the Service de l'habitation et du développement urbain, Ville de Montréal, June 1989.
2. Thompson, Elizabeth, "It's all there — piled high in a corner closet," *The Gazette*, August 29, 1992, p. B2.
3. Statistics from *Annual Report 1990*, Communauté urbaine de Montréal, General Management — Communications, 2nd quarter, 1991, and the *Cahier d'information économique et budgétaire, 1991*,Ville de Montréal, Service de planification et de la concertation, Module des communications, 1990.
4. Ville de Montréal, *Les orientations et les stratégies du Plan d'urbanisme de Montréal*, Service de l'habitation et du développement urbain, Bureau du plan d'urbanisme, 2nd Quarter, 1992.
5. Herland, Karen, "Urban Shuffle," *The Montreal Mirror*, April 2-April 9, 1992, p. 8.
6. Ville de Montréal, *Cahier d'information économique et budgétaire, 1992*,Service de planification et de la concertation, Module des communications, 4th Quarter, 1991.
7. *The Gazette*, "How the city spends your money," November 16, 1991. p. A1
8. McIntosh, Andrew, "A buffer of highly paid bureaucrats," *The Gazette*, November 16, 1991. p. B5
9. *The Gazette*, "Longterm debt at the start of 1991," November 16, 1991. p. B5. Communauté urbaine de Montréal, *Annual Report 1990*, General Management — Communications, 2nd Quarter, 1991.

REFERENCES

Boskey, Sam, Democratic Coalition Councillor, private conversation, July, 1992.

The Gazette, "How the city spends your money," November 16, 1991. p. A1

The Gazette, "Longterm debt at the start of 1991," November 16, 1991. p. B5

GIUM, *Dossier Urbain: Arrondissement Rosemont/Petite-Patrie,* Prepared for the Service de l'habitation et du développement urbain, Ville de Montréal, June 1989.

Herland, Karen, "Urban Shuffle," *The Montreal Mirror,* April 2-April 9, 1992, p. 8.

Laberge, Léon, Montréal City Clerk, private conversation Sept. 5, 1992.

McIntosh, Andrew, "A buffer of highly paid bureaucrats," *The Gazette,* November 16, 1991. p. B5

Thompson, Elizabeth, "It's all there — piled high in a corner closet," *The Gazette,* August 29, 1992, p. B2.

Ville de Montréal, *Cahier d'information économique et budgétaire, 1991,* Service de planification et de la concertation, Module des communications, 4th Quarter, 1990.

Ville de Montréal, *Cahier d'information économique et budgétaire, 1992,*Service de planification et de la concertation, Module des communications, 4th Quarter, 1991.

Ville de Montréal, *Les orientations et les stratégies du Plan d'urbanisme de Montréal,* Service de l'habitation et du développement urbain, Bureau du plan d'urbanisme, 2nd Quarter, 1992.

1.2 PARTY POLITICS

The MCM — From grass roots to green space

Until recently, the only thing most Montréalers knew about municipal politics was that Jean Drapeau ran this city for the better part of thirty years as leader of the Civic Party (CPM), until his retirement in 1986. Much has been made of Drapeau's penchant for grandiose schemes (Expo 67, the Olympics) with enormous bills passed on to taxpayers, and the fact that membership in his CPM was by private invitation, with the expectation of total loyalty.

Fewer people knew that party politics at the municipal level only existed officially since the seventies, through a provincial dictum. Until then, Drapeau's unified (if elite) crew were considered an anomaly. A team was probably perceived as a comforting and efficient alternative to a mishmash of individual interests and alliances. Yet Drapeau's reign was marked by secrecy, with decisions favouring corporate interests over individuals and development over neighbourhoods.

Montréal is now ruled by the Montréal Citizen's Movement (MCM), a party created in direct response to Drapeau's anti-democratic, extravagant bureaucracy. The MCM won most seats in Council in both 1986 and 1990, essentially giving it carte blanche in City Hall. Far away from its original grass-roots base, the MCM threw one of the biggest and most expensive parties ever in the summer of 1992, to mark the 350th year since the "discovery" of Montréal by white Europeans. Although nearly a third of Montréal's population lives below the poverty line, Executive Committee chair Léa Cousineau was quoted as saying that she didn't think Montréalers would have opposed the $23 million renovation project for City Hall, had they been asked. We weren't. The tune may have changed but the (MCM's) record remains much the same as before.

The party is also at a crossroads. Mayor Jean Doré was forced to make a statement on behalf of the MCM and the city's government in September 1992 to stop nearly one-third of the MCM Councillors from leaving the party or calling for a new leadership. Although Michel Prescott, who had been a Councillor with the MCM left the party anyway, and denounced the proclamation as rehashed promises, the other Councillors returned to a wait-and-see attitude, and the dissension appears to be temporarily quieted. With the right-wing Civic Party gaining support, and the parties on the left of the MCM facing turning points of their own, municipal politics are leaving room for potential change.

Challenge from the Left

The MCM emerged from the ashes of the Front d'Action Politique (FRAP) as a credible opposition to the CPM in the early seventies. FRAP was an alliance of far-left militants and community organizations that wanted City Hall returned to the people. The coalition worked through existing community groups and unions to encourage members to take an active role in municipal government. FRAP threatened to be a force to be reckoned with in the 1970 election, but was discredited by Jean Marchand, then a federal cabinet minister, who suggested they were connected to the FLQ. Montréal was occupied by the army during the "October Crisis" of that year. Within a context of right-wing induced panic, Drapeau's re-election was assured. By 1973, some of FRAP's more radical elements left to make way for Parti Québécois supporters (like Jean Doré) and a more moderate MCM emerged.

During the next year, the MCM was constituted as a political party. Although it retained community links and a union-based membership, it also developed a program and a profile more in keeping with electoralism. The MCM's party program, titled "Une ville pour nous," still promised to deliver the city into the hands of the people.

The MCM loosened the Drapeau stranglehold on City Hall in 1974 by winning 18 of the 54 seats in Council. New parties emerged between 1974 and the next election, significantly the Municipal Action Group (MAG) led by some higher profile, capital "L" Liberal candidates, including Serge Joyal and MCM discontents like Nick Auf der Maur. The media seized on MAG as a "credible" alternative to both the bloated Civic Party and the "radical" MCM. Montréalers split the vote in several ridings, reducing the MCM to a single elected Councillor, Michael Fainstat, in 1978.

During Fainstat's term, many of the left-wing elements of the party's program were dropped altogether, or relegated to the realm of the very distant future and watered down. The MCM continued to promise more access to City Hall for Montréalers, through a series of local decision-making mini-Councils, a more open, democratic administration, and social issues like housing, various "minority" interests, and improved, low-cost public transportation. However, in the program, most of the issues were described vaguely as "a commitment to," instead of outlined in concrete terms. This drove many of the left-wing community-based members to abandon the MCM, leaving it in the hands of its more centrist members.

The MCM's battle was finally won in 1986 when the party swept 55 of the 58 seats in Council. The CPM was left in a shambles, while a clear majority gave the MCM all the room they needed to implement the changes they'd been promising for a dozen years. Although some wheels were set in motion, the pace was so slow, with some ideals dropped altogether, that four MCM Councillors defected before their first term was up. Citing overwhelming pressure to follow the party line and the silencing of debate within the party, they formed their own party, the Democratic Coalition of Montréal (DCM). This party, they felt, was truer to the original ideals of the MCM.

The MCM currently runs the show, with 37 of the 51 seats on Council. Their most recent party program no longer promises "Une ville pour nous" but, instead, very clearly indicates who's in charge with "La Ville que nous voulons." The CPM is now the official opposition, with five seats. Although only one seat was actually won in the 1990 election, two Municipal Party (MPM) Councillors and one MCM Councillor jumped to the party within two years. This left the fairly new MPM with only one seat, that of their mayoral candidate, Alain André. By the summer of 1992, the two parties merged, giving André the fifth seat in the "new" CPM. A by-election in St-Jacques in November gave the party another seat. The DCM won three seats in the last election, and then gained a fourth in a 1991 by-election. In June 1992, two of those Councillors left the party to sit as independents. They joined one Councillor who ran as an independent, one who left the MCM in early 1992 and another who left in September of that year.

If this game of municipal musical chairs isn't confusing enough, consider the irony of an official opposition with only one more Councillors than those who reject all parties by sitting as independents. Hardly a rousing endorsement for a clear path to change. A municipal version of the "Green Party," Ecology Montréal (EM), has also emerged as a left-of-centre alternative, although they won no seats on Council. An anti-party exists in the guise of Montréal's White Elephant Party, which has served to punctuate election campaigns with sometimes pointed humour, and runs a substantial slate of candidates, but has yet to be taken really seriously by voters. A new party, the Bloc Municipal, emerged just before the 1992 Saint-Jacques by-election, as a right-wing alternative to the Civic Party. It remains to be seen if the party is a new force to be reckoned with, or if it will disappear before the next general election in 1994. A more complete profile of the MCM and the parties to the left and right follows. For a scorecard of who jumped where and when, refer to Appendices A and B.

The MCM in Action

Critics on both the left and right of the MCM cite problem after problem within the current government: style over substance, irresponsible spending, and reforms, quotas and principles without strong legislation to back them up. Decisions are made under a veneer of openness with certain key doors remaining locked. The names of these issues (Overdale, urban planning, waste disposal, 350th birthday party, Anti-Apartheid policy) may change, but the basic disagreements remain the same.

> *"Quant à la discipline du parti au conseil, les statistiques sont fort éloquentes. De plus, la règle est claire: les représentants du PCM doivent appuyer sans restriction toutes les propositions du comité exécutif, formé de six hommes de confiance, la règle de l'unanimité prévaut également, puisque les propositions qui ne font pas consensus sont reportées."[1]*

Although it may seem strange to start a discussion of the MCM with a reference to the autocratic CPM, the truth is that although the Executive Committee referred to in the above quote is no longer six men, but now made up of an equal number of men and women, the outcome is the same. No matter what happens in City Hall, or the various new bodies created by the MCM, the final decision is always made by the Executive Committee. Since this Committee is made up exclusively of MCM Councillors, and MCM party solidarity is required, in the final analysis the MCM rules.

DCM Councillors left the MCM as they realized that the MCM's original goal of opening the city up to its citizens was slowly being eroded, even as the MCM put the appropriate mechanisms in place. Although promises were kept, the consultative bodies that were created to allow average Montréalers a voice at City Hall had no real power or authority. Each and every one still depended on the Executive Committee for approval and endorsement. Even as Councillors, they could not challenge the discrepancy between what they had originally understood "access" to mean, and the powerless reforms that were instituted by the MCM in its name. It became more and more apparent during the MCM's first term that disagreement should be confined to the party, behind the closed doors of the party's private caucuses (held two hours before each Council meeting) and only be made public afterwards. Thus, in Montréal: A Citizen's Guide to Politics, Sam Boskey is quoted as saying the right to dissent "only exists between 5:00 and 7:00."[2] Voting against your party was often followed by a "motion of censure" from the caucus. So much for free speech or voting with your conscience.

This blind adherence to appearances is what leads to comparisons with Jean Drapeau's monopolistic rule. Luc Chartrand sums up the charges against Jean Doré: *"On lui reproche ce qu'on reprochait à Jean Drapeau: de concentrer le pouvoir dans les mains du comité exécutif, de ne pas laisser le conseil...discuter des questions importantes et de ne pas permettre aux conseillers de prendre des positions personelles plutôt que de suivre la politique du parti."[3]*

The practice remains true today. It is very rare for an MCM Councillor to vote against the party. There are no provisions in Council regulations for abstentions. Disagreement can be demonstrated in other ways. Councillors can leave the room during a vote. This move runs them the risk of a $100 fine for missing a meeting. The most recent example occurred during the vote to pass the 1992 budget, when five MCM Councillors left the room, and two others voted against the budget outright. Budgets do not vary that much from year to year, but they can be useful in determining the priorities for a government, and the MCM's decision to heavily tax businesses in order to maintain revenue was at issue. By the spring of 1992, two of those Councillors had left the party: Michel Benoit jumped to the CPM and Marcel Sévigny, who had long held a fairly dissident position within the MCM, finally chose to sit as an independent. Michel Prescott joined the defectors in the fall of that year, although he also chose to remain independent.

The combination of the by-election loss in an MCM enclave, public disagreement over the key issue of the budget, and the party defections were the beginning of the largest crisis in the MCM's history. Although a handful of Councillors left the party to eventually form the Democratic Coalition in 1989, by June 1992 almost a third of the MCM Councillors were grumbling openly. This time, it was not just a well-defined left-wing attack. Party faithfuls, including former Executive Committee member and MUC Transit Corporation Chair Robert Perrault, and Council Chair André Berthelet, criticized spending decisions, lack of leadership and the government's disregard of the needs of ordinary citizens and Councillors themselves. Many felt these concerns demonstrated a shift away from Montréalers and towards the trappings of power concentrated in the hands of a few bureaucrats and party elite. Perrault went so far as to publish a scathing critique of the MCM in the op ed pages of *La Presse*.

A series of tense private meetings between the Mayor and disgruntled Councillors were held over the summer. Disagreement dissipated after a five-hour party meeting in September 1992. Mayor Doré promised to increase Councillor power through local District Advisory Councils (DACs), take tighter control of the City reins, improve civil service efficiency and improve service delivery. The plan also included more support for economic development, and a lift of the MCM freeze on condo conversions. It remains to be seen whether these decisions will in fact help Montréal's citizens or simply reinforce the MCM's base amongst the economic elite. The speech was also peppered with references to the current malaise with the MCM and Montréal's government as being typical of the one faced by all governments and businesses in the 1990s, with no distinction being made between the roles of the public and private sector.

Only Michel Prescott, who'd threatened to leave the MCM in May, was not immediately won over, and he eventually opted for independence, charging that Doré and the party had lost contact with the everyday reality of Montréalers. He further charged that the "reforms" delivered by Doré to placate dissension were nothing more than rewarmed promises that had been made long ago. Other Councillors accepted the new deal and agreed to wait and watch for the proposed changes. Montréalers will be watching as well.

The MCM's Record

Accessibility

To the MCM's credit, they have set up a variety of ways for citizens to approach City Hall. If you're concerned about a new bar opening on the corner of your street, you can go to your local Access-Montréal office and find out about current zoning laws in your neighbourhood. You can register there to ask a question about those zoning policies at your local District Advisory Council (DAC) meeting. If you are still not satisfied, you can address a question about the zoning problem at a city Council meeting. If the problem is big enough, one of the city's five standing Committees may hold hearings on the zone, where you can present a brief. Finally, if the area in question is really controversial (say a part of Mount Royal) the city's public consultation office (BCM) may investigate the problem and you can present a brief there. All of these outlets are MCM initiatives. However, these same bodies all report to, and take direction from the Executive Committee, which meets behind closed doors once a week to pass judgement on issues as small as zoning or as large as political orientation and multi-million dollar city contracts. The buck still stops there. A more detailed explanation of some of these initiatives is available in the chapter on Montréal government, but their overall effects will be addressed here.

Consultation is a big catchword for the MCM. DACs, Standing Committees, special Committees, and the BCM were established to allow for public input. Yet the Executive Committee determines the mandate and scope of each of these bodies. Layers of administration mean that citizen input is heard at public meetings, interpreted by those in charge of the consultation process, and drafted into watered down reports to the Executive Committee. Executive Committee members have the freedom to respond only to what they want to hear, and to bring their own version of events to City Council for a final rubber stamp. At every stage of the process, there is so much room for reinterpretation that individual complaints or problems can easily be lost in the paper shuffle. In short, it is the Executive Committee that stacks the deck and deals the cards, and then tallies up the score. Perhaps the concept of "consultation" itself is the problem.

"*Dans la concertation, le décideur va voir les gens directement concernés. On discute, on fait des compromis et on aboutit à une décision qui tient compte de l'ensemble des points de vue exprimés. La consultation, par contre, est loin d'impliquer un partage du pouvoir. Il ne s'agit, pour le décideur, que de prendre le pouls de la population et, ensuite, de décider seul,*" said Jean-François Léonard, a political science professor at the Université du Québec à Montréal (UQAM) and co-author of several books on Montréal politics.[4] This comment succinctly captures the frustration with the consultation process to date. The right-wing recognizes that the city has established a series of ways to let the public be heard without really having to listen, and in the interests of expediency and cost-efficiency, recommends that the process be dropped altogether. The left-wing has no guarantees that the process will legitimately open up and feels cheated by the current system.

Even those with no stated position in terms of city government are still mystified, if not unimpressed by the structure established by the MCM. A CROP Poll commissioned by *La Presse* just before the 1990 election underlines some obvious problems. A full 68% of those surveyed felt that the city's consultation process had not improved. Of those, 33% felt it was the same as under the Drapeau regime, and 11% considered it worse than before. In that same poll, 63% felt that the ability of the current administration to keep them adequately informed had not improved[5] — fairly damning for an administration that promised (and prides itself on) open and accessible government.

An alternative system is possible, but would require major restructuring. There are those who feel that the final nail in the CPM's coffin was hammered in 1984, when they proposed building a huge shopping mall over McGill College Avenue. They tried to ram the project through Council in four days but reaction was swift and the project was shelved. At the time, Mark London, Executive Director of Heritage Montréal, produced a series of criteria for the ideal consultation process. The first was that it must be carried out by a neutral agency, not the organization promoting the project.[6] The last was that the process must be binding. The MCM strikes out on both counts.

Susan Ruddick provides an in-depth analysis of the MCM from its inception today in *Fire in the Hearth: The Radical Politics of Place in America*. She explains the frustration on both sides as a result of the MCM's "having raised expectations around the possibility of public consultation, while the administration risks dashing them by holding power too tightly with the ranks of the Executive Committee."[7]

Spending

The 1992 budget that nearly caused a near mutiny within the ranks of the MCM was firmly opposed by all opposition Councillors. It saw municipal spending jump by 9%, to nearly $2 billion. The Executive Committee argued that the main reason for the large increase was the provincial government's decision to end transfer payments to municipalities to help finance public transit — a move that cost Montréal $75 million. A series of other minor changes to the process of municipalities collecting revenues through school and amusement taxes cost the city another $25 million. The MCM Executive repeatedly pointed out that without that unexpected cost, the city's budget only rose by just under 5%, in keeping with the cost of living.

What enraged opposition Councillors and taxpayers alike was that the city chose to recover the money by imposing an immediate 14.6% surtax on commercial and industrial buildings. Right-wing Councillors deplored this move made in the wake of an economic recession and record bankruptcies. Left-wing Councillors argued that the increase should have been introduced gradually over several years. Taxpayers responded by demanding reevaluations of their properties, effectively slowing the tax collection process to a near standstill. They also circulated petitions, crowded City Council question periods and generally made a fuss. By April 1992, the city finally responded by cutting the budget by nearly $20 million, mostly in public works and fire prevention services.[8] Three months later, the city announced another $12.5 million in cuts, made possible by letting employee contracts run out without renewing them.[9] But what is the city actually spending money on?

In the last two years, the MCM financed a series of cosmetic projects that have left Montréalers frustrated and somewhat baffled. Although the City Hall building was in need of repairs for safety reasons, the $23 million spent in renovations included the $1.2 million installation of infra-red lights in men's urinals that activate them them to flush automatically. Also included are a $300,000 bullet-proof window for Mayor Doré's office and gold and crystal fixtures in some bathrooms. The city also forked over $29 million to repave certain public squares and a street in Old Montréal in granite. The lighting on the cross on Mount Royal has been refitted with a high-fibre optic system which allows the cross to flash blue and red. In the event of the Pope dying, the cross will also be able to glow purple. This innovation cost some $300,000. The city has also contributed several million dollars to the refurbishing or rebuilding of nearly a dozen museums and cultural centres since 1989.

Most of these projects are indirectly connected to the 1992 350th birthday party for the city. The MCM had decided that despite growing poverty, economic recession and record unemployment, an all-out party was just what Montréalers needed to keep their spirits up. They also argued that a sumptuous party would bring financial benefits through increased tourism. Hence, the renovations, museums and a public relations campaign likened to Drapeau's heyday. Nearly every summertime festival, event or attraction (including the fireworks festival, jazz festival, world film festival, etc.) was announced as bigger than ever in 1992, and most have been given an extra shot in the arm by the city to promote the party.

The celebration involved community initiatives as well as corporate sponsorship, as well. Thus Mayor Doré grins amidst happy Montréalers in a Coke ad — Coca-Cola is a major sponsor, as are Ford, Molson and Esso. Promotions include the 350th birthday logo on Molson beer caps, and "Celebrate Montréal" bus shelter and billboard ads written in the distinctive Coca-Cola trademark signature. Looking back on the summer of 1992, we'll all be hard-pressed to remember if there was more hype around the birthday party or the release of *Batman Returns*.

As for Montréalers who need more than a party, the MCM's response has been far less impressive. After closing down the city-financed centre (serving the estimated 15,000 homeless in Montréal), during a labour dispute in 1991, the city shelved plans to open a new one when shopkeepers in the area balked over potential problems. To add insult to injury, homeless rights groups charged the City with encouraging the police to keep Montréal clean by harassing homeless off the streets over the course of the summer-long party.[10] The city has issued statements denouncing federal cuts to subsidized housing programs, without really exploring creative alternatives. When asked to join a coalition protesting changes to the provincial welfare system's various workfare programs, the city's most eloquent response was to announce the creation of 1,000 temporary municipal jobs under those very programs.[11]

Ignoring the real needs of Montréalers while throwing an enormous party has clearly alienated the left-wing, both in and outside of City Hall. Lavish spending, however, has encouraged a more ironic response, the CPM, which the MCM often criticized for grandiose schemes, is now accusing the MCM of the same.

Style over Substance

Another major criticism of the MCM concerns the city administration's preference for style over substance. The results are not only frustrating, they may be damaging in the long run.

During the summer of 1992, the MCM introduced the $58 million Biodome. Located in the Velodrome, the space has been transformed into a type of museum showcasing four distinct ecosystems, all under glass. Nearly 2,000 different species of animal, fish and bird life have been set free under the dome, where eventually, beluga whales will swim. Thousands of different plant species are also on display to anyone for the $8.50 admission price. Many critics have called the structure a glorified laboratory for bioresearchers.[12] While the spectre of taking children to a museum to see "nature" is frightening, the split between image and reality is even wider. As Jacques Cordeau, a city blue collar worker and member of its union's Environmental Committee, pointed out, while the city spent millions on the Biodome, "They've ignored Mount Royal and a study on how to protect it for two years now. So they're spending money on an unnatural environment and ignoring the real one."[13] The DCM launched a campaign in August 1992 to stop the city from bringing in beluga whales. Arguing that these mammals have never survived in captivity, they claim that a decision to bring them to the Biodome would amount to contributing to the extinction of a species for the sake of the museum. Equally contradictory is the fact that the "northern" aspects of the dome are kept cold using CFC technology, only months after the city announced a reduced CFC policy for Montréal. Alternatives to the CFC cooling system were available, but considered too expensive.[14] The city government has also recently approved a $13 million Golfodrome, seven stories of indoor recreation including a golf-course, underlining the MCM's preference for nature-under-glass.

This gap between practice and policy has haunted the MCM throughout its administration. "So far, (the MCM) has relegated radical politics to the symbolic realm, with public events like the naming of Mandela Park, and made economic concessions only under duress, the latter largely to low-income housing — the forté of community organizations. In the less-tread terrain of economic development, however, it has sided with federal Conservative policy, hoping to transform Montréal into a Cape Canaveral of the north through aerospace and high-tech federal contracts," wrote Ruddick in 1990. For instance, in 1987, the MCM declared Montréal a Nuclear-Free Zone, amidst much pomp and circumstance. Signs were put up all over the city, and the policy was even declared in a special floral arrangement on the lawn of City Hall. "Party policy has been disregarded as the administration hides behind the letter of the MCM electoral platform, hairsplitting distinctions between the military, nuclear and nuclear weapons industries in order to assist [Montréal-based] Vickers secure a contract for nuclear submarines."[15]

Such inconsistency has disenchanted many former supporters of the MCM. An anti-apartheid policy and the recently renamed Mandela Park exist alongside the MCM's continued willingness to work with companies that do business in South Africa, for example co-sponsoring events with questionable multinationals including Shell and Benson and Hedges. A year and a half after its establishment, the policy was watered down to allow the city to do business with corporations that had up to a 50% interest in South Africa and not the original limit of 10%.[16]

The MCM's 1986 promises to make Montréal a safer place for women included plans for creating special teams within the MUC police force to deal with domestic violence, decriminalizing prostitution to help women working in the sex industry, and improving safety for women on city streets by paying attention to walkways and lighting. These commitments, if implemented, would have made concrete changes in the lives of women. The presence of feminist Léa Cousineau as the head of the city's Executive Committee should have ensured that these issues were quickly attended to. Cousineau had earned her political stripes as attaché to Lise Payette, one of the first strong feminists in the provincial government. Yet Cousineau, herself, insists that her title is "Chairman" of the Executive Committee and ascribes to a liberal brand of feminism more concerned with the number of women in administrative positions than the social inequalities that keep women from attaining them.

The first promise the city kept was the 1991 passage of a by-law against public billboards displaying naked women outside of what they termed "erotic establishments." This proposal was certainly the most likely to gain widespread approval (satisfying moralists as well as some women's groups). Even so, it could easily be used to push the sex trade underground, pushing the very women the 1986 program promised to protect into even greater danger. The city's use of the term "erotic establishments" was also problematic. Although it technically meant strip clubs, the possibility that the by-law could be used against businesses like L'Androgyne, Montréal's gay and lesbian bookstore, existed. The by-law was judged unconstitutional almost exactly one year after its adoption by Justice Ginette Piché of Québec's Superior Court. She ruled that a municipality could not regulate signs for the sex industry, since the industry itself was not prohibited under federal law. The city government is considering a new by-law to address the issue.

In July 1992, the city government announced a second initiative on behalf of Montréal's women. To address problems of street safety for women, it declared it would monitor a group of women's responses to a "typical" neighbourhood and implement their safety recommendations. The plan would see changes in one pocket of the city about a year after the announcement. No deadlines have been set for the rest of the city.

Meanwhile, complaints against the MUC police force concerning their response to questions of women's safety are growing. Over the last few years, police have consistently waited days, even weeks before publicizing information about serial rapists when they have struck on different parts of the island. After news of four rapes of teenagers in one east-end park went public in 1991, an officer suggested that "girls should know not to be there" and that announcing information about their attacker would have "frightened the public over a situation that wasn't that serious."[17] This misplaced fear that women cannot handle information that could protect them is paternalism at its worst. MUC Police Chief moved into the realm of hypocrisy after he was named head of the Canadian Association of Police Chiefs in September 1992. Despite complaints from women in his home town, he vowed to use his new position to particularly address crimes against women and children.

Signs remain a favourite theme of the MCM. AIDS is easily one of the greatest social problems effecting this generation. City Council lost a member, Raymond Blain, to the disease in 1992. In 1991, the MCM made it mandatory for a grand total of 1,400 bars, restaurants and arcades to post eight-inch square signs displaying a condom and declaring Montréal a "healthy city" somewhere near their bathrooms. The signs offer no phone numbers for people who want more information. Compare this "prevention" campaign with the $1.2 million that Toronto gave to community groups specifically dealing with AIDS in 1991.

The MCM also falls short on the recycling front. In March 1991, Executive Committee member Richard Brunelle termed the three year-old project "still at the experimental stage."[18] Currently, only 29% of Montréal's residents have access to curbside recycling, compared to some 91% of Toronto residents. In fact, 3% of all domestic waste produced in the city is actually recycled; commercial and industrial initiatives (and the waste they produce) are not part of the equation. The city hopes to have full residential recycling in place by 1994, just in time for the election.[19]

The MCM made a big deal of their introduction of home pick-up for dangerous and toxic wastes. They listed it as a major accomplishment in *Sommaire des Réalisations: Novembre 1986 à Décembre 1989*, an extensive document released just before the 1990 election. The fact that this was actually an initiative taken at the MUC level is downplayed — in fact, the MCM opted out of the collection program in 1991, citing high costs. They promised their own version of collection for fall 1992.

Shifting Support

An article that appeared in *the Gazette* before the 1990 municipal election outlined the situation by interviewing ten community, business and development leaders on their opinions on the MCM's first term. The author concluded that there had been a "flip-flop" in support for the MCM. Their original supporters were now disappointed, and groups who were worried about the *carte blanche* the MCM was handed in 1986 were more than pleased with the way things had turned out.

On the question of housing, FRAPRU member Pierre Gaudreau has said — which many have called the MCM's most consistently progressive dossier — "Its big objectives are laudable. In its practice, we're very disappointed." On the flip side, the secretary of the Urban Development Institute, a developer's lobby group, David Powell said, "...[T]here were concerns over what would happen with the MCM. On balance, we were pleasantly surprised."[20]

The reasons for the shift in the MCM's direction (and subsequent shift in support) are not immediately apparent. Although the MCM has clearly managed to contradict it's original programs, and betray many of its original ideals, the shift has been gradual. As waves of more militant members left at turning points in the party's history, room was left to put previous priorities onto the back burner and subsequently, to continually adopt a more watered-down, centrist position, until little of what once fired the party remains. Ruddick describes the MCM as having "seriously diluted the original program of the party, moving from a stance of social mobilization and citizen empowerment to one of beneficent service delivery."[21] By 1992, "services" was the buzzword of the MCM, and their protection was the oft-cited reason for the ballooning municipal budget. The control the provincial government has over municipal governments, in terms of setting financial policy and revenue collection (see next chapter), have forced cities to make tough choices in terms of spending. "As the financial burden falls to city governments, they have to make political decisions, they should be fighting for more powers," said Andrea Levy, who had been active in the MCM for 12 years before moving to EM. "The MCM set out to defeat the idea that 'municipal government is not political, it simply provides services' and now they pander to it."[22] The city's most recent annual report is introduced with the disquieting assurance that city workers are bent on "the pursuit of our corporate objective: making Montréal a genuine public service enterprise."[23] Given the MCM's original mandate and program, the shift from reform to paternalism is discouraging.

Overall, the MCM seems to be learning the political lessons of promises over performance, and the party continues to swear by populist ideals while moving further and further away from them in practice. The ambitious master urban plan introduced in 1992 promised improved quality of life, residential and community services, green space and future development on a human scale for most of the city. Yet the only specific information offered are technical changes to zoning by-laws and guidelines for building construction, while the other promises involving improved quality of life are given no deadlines or concrete means of implementation.

The discontent within the party that finally came to the surface in 1992 will probably not be the push for change the party needs. Voters sent a clear message to the party in the 1991 by-election. Almost a dozen candidates vied for the seat available in 1992. The free-for-all was a clear indication that just about everybody thought that they could do better than the party in power. When Civic Party candidate Sammy Forcillo won that seat, Mayor Doré insisted that the 30% voter turnout meant that interest was low, and that the vote could not be counted as a vote against his party. Yet, the turnout was consistent with turnout during the last general election in 1990 (which was not vying for news coverage with the constitutional referendum) and the fact remains that the MCM has lost all of the last four by-elections.

The MCM's concentration on appearances over real direction and political change is pleasing fewer and fewer people, all across the political and economic map. Individuals within the party should be able to follow their constituents" consciences, instead of bowing to pressure to present the seamless appearance of one party one vote. Consultation should be built around citizen participation, instead of wasting time and money on appearing to listen, without ever really hearing. The city needs more consistent policies which would force it to comply with recommendations from it's own consultation office and committees, instead of adhering to a top-down model of government.

It is possible that the 1993 budget will reveal a change in direction, as promised by Mayor Doré. Increased funds for DACs, to allow them to wield more power and stricter budgets in terms of purely bureaucratic services vs. money allotted for citizen-directed services would also be an indication of a shift. Some departments found their budgets inflated to handle the 350th Birthday Party, it will be interesting to note whether these budgets will remain enormous, or be cut back down to size.

If not, Montréalers will realize that the MCM is a carefully constructed magic act that may disappear in a puff of smoke. Adding to the mirage, was Doré's response to losing a political attaché in November 1990 (after it was revealed several municipal employees were illegally working on the MCM campaign): he replaced her with Benôit Gignac, whose previous publicity experience was with the Cirque du Soleil.[24]

MCM
85 Ste. Catherine West,
8th floor,
Montréal, QC
H2X 3P4
284-2116

NOTES

1. Louise Quesnel-Ouellet, Political Science professor at the Université Laval, as quoted in Baccigalupo, Alain avec Luc Rhéaume, *Les Administration municipales québécoises des origines à nos jours*, Tome II, Editions ARC, Ottawa, 1984.
2. Roy, Jean-Hugues and Brendan Weston, Montréal: A Citizen's Guide to Politics, Montréal; Black Rose Books Ltd, 1990.
3. Chartrand, Luc, "Où va Jean Doré?" *L'Actualité*, April 1989 p. 39.
4. Roy, Jean-Hugues, "Les deux pieds sur terre," *Voir*, November 1-November 7, 1990.
5. *La Presse*, Rapport sur un sondage CROP, 19 October, 1990 p. A6.
6. *Downtowner*, Two page ad re downtown master plan. May 30, 1990.
7. Ruddick, Sarah, "The Montréal Citizen's Movement: The Realpolitik of the 1990s?" in *Fire in the Hearth: The Radical Politics of Place*, Davis, M. et al, eds. London; Verso, 1990 pp 287-316.
8. Kumar, Nantha, "New Cuts, *The Montreal Mirror*, April 30 - May 7, 1992, p. 8.
9. *The Gazette*, "City plans $12.5 million budget cut," July 14, 1992.
10. Kumar, Nantha, "No Can Go," *The Montreal Mirror*, July 9-July 16, 1992, p. 8
11. Herland, Karen, "Make Work, Not Jobs," *The Montreal Mirror*, May 28-June 4, 1992, p. 7.
12. Kumar, Nantha, "Naturally Domed," *The Montreal Mirror*, April 2-April 9, 1992, p. 7.
13. Herland, Karen, "What Next," *The Montreal Mirror*, January 9-January 16, 1992, p. 6
14. Kumar, Nantha, "Under the Dome," *The Montreal Mirror*, April 9-April 16, 1992, p. 8.
15. Ruddick, op. cit.
16. Kumar, Nantha, "Diluted Policy," *The Montreal Mirror*,, April 16-April 23, 1992, p. 8.
17. *The Montreal Mirror*, "No News is.. Dangerous," December 26, 199-January 9, 1992, p. 19.
18. Lamarche, Robert, "La Famille Slomo," *Voir*, March 21-27, 1991, p. 5.
19. Ville de Montréal, *Annual Report 1991*, Secrétariat général, Service de la planification et de la concertation, Bureau des Communications, 2nd quarter, 1992.
20. Peritz, Ingrid, "Flip-flop on the MCM," *The Gazette*, October 29, 1990, p. A1.
21. Ruddick, op. cit.
22. Private conversation, Andrea Levy, September 23, 1992.
23. Ville de Montréal, *Annual Report 1991*, op. cit.
24. Herland, Karen, "Expanding to fill the space," *The Montreal Mirror*, December 26, 1991-January 9, 1992, p. 7.

REFERENCES

Baccigalupo, Alain avec Luc Rhéaume, *Les Administration municipales québécoises des origines à nos jours*, Tomes I et II, Editions ARC, Ottawa, 1984.
Buckie, Catherine, "Montréal erotic-sign bylaw is judged unconstitutional," *The Gazette*, September 2, 1992, p. A1.
Chartrand, Luc, "Où va Jean Doré?" *L'Actualité*, April 1989 p. 39.
Doré, Jean, *Résumé de la présentation du plan d'action 1992-1993 proposé par le Maire de Montréal*, September 23, 1992. Unbound report.
Downtowner, Two page ad re downtown master plan. May 30, 1990.
The Gazette, "City plans $12.5 million budget cut," July 14, 1992.
The Gazette, "The four day gap," editorial, August 2, 1992, p. B2.
Hamilton, Graeme "Montréal dumps toxic waste pickup," *The Gazette*, April 23, 1991 p. A4.
Herland, Karen, "Budget Won't Budge," *The Montreal Mirror*, December 5-December 12, 1991, p. 8.
Herland, Karen, "Council Costs," *The Montreal Mirror*, April 23-April 30, 1992, p. 9.

Herland, Karen, "Expanding to fill the space," *The Montreal Mirror*, December 26, 1991-January 9, 1992, p. 7.

Herland, Karen, "Make Work, Not Jobs," *The Montreal Mirror*, May 28-June 4, 1992, p. 7.

Herland, Karen, "MCM from ashes to auction block," *The McGill Daily*, November 1, 1990, p. 3

Herland, Karen, "Parting Politics," *The Montreal Mirror*, March 19-March 26, 1992, p. 8.

Herland, Karen, "The Real Thing," *The Montreal Mirror*, May 7-May 14, 1992 p. 9.

Herland, Karen, "Strange Staff," Scuttlebutt, *The Montreal Mirror*, December 5-December 12, 1991, p. 9.

Herland, Karen, "What Next," *The Montreal Mirror*, January 9-January 16, 1992, p. 6.

King, Mike, "Civic Party absorbs Municipal Party," *The Gazette*, July 15, 1992, p. A3.

Kumar, Nantha, "Diluted Policy," *The Montreal Mirror*,, April 16-April 23, 1992, p. 8.

Kumar, Nantha, "Naturally Domed," *The Montreal Mirror*, April 2-April 9, 1992, p. 7.

Kumar, Nantha, "New Cuts, *The Montreal Mirror*, April 30-May 7, 1992, p. 8.

Lamarche, Robert, "La Famille Slomo," *Voir*, March 21-27, 1991, p. 5

The Montreal Mirror, "No News is...Dangerous," December 26, 199-January 9, 1992, p. 19.

Peritz, Ingrid, "Flip-flop on the MCM," *The Gazette*, October 29, 1990, p. A1.

La Presse, "Marielle Séguin quitte le cabinet du maire Doré," November 28, 1990, A14.

La Presse, Rapport sur un sondage CROP, October 19, 1990 p. A6.

Private conversation, with Mi'chel Prescott upon his resignation from the MCM, October 2, 1992.

Roy, Jean-Hugues, "Les deux pieds sur terre," *Voir*, November 1-November 7, 1990.

Roy, Jean-Hugues and Brendan Weston, *Montréal: A Citizen's Guide to Politics*, Montréal; Black Rose Books Ltd, 1990. (Several articles including Hiltz, Weston, Wheeland).

Ruddick, Sarah, "The Montréal Citizen's Movement: The Realpolitik of the 1990s?" in *Fire in the Hearth: The Radical Politics of Place*, Davis, M. et al, eds. London; Verso, 1990 pp 287-316.

Scott, Sarah, "Has democracy worked in Jean Doré's City Hall?," *The Gazette*, October 20, 1990, p. B1.

Thompson, Elizabeth, "City set to lift ban on condo conversion, Doré says," *The Gazette*, September 24, 1992, p. A3.

Thompson, Elizabeth, "Doré faces a palace revolt tomorrow," *The Gazette*, September 19, 1992, p. B1.

Thompson, Elizabeth, "Doré pledge of reform soothes MCM caucus," *The Gazette*, September 21, 1992, p. A3.

Thompson, Elizabeth, "Perrault's attack drops a bomb on MCM," *The Gazette*, August 10, 1992, p. A3.

Ville de Montréal, *Annual Report 1991*, Secrétariat général, Service de la planification et de la concertation, Bureau des Communications, 2nd quarter, 1992.

Ville de Montréal, *Sommaire des Réalisations: Novembre 1986 à Décembre 1989*, Cabinet du Comité exécutif, January 1990.

Wallace, Catherine, "City consulting women on street safety,: *The Gazette*, July 15, 1992, p. A1.

1.3 TELLING LEFT FROM RIGHT

Parties on the Left

The two parties to the left of the MCM were both established just before the 1990 election. Both the Democratic Coalition and Ecology Montréal are direct products of dissatisfaction with the MCM's inability to hold on to its grass-roots principles. The parties share a commitment to the environment, and a philosophy that would see Montréal emerge as a city dedicated to its citizens, not necessarily as simply an economic cog in a corporate or multinational machine. Recognizing that their philosophies were similar, they chose not to run against each other in all but two ridings in the 1990 election.

As was previously discussed, the DCM was created by a handful of ex-MCM Councillors who broke away from the party specifically because they felt the MCM no longer fulfilled its original mandate. They split with the MCM during their 1986-1990 terms in Council, staying on as independent Councillors to act as watchdogs on the current administration. They also proposed several private bills, some of which were actually passed. Less than a year before the 1990 election, they officially announced the creation of the DCM, and began to organize in ridings around the city.

DCM members have consistently called the MCM on a number of government decisions, both large and small. The 1990 party program shows a clear understanding of the way the administration works (based on longstanding experience) and includes several concrete proposals for opening up City Hall. It provides plans for direct attacks on poverty, promises to develop low-cost housing, but most importantly, includes a commitment to decentralization: "We can no longer make administrative and political decisions that apply uniformly to all of Montréal…this is why we advocate a true decentralisation towards the neighbourhoods" reads the introduction to the DCM party program.[1] This tone echoes early material produced by the MCM.

The DCM has done very well in the west of the city. Not only were two of its three incumbents re-elected there in 1990, the party gained a fourth seat there in a 1991 by-election. That vote was particularly telling. All municipal parties kicked into election gear, following Michael Fainstat's decision to retire from active politics after four and a half elected terms with the MCM. The ballot for this by-election sent a clear message to the MCM. Two of the candidates had been members of the MCM and a third worked for them in the corporation that organized the city's 1992 party. The only candidates that had never worked with the party before were those presented by EM and the MCM itself.

The DCM's candidate, Claudette Demers-Godley, won the seat far ahead of the pack, with over 40% of votes cast.[2] The victory was doubly important because it broke the longstanding MCM stronghold in that riding. It also gave the DCM official opposition status (given to the party with the second highest number of Councillors), at least briefly, until party-jumping to the right-wing gave the CPM more Councillors.

Unfortunately, the by-election pre-empted wrangling over internal structures that had been going on in the party after its hasty constitution before the 1990 election. Decisions around party voting, particularly how to properly represent the constituents of Councillors who relied heavily on creating local chapters as opposed to those who chose to devote their efforts to issues, not internal organizing, were never properly resolved in a string of meetings from late 1991 through the summer of 1992.[3] The debate was viewed by the media as a split between anglophone and francophone interests, although electoral politics were more clearly to blame. By June 1992, both Demers-Godley and Pierre Goyer, the one DCM Councillor not elected in the west end, had decided to leave the party and retain their seats as independent Councillors.[4] Attempts to establish yet another party out of the ashes never took hold. Thus the DCM chose not to field a candidate in the 1992 by-election in the St-Jacques district. This leaves them with two anglophone representatives, a public face that will have to change if the party is to emerge as a valid left-wing alternative.

DCM
P.O. Box
Succ. Youville
Montréal, QC
H2P 2V5
481-6427

Ecology Montréal is not necessarily the one-issue party its name would imply. The concept of a locally-based, municipal green party originated with Dimitri Roussopoulos. He, like the founders of the DCM, had been an MCM member and his dissatisfaction with the party drove him to organize with others and form EM in 1989. After discussions around whether to form a party, or a movement of community-based groups similar to FRAP's original structure, EM eventually fielded 21 candidates in the 1990 election. A commitment to gender equality dictated that 10 women and 11 men ran and the party is currently co-chaired by Bernard Bourbonnais and Lucie Dufresne. Members also chose not to present a mayoral candidate.

Although EM did well in parts of Plateau Mont-Royal, its overall results were weak, with rarely over 10% of votes in any district.

EM's base remains in the Plateau, but local associations exist in NDG, Centre-Sud and elsewhere. It has participated in both by-elections since 1990. EM has worked towards coalition-building with groups with similar interests in cities and elsewhere. Members have also been active locally in organizations like Action Rébuts and consultations around waste management issues.

By the fall of 1992, EM had formalized its constitution and program. Besides a commitment to environmentally-sound cities, the program considers decentralization and the organization of neighbourhood councils, a more human scale of development with community and cultural resources as integral to a thriving populace. Recognizing that local government is political in terms of the direction it provides in all aspects of planning and policy-making, it has made tools for greater citizen control of the entire parliamentary system part of its platform. Direct access through population-mandated referenda, mechanisms to call for the resignation of Councillors and a two-term maximum for municipal office-holders have been worked into its program. The EM also defines its role on the municipal front as educational, and seeks to raise issues at the municipal level, taking its cue from the green saying, "think globally, act locally." Bourbonnais chose to run for the EM in the 1992 by-election, and came in a respectable third, immediately behind the MCM candidate.

Ecology Montréal
P.O. Box 235
Succ. Place du Parc
Montréal, QC
H2W 2M9
281-VERT (8378) Fax: 271-3655.

Parties on the Right

The Civic and Municipal Parties finally merged in 1992. They had remained outwardly independent of each other until then, negotiating behind the scenes. The parties had always shared many of the same philosophies: cutting government spending, aiding business and development, a nostalgic respect for the way things were under Drapeau and a desire to put Montréal on the international map were common concerns, in keeping with ideals espoused by the right of the political spectrum. In its 1990 program, the MPM proclaimed that *"Montréal doit devenir la plaque tournante des échanges nord-sud"* on a continental scale.[5]

Unlike their left-leaning counterparts, the MPM and CPM were committed enough to both their vision of the city and the spirit of free-market competition to run full slates in 1990. The result, particularly in the north and east of the city, was that they split the vote and allowed the MCM to retain its seats.

The CPM gained more of the popular vote, but won only one seat in 1990. Although it had a recognizable name, it chose to run on its past achievements. On the one hand, because little of the old guard remained, and on the other, since little trust was left for what the party had represented, it proved a counter-productive strategy.

The MPM ran a more media-influenced campaign. Many of its chosen candidates were local "stars" hoping to win on charisma. In keeping with its stated principles, its style verged on the paternalistic, with mayoral candidate Alain André promising to "spoil" Montréalers.[6]

By early 1991, negotiations had begun for the two parties to merge. Differences over leadership kept slowing the process. By the fall of 1991, Municipal Party Councillor Nick Auf der Maur leapt to the CPM hours before the merger was finally to be made official, effectively blocking it. Pierre Gagnier, also elected as a MPM Councillor in 1990, followed Auf der Maur in January 1992. MCM Councillor Michel Benoit joined the two in March. Add these three to the one Councillor elected with the CPM in 1990, and the party had four seats and status as the official opposition. All this left the MPM with André as their lone Councillor.[7] Yet all was forgiven when the two parties finally merged in July 1992, and André became the fifth CPM Councillor.

Councillor-leaping has thus redefined the face of municipal politics. Voters roundly rejected the CPM after Drapeau's resignation in the 1986 elections, and continued to vote against its excesses, electing only one Councillor from the party in 1990. Elected Councillors have managed to redefine the balance of power by turning to the CPM during their terms and creating an opposition that was never elected as such. Current dissatisfaction with the MCM has left voters seeking alternatives and the clear majority for the CPM in the 1992 by-election is an indication of this. Sammy Forcillo became the sixth CPM Councillor when he regained the seat he had lost to Raymond Blain in the MCM's sweep of 1986.

CPM
3341 Jean-Talon East,
Montréal, QC
H2A 1W6
723-1000

NOTES

1. *Political Program of the Democratic Coalition of Montréal*, September 1990, Working papers.
2. Kumar, Nantha, "Opposition Official," *The Montreal Mirror*, November 7-November 14, 1991, p. 10.
3. Boskey, Sam, private conversation, July 3, 1992.
4. Adolph, Carolyn, "2 Councillors exit Democratic Coalition, say party too rigid, too anglo," *The Gazette*, June 21, 1992, p. A2.
5. Parti Municipal de Montréal, *Program Politique*, 26 août, 1990.
6. Favreau, Mariane, "Gater les Montréalais," *La Presse*, November 2, 1990, p. A11.
7. Herland, Karen, "Parting Politics," *The Montreal Mirror*, March 19-March 26, 1992, p. 8.

REFERENCES

Adolph, Carolyn, "2 Councillors exit Democratic Coalition, say party too rigid, too anglo,"
The Gazette, June 21, 1992, p. A2.
Block, Irwin, "Campaign '90 has been short on promises," *The Gazette*, November 3, 1990, p. A8.
Boskey, Sam, private conversation, July 3, 1992.
Favreau, Mariane, "Gater les Montréalais," *La Presse*, November 2, 1990, p. A11.
Harris, Lewis, "I'll act first and talk later, Civic Party mayoral candidate says," *The Gazette*, September 17, 1990, p. A3.
Harris, Lewis, "Municipal Party proposes tax deferments for elderly," *The Gazette*, August 27, 1990, p. A3.
Herland, Karen, "Parting Politics," *The Montreal Mirror*, March 19-March 26, 1992, p. 8.
Hickey, Kathleen, "Parties come and go but rhetoric is forever," *The McGill Daily*, November 1, 1990, p. 8.
Kumar, Nantha, "Opposition Official," *The Montreal Mirror*, November 7-November 14, 1991, p. 10.
The Montreal Mirror, "DemCo's Woes," August 6, August 13, 1992, p. 10
Pavelich, M.D. and Carl Wilson, "Marrying democracy and ecology," *The McGill Daily*, November 1, 1990, p. 5.
Parti Municipal de Montréal, *Program Politique*, August 26, 1990.
Platform of the Civic Party, election 1990.
Political Program of the Democratic Coalition of Montréal, September 1990, Working papers.
Program Principles of Ecology Montréal, election 1990.
Roslin, Alex, "Change is in the Air," *The Montreal Mirror*, July 23-July 30, 1992, p. 7.
Thompson, Elizabeth, "Civic Party chief spurns deadline for deciding on proposed merger," *The Gazette*, March 12, 1991, p. A3.
Thompson, Elizabeth, "Municipal, Civic parties reach agreement to merge," *The Gazette*, March 16, 1991, p. A3.
Thompson, Elizabeth, "Municipal Party members demand leader resign," *The Gazette*, May 14, 1991, p. E8.

Section II

Inside City Hall: Political and Bureaucratic Structure

Political and Administrative Structure

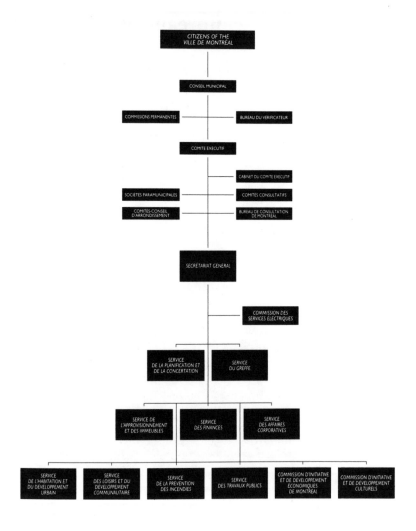

CITIZENS OF THE
VILLE DE MONTRÉAL

CONSEIL MUNICIPAL

COMMISSIONS PERMANENTES

BUREAU DU VERIFICATEUR

COMITE EXECUTIF

CABINET DU COMITE EXECUTIF

SOCIÉTÉS PARAMUNICIPALES

COMITES CONSULTATIFS

COMITES-CONSEIL
D'ARRONDISSEMENT

BUREAU DE CONSULTATION
DE MONTRÉAL

SECRÉTARIAT GÉNÉRAL

COMMISSION DES
SERVICES ÉLECTRIQUES

SERVICE
DE LA PLANIFICATION ET
DE LA CONCERTATION

SERVICE
DU GREFFE

SERVICE DE
L'APPROVISIONNEMENT
ET DES IMMEUBLES

SERVICE
DES FINANCES

SERVICE
DES AFFAIRES
CORPORATIVES

SERVICE
DE L'HABITATION ET
DU DÉVELOPPEMENT
URBAIN

SERVICE
DES LOISIRS ET DU
DÉVELOPPEMENT
COMMUNAUTAIRE

SERVICE
DE LA PRÉVENTION
DES INCENDIES

SERVICE
DES TRAVAUX PUBLICS

COMMISSION D'INITIATIVE
ET DE DÉVELOPPEMENT
ÉCONOMIQUES
DE MONTRÉAL

COMMISSION D'INITIATIVE
ET DE DÉVELOPPEMENT
CULTURELS

From Ville de Montréal, Annual Report 1991, Secrétariat Général, Service de la planification et de la concertation, Bureau des communications, 2nd quarter 1992, p. 31.

2.1 THE EXECUTIVE COMMITTEE AND EVERYONE ELSE

Responsibilities

Montréal's powers are determined by the Québec government and the city charter is in fact a provincial law. The province has passed several laws (each one book-length) that detail the management of municipalities. The powers and regulations governing small villages are determined by one, another governs cities and towns, and another sets municipal fiscal policy. Each of these laws has hundreds of amendments that refer to Québec's 300 municipalities. Because of their size and scope, Montréal and Québec City have their own specific charters. Every time any city government decides to amend, extend or reinterpret its powers, it has to get provincial approval. Politicians must make an annual pilgrimage to Québec City to revise Montréal's Charter. Usually it's a fairly uncontested process to clarify questions of interpretation. The city also brings the specific wording of newly enacted by-laws that further detail already existing powers, such as changes in zoning regulations, for example.

Most of this legislation goes through Québec's Ministry of Municipal Affairs. In the last few years, the Ministry has taken it upon itself to update and consolidate management of municipalities. The law on fiscal policy is relatively new, and supercedes Montréal's Charter. The same applies for a new law governing management of municipal elections and referenda. According to Montréal's City Clerk, Léon Laberge, the province is currently upgrading the law on cities and towns, and the new version, expected by the end of the decade, will in fact include Montréal and Québec City, rendering their separate charters unnecessary. The province is also considering extending its powers beyond mere municipal management to include guidelines for environmental management and cultural development at the municipal level.

Many groups protesting business tax hikes in the city's 1992 budget were frustrated to discover that, unlike smaller municipalities governed by the general cities and towns law, Montréal's Charter does not allow city-wide referenda to be held on issues concerning zoning or loans. City politicians would need to get provincial approval to institute such powers. The city seems unlikely to do that in the near future. In fact, any issue can be brought to Council for a referendum as long as a petition with 500 signatures is presented. However, Council can still refuse to honour the demand for a referendum, forcing the challenge to go to the court system, a far more costly situation.

What follows is a list of the current powers of the city. Some of these spheres of responsibility are not the exclusive jurisdiction of the city, but can be shared with private concerns, other municipalities or the provincial and federal governments. The next chapter provides a more detailed description of the civil service that manages these responsibilities.

Finances: budget, property evaluation, city finances (loans, etc.) and taxes (imposition, collection).

Administrative: Acquisition of property, archives, city offices, municipal court, Committees, contracts, intermunicipal relations, expropriations, referenda, socio-economic data.

Public Hygiene: Water supply, sewage system, collection and disposal of waste, waterworks, public markets, public nuisances (this is a fairly broad category. The city has defined this to include things like distribution of circulars or smoking in public spaces; it could potentially be used to control traffic in congested areas), housing conditions.

Recreation and Culture: Libraries, museums, exhibits, fairs, parks, playing fields.

Territory: Annexations, reorganization.

Public Security: fire prevention, emergency measures, animal surveillance.

Health and Safety: Administration of provincial welfare, public health campaigns, daycare.

Transportation: Traffic and parking, snow removal, roads and public spaces.

Urban Planning: Cultural properties, construction, demolition, lighting, industrial and commercial development, zoning, beautification programs.

Mayor

The Mayor is elected on a separate ballot during municipal elections. This is the only office that can claim to represent the entire city and not just a single electoral district. This system was critiqued with the emergence of party politics at the municipal level; theoretically, a Mayor elected from one party could head a government made up of a majority of Councillors representing another. This has never happened, and the psychological advantage of total voter support has discouraged Mayors from changing the system.

Through the charter, the Mayor is an equal member of the Executive Committee and any other Committee (standing or ad hoc) of Council, as well as of the MUC Council. The next section deals more completely with the relationship between Montréal and the MUC.

The Mayor can call a Council meeting at any time and set its agenda. In cases of emergency, the Mayor can approve spending public funds, and get Council approval after the fact. The Mayor can control the full range of municipal activities. The Mayor can question any decision, fire any city employee, enforce any regulation or call for an investigation. The Mayor has no direct veto power, but any contract, decision, regulation or report must be signed by the Mayor within four work days after approval by Council. Technically, if the Mayor refuses to sign, the refusal along with a written explanation is then returned to Council to reopen debate. The refusal is essentially an invitation to reconsider. If Council maintains its decision after a second evaluation, it goes into effect with or without the Mayor's approval. Since Mayor Doré is a member of the MCM which, as of 1992, holds all positions on the Executive Committee and the vast majority of seats on the five Standing Committees and nearly four out of five seats in Council, veto powers have never been used.

The Mayor's current salary is about $103,000. This is based on a $60,000 base plus extra for work on various Committees (including the MUC Council), expenses and so on. Every three months, the Mayor selects a different Councillor to act as deputy Mayor. Usually this Councillor acts as the Mayor's proxy at ribbon-cutting ceremonies or other official functions that require a Mayoral presence. The deputy Mayor is paid an extra $1,000 per month for this role.

Executive Committee

The Executive Committee is comprised of the Mayor and six other Councillors, named by the Mayor and approved by Council, usually within a week after an election. This body elects a Chair and Vice-Chair from among themselves.

The Executive Committee holds weekly, closed meetings. Other Councillors are not allowed to attend. Quorum is four and the Chair's vote is used as a tiebreaker. Decisions are made public the next day.

Its members retain their regular positions as Councillors and/or on other Committees of the city or the MUC. Each member is responsible for specific issues, which generally means they sit on related Standing Committees and act as spokespeople during Council meetings. To find out which Councillors sit on the Executive Committee, refer to Appendix A.

The Executive Committee ultimately determines how issues are presented to Council. In practice, nearly every motion presented to Council is prepared by the Executive Committee. Reading through Council minutes shows motion after motion presented by the Chair of the Executive Committee and seconded by the Vice-Chair. This makes the scope of the Committee's power all too clear.

The Executive Committee has the power to approve any contract worth up to $100,000. For larger contracts, it accepts tenders and decides which one is best, presenting only that option to Council for official approval. It can skip Council approval in cases where the contract will mean spending less money than was budgeted. The $100,000 ceiling represents a 200% increase over Executive Committee powers over the beginning of the MCM mandate. According to Committee Chair Léa Cousineau, the provincial government suggested the latest increase. While contracts to be approved by Councillors are made readily available to them, Councillors have to do their own digging to find out what contracts have been approved by the Executive Committee, this based on the minutes of meetings that are released weeks after decisions were taken. The Executive Committee also reviews all financial arrangements involving the city or city property, such as the purchase, sale and rental of space, loans, franchises, contracts and payments due from the city. It has the power to sell city property worth less than $10,000.

The city charter gives the Executive Committee the power to reallocate public space, name public sites, suspend permits if zoning is under review, and handle similar requests on behalf of the directors of municipal services.

All reports from public consultations, DAC meetings, Standing Committees and city departments are submitted directly to the Executive Committee. Usually, the committee has 60 days to respond to the document. The charter defines which issues require Council approval, but since the Executive Committee sets the agenda for Council meetings, how issues are presented remains at its discretion. In practice, this means that if a Standing Committee reports on an issue of public concern, with recommendations for new or revised legislation, the Executive Committee can define the wording of the legislation that is presented to Council.

The Executive Committee is also responsible for determining the city's financial priorities by overseeing and presenting the annual budget for operations as well as the triennial capital-works plan. Although property value assessments are determined every three years by the MUC, using formulas determined by the province, it is the Executive Committee, through the budget, that determines the level of taxation. It is also ultimately responsible for reporting on the collection of taxes.

Council

According to Montréal's charter, the powers of City Council rest entirely within the forum of Council meetings. Council is made up of the 50 elected Councillors, and the Mayor. The meetings are chaired by an elected non-voting member of Council. During Jean Drapeau's term, he held this position himself.

Council meets on the first Monday of every month, with a break over the summer. Since agendas tend to be long, meetings are often continued over the next few afternoons and evenings. The Charter outlines the types of decisions that require Council approval: adoption of the municipal budget, adoption of by-laws (to be enforced through municipal court) or resolutions (policies, positions, decisions meant to reflect Council's priorities), approval of Executive Committee reports, and approval of contracts and spending that exceed the Executive Committee's decision-making powers.

Since Council runs on a system of parliamentary democracy, all of these issues are screened and presented by the Executive Committee. That party strongly discourages public disagreement and the party line is handed down in caucus meetings of MCM Councillors held just before Council meetings — so the MCM almost always votes *en bloc.* The presumption that the MCM will vote for the Executive Committee is so strong that often only opposition members are asked to register their votes in Council.

Exceptions to this rule are always noteworthy, and often funny. In September 1991, MCM Councillor Vittorio Capparelli voted against the city's inch thick three-year capital works budget, representing some $586.3 million in spending. He rejected the budget saying that not enough discussion had been devoted to it, although he did admit that this budget generally receives very little debate. "Usually the opposition demands more discussion so we can modify the budget with civil servants before approving it," he said at the time.[1]

The MCM majority is such that even with opposing votes from the entire opposition, and seven MCM Councillors either voting against the budget or refusing to vote at all, the vote still passed. This absolute control of Council is not uncommon as a "democratic" form of government. Yet Capparelli is not the only one who became concerned with the amount of power the MCM held in the hands of the Executive Committee and bureaucratic elite. Mayor Doré was forced to answer to a dozen of his own Councillors in the summer of 1992 when they charged that even as elected MCM Councillors, they felt excluded by the decision-making process. Doré promised that changes would be in evidence by the end of 1992.

Under the current government, Councillors saw the bulk of the agenda (particularly motions involving municipal contracts or tenders) just before the meetings, so that any kind of research into other options or the background of the firms in question was impossible. The Charter states that agendas must be made available at least two working days in advance. Often only public reports to be approved or general motions were handed out ahead of time. Only this year was enough information made available to Councillors the Monday before Council meetings so that they could review it. Even so, the provincial regulations fall short in terms of the sheer volume of material to be examined before meetings.

Opposition Councillors can submit their own agenda items — similar to private members" bills in a parliamentary system — as a way to introduce different issues into Council meetings. However, they only have the power to present resolutions, which must then be endorsed by an Executive Committee approved by-law to become enforceable. The DCM frequently takes advantage of this privilege. However, opposition members claim that unless the bills are uncontroversial resolutions (a commitment to use more recycled paper in City Hall, for instance), or involve little or no expenditures, they are usually voted down by the MCM majority.

Opposition members are perhaps most vocal during the hour they can question each other early in every Council meeting. They use this forum often, to challenge the Mayor or Executive Committee members on issues raised by the media, or those revealed through their own investigations.

A public question period begins every Council meeting, prior to the Councillor's opportunity to question Council members. This initiative is often used by the MCM as an indication of their commitment to democracy, since the practice was introduced during their first term in office. What the MCM failed to acknowledge was that the provincial charter for cities and towns requires this of all municipalities it governs. It was either by oversight or expediency that this clause was left out of Montréal's original charter. This "innovation" only served to provide Montréalers with the same opportunity that residents of Pierrefonds and Verdun had enjoyed for years. Citizens must register their questions an hour in advance with the city clerk. A full hour is devoted to these questions during each meeting. Each person is allowed one supplemental question, and then must step down, whether or not they feel they have received an adequate response.

The meeting schedule is prepared at the beginning of each year, and is available through the city clerk's office. Usually a general announcement appears in major newspapers two weeks before each meeting. On the Saturday before a Monday night meeting, another ad appears outlining highlights of the agenda.

Councillors

Montréal City Councillors are elected every four years in electoral districts determined by the city. Their seat on Montréal's Council automatically makes them members of the MUC Council. The Councillors' only power is to vote at Council meetings. They are obliged to participate in every vote that they are present for. If they miss a Council meeting (i.e. don't appear for at least 10 minutes) they must forfeit $100 of their annual stipend. Councillors must declare all financial holdings annually and announce when a vote implies a potential conflict of interest.

Their annual stipend is based on a salary of $33,000/yr, one-third of which is non-taxable income. This includes $5,000 for sitting on the MUC Council. A whole series of extra payments can be added to reflect a Councillor's position on Standing Committees of the city or the MUC, or various other titles. These amounts range from another $45,000 for Chair of the Executive Committee to $1,000/month, for the deputy Mayor.

A code of ethics was established for all Councillors in July 1990. A Standing Committee on Ethics is made up of five non-Executive Committee members of Council, and is chaired by the City Council's Chair. This Committee can only meet when asked to because of a charge against a Councillor. It has never met.

Standing Committees

There are now five Standing Committees of Council (see below). Once established, the Committee sets its own agenda (pending Council approval), and must respond to requests for study from the Executive Committee. It can hold public consultations. Each Committee must hold at least four meetings per year, all of which are public and include a 20 minute question period.

Along with studying and reporting on specific subjects, as mandated, each Committee is required to be familiar with the operations and budgets of related city departments, and meets with these administrators on an annual basis.

The MCM-controlled Executive Committee only named two opposition Councillors to any of the Committees (Nick Auf der Maur on Planning and Housing, and Pasquale Compierchio on Environment and Public Works). Although both Councillors are now with the Civic Party, Auf der Maur represented the Municipal Party when he was given the seat. This is one example of how the MCM has expanded the power it holds as the ruling party. Although its control of the Executive Committee is standard practice in many governments, that control extending to what are essentially advisory bodies is unnecessary. After this decision, the DCM chose to boycott the Committees. Sam Boskey, who was a member of the old Cultural Development Committee, declared that the current structure, which denies any space for minority reports, is unworkable, "The whole purpose of (a Committee) is for ideas to be played out. All the accepted norms of parliamentary democracy are being ignored."[2] Since 1990, two other MCM Councillors sitting on Committees have left the party, while retaining their membership in the Committees. The death of Councillor Raymond Blain left another seat open.

The Committees themselves were created as part of the MCM's attempt to make Montréal more accessible to it's citizens. However, since their power is limited solely to making recommendations to the Executive Committee, they became a symbol for disillusionment amongst the remaining left-wing members of the MCM. The very month that the MCM came into power in 1986, a proposal to raze a residential block, Overdale, and replace it with luxury condos, was made. The tight-knit community reacted immediately to the threat and rallied the residents of the 107 households that would be effected into what amounted to the first grass-roots challenge that the MCM government faced. Using arguments like the historical significance of the dwellings on the block and the fact that it remained one of the few low-income enclaves in an increasingly gentrified downtown core, they quickly gained the support of heritage groups and housing activists. They also eventually won over the city's (then called) Housing and Urban Planning Committee, whose final report on the project suggested that the residents should be allowed to retain their homes. In 1987, the MCM government chose to ignore its Committees recommendation and gave the development the green light, anyway. Several party members were discouraged by the government's complete disregard for its own Committee. Many of the eventual members of the DCM cite this as the beginning of the end of their involvement with the MCM.

Below is a description of the Committees, their work, and the city departments and the paramunicipal corporations under their jurisdiction. Their responsibility is to review the budgets of these bodies and make recommendations. Detailed descriptions of the role of these bodies will appear in the next two chapters. A full schedule of forthcoming annual Committee meeting dates and subjects is prepared at the end of each year. This information is available through a special division of the clerk's office at 872-3770.

Administration and Quality of Services Committee
This Committee is mandated to oversee questions of financial and administrative management. For several years the Committee studied and reported on equal access employment programs for the city government. In 1987, the Administration and Finance Committee was charged with hiring more "minority" employees (defined as non-anglophone, non-francophone and non-Native people, for example Italians, Por-

tuguese, Vietnamese and Jamaicans would all be considered "cultural communities"). A program defined in 1989 still applies. It called for 25% targets for hiring, yet every year since then, the city could only claim 10% hiring from cultural communities, with a total representation of 1% of the city's bureaucracy staffed by members of visible minorities. The government claims that this reflects the lack of applicants for positions, while critics counter that the city has not been aggressive enough in meeting its goals.[3] By 1992, the Committee had recommended tougher guidelines to enforce the policy, including repositing jobs if fewer than one-quarter of the applicants are members of visible or ethnic minorities. This year, it will review the results of an "self-identification survey" that it handed out to all municipal employees in August of 1991, this in order to fully assess the cultural/ethnic composition of the city's administration.

The Committee has also reviewed amendments to the legislation governing DACs (see below), contractual obligations of firms that do business with the city, as well as various internal structures, including the means by which municipal taxes are collected and computerizing administration procedures.

Currently, the Committee is hoping to review and report on the quality of services available to Montréalers, starting with a general review of the bureaucracy. The Committee will also begin to study how well the district system has worked in terms of decentralizing front-line services within the districts. It will probably not be holding public meetings on these subjects until early 1993. This is five years after the districts were originally defined, with the primary goal of decentralizing city services.

Chair Jean Durivage/V-C Sylvie Lantier
City Budget
Auditor's report
Finance
Planning and Coordination
Secretary General
Supplies and Properties

Planning and Housing Committee
Generally responsible for regulations and policies regarding urban planning, housing and the use of city property. Since its inception, it has reported on issues like urban safety for women, the city's housing goals, urban beautification policies, and guidelines for roof antennae and mechanically ventilated office buildings.

Among its current files are policies on abandoned buildings, unoccupied space and heritage sites. It has also devoted time to reviewing the full-scale city-wide urban plan.

In 1992, the Committee released an update on the 27-year-old housing code. Although rental disagreements are within the provincial jurisdiction of the Régie du logement, standards for building repair and maintenance are monitored by the city's 17 inspectors and regulated through municipal court. One major change in the code was to increase first fines levied against irresponsible landlords from $300 to $1,000. Housing activists complained that either way, that was only a ceiling, and in reality fines were usually very low. They counter that landlords intent on speculation will usually allow a building to fall slowly into disrepair, paying minimal fines whenever inspectors catch up. Eventually they can apply to the city for a huge grant to subsidize half of the necessary renovations, gentrifying the building in the process, or sell the building to another landlord — who will do the same thing. The code also allows each new landlord to start with a clean slate — by changing a property's ownership, previous charges are dropped and the new landlord is given a new deadline to do necessary repairs, while tenants suffer. These loopholes in the new code disappointed housing-rights advocates: "our main concern is to create a code that favours the constant maintenance of buildings," said Pierre Marquis, director of the Comité logement de St-Louis.[4]

Chair Pierre Lachapelle/V-C Nick Auf der Maur
Corporation des habitations Jeanne-Mance (CHJM)
Office Municipal d'habitation de Montréal (OMHM)
Service de l'habitation et du développement urbain (SHDU)
Société d'habitation et de développement de Montréal (SHDM)
Société des terrains Angus (SOTAN)
Société immobilière du patrimoine architectural de Montréal (SIMPA)

Environment and Public Works Committee
Generally concerned with environmental issues involving city methods and planning. The Committee was involved in creating the city's policy on reducing the use of CFCs. It has also worked on areas as diverse as streamlining inspection procedures and controlling dogs in public spaces. The Committee studied safety issues involving the Des Carrières incinerator, and recommended that the incinerator continue to function, with some structural improvements to better clean-up emissions.

The Committee has also studied two different reports produced by the city in 1990 and 1991, reviewing the administration's environmental track record for each year. Both reports are filled with pages of anything and everything that might be considered "environmental," including participation in public relations events, studies on snow removal, initiatives for reducing and recycling in particular government offices and references to participation in other projects initiated through the MUC or the province.

Recognizing the uneven tone of the reports, the Committee has recommended that future reports provide more concrete information, and that an inter-departmental Committee on environmental issues within the city government be re-established. It is currently examining a long-overdue policy on a municipal commitment to environmental purchasing. This would cover everything from recycled paper (which the Committee itself doesn't use) to using non-toxic pesticides on public green space. Most other area municipalities already do so and the city's own blue collar worker's environmental committee has been urging it to do the same for years. [6] The Committee will also be exploring ways for the city to reduce energy consumption.

Chair Konstatinos Georgoulis/V-C Diane Barbeau
Electrical Services
Public Works

Economic Development Committee

This Committee studies the city's role in economic development. It's priorities are defined as job creation and fighting poverty. One of its early areas of study was the city's large fashion industry. It has also explored the local impact of federal and provincial spending, tourism and the free-trade deal. It helped to formulate the original plans and directions of the network of Corporations de développement économique communautaires (CDECs) in the city.

Its general concern with development has given it divided priorities, on the one hand exploring issues like racism and education as they effect employment, and on the other, encouraging heavy industry and studying research in biotechnology as a potential local frontier. One of its current priorities is the encouragement of "green" industries in Montréal. With this in mind, it is monitoring the progress of the current public consultation on solid waste disposal.

Yet, over the course of the consultation, at least one glass recycling plant in greater Montréal had to close down, and in the spring of 1992, it was revealed that a company commissioned by a suburban municipality to collect recyclables was actually dumping it, unsorted, in a local landfill. Ecology Montréal spokesperson Dimitri Roussopoulos stated that concentration on private industry and market fluctuations to handle the potential gold mine involved in sorting and recycling garbage is the wrong way to go. "There are huge profits to be made privately in management and recycling of waste." He suggests that the city government should take on the task itself, providing jobs and plants, using Montréal as its own market. In Salzberg, Austria, the city collects organic waste which it uses as compost in public parks. A city could also produce the paper pulp it needed through de-inking and paper recycling plants.[7]

Chair Abe Limonchik/V-C André Cardinal
Commission d'initiative et de développement économiques de Montréal
(CIDEM)
Société de développement industriel de Montréal (SODIM)

Culture and Community Development Committee
Its very large mandate includes art, culture, recreation, social development and public safety. The Committee has been involved in public consultations around services like fire prevention, the network of Maisons de la culture (municipally run community art/culture galleries), public libraries, community development and the role of youth in Montréal society. It has also reported on Commission d'initiative et de développement culturels (CIDEC) initiatives including the report they submitted on support for cultural industries and other initiatives like the Biodome.

It was responsible for public consultations on the legislation of signs for "erotic establishments." This law was eventually struck down in Québec Superior Court.

Recently, the Committee helped to prepare legislation governing artists selling their wares on public streets. Currently, they are preparing final reports on many of the issues raised above.

Chair Martine Blanc/V-C open
Association montréalaise d'action récréative et culturelle (AMARC)
Commission d'initiative et de développement culturels (CIDEC)
Fire Prevention Department
Recreation and Community Development Service
Société du palais de la civilisation (SOPAC)

Consultative Committees

Besides the regular Standing Committees of Council, occasionally special Committees are created to examine key issues, usually ones that need one-time study. Currently one has been established to study the city's master urban plan.

Their track records vis-à-vis administration promises are not much better than those of the Standing Committees. Like the Standing Committees, they can only make recommendations to the Executive Committee. Both the policies around apartheid and making Montréal a nuclear-free zone emerged from this type of Committee, and both were watered down or ignored months after they were enacted.

District Advisory Councils

The city institutionalized more local participation with District Advisory Councils (DACs — often referred to by their French name; Comité-conseil d'arrondissement, CCA). In the mid-seventies, while the MCM was just starting out, neighbourhood Councils were an important element in their program, envisaged as a way to decentralize city government. The idea was to create local Councils to deal with specific political and economic concerns from a grassroots perspective. The concept was described in the 1976 party program as "never another government within the capitalist society [but] rather...an alternative to the present state at all levels...[one which] must never be imposed from above by legislative act or party dictate."[8]

Once defined as a tool for grassroots democracy and struggle, today's DACs reflect little of the original concept. By the time the MCM wrote their 1986 party program, neighbourhood city offices were described as a way to "decentralize those municipal services which most closely affect everyday living to ten neighbourhoods...directed by a decision-making neighbourhood Council...[they] will provide decentralized...city services," or, simply, another level of government. Nine such DACs were established in 1987 after the MCM came into power; though with the much more formal title District (not neighbourhood) Advisory (not decision-making) Council. The city defined the districts without consultation, sometimes dividing the jurisdictions of particular community centres. The areas covered were also much larger than those suggested as tools for grassroots participation, representing up to 150,000 people.

In the by-law establishing DACs, their role is defined as, *"un lieu de consultation plus proche de la population,"* and all pretence of decision-making and direction from below instead of above is dropped altogether. Recently, the MCM has announced that the DAC's role would be expanded and Councillors would have more say. An earlier attempt to do this in 1991 simply led to more civil servants. There is no reason, given the careful wording of current definitions of DAC jurisdictions, that expanded powers will lead to any political decision-making.

Each DAC, with the exception of downtown's Ville-Marie, represents 4 to 7 electoral ridings and those city Councillors are also DAC Councillors. Because Ville-Marie's territory has only two Councillors, extra members are elected by Council upon recommendation of the Executive Committee. Each DAC elects its own Chair and Vice-Chair.

The initial premise was that this level of consultation could screen local issues and iron them out before they were presented to the Executive Committee and Council as a whole (i.e. based on local concerns, they would deal with minor zoning changes, parking problems, use of public buildings, demolitions etc.), but final decisions would still be made at other levels with the DAC's playing only an advisory role. As Jean Panet-Raymond wrote in *Montréal: A Citizen's Guide to Politics*: "their agenda is still set by the Executive Committee, and the only occasion for the population to show any initiative is during question period. The DAC's composition is limited to local Councillors. They are thus simply conveyor belts of administrative priorities."[9] In the MCM's 1990 party programme, the DAC's role is described as developing "socio-cultural" activities and "promoting quality of life." In 1990, the DAC's powers were expanded to include approval of a new coat of paint for public facilities.

DACs have become a place where local and individual concerns can be raised, but are then easily lost in the subsequent paper-shuffle. Opposition Councillor Sam Boskey said, "DACs aren't trusted with establishing priorities. They just handle individual requests as they come in, so the squeaky wheel gets the most."[10]

All meetings must take place within the district and must be advertised in local and city newspapers at least four days in advance. All pertinent documentation must be made available at local Access-Montréal offices.

Each meeting has a period for questions from the public, requests (briefs) from the public and requests from member-Councillors. Citizens can register for the question period on the night of a meeting. Those wishing to make a request must sign up at their local Access-Montréal office the Friday before a meeting, stating the nature of their request. Councillors can respond immediately (if it is within their jurisdiction) or send the matter off to the appropriate city department (if the DAC has the power to agree but not to do whatever is being asked) or to the Executive Committee (if the DAC does not have decision-making power on the matter in question.) They can also refuse outright. The DAC must write a report to the Executive Committee within five days; the Executive Committee has 60 days to respond.

The Executive members and phone numbers for each DAC are listed here. For more information on their population and territory, refer to the district profiles.

Ahuntsic/Cartierville DAC I Chair Gérard Legault/V-C Michel Benoît (6742).
Villeray/Saint-Michel/Park Extension DAC II Chair André Berthelet/ V-C Micheline Daigle (6375)
Rosemont/Petite-Patrie DAC III Chair Diane Martin/V-C Réal Charest (6375)

Mercier/Hochelaga-Maisonneuve DAC IV Chair Diane Barbeau/V-C Nicole Milhomme (6716)

Plateau Mont-Royal/Centre-Sud DAC V Chair Manon Forget/V-C Serge Lajeunesse (6752)

Centre DAC VI Chair Hubert Simard/V-C open (6395).

Côte-des-Neiges/Notre-Dame-de-Grace DAC VII Chair Abe Limonchik/V-C Sharon Leslie (6732)

Sud-Ouest DAC VIII Chair Jean Durivage/V-C Marcel Sévigny (6519)

Rivière-des-Prairies/Pointe-aux-Trembles DAC IX Chair Giovanni De Michele/V-C Ghislaine Boisvert (6618)

Access-Montréal Offices

One of the first major changes introduced by the current government was the creation of Access-Montréal offices (known by their French acronym, BAM). A network of 13 such offices were scattered across the city with the stated intention of acting as "des 'guichets uniques' qui contribuent à la fois à activer la déconcentration des services municipaux et à simplifier les démarches des citoyens et des citoyennes."[11]

In particular, Access-Montréal offices were designed as a way to make city departments that deal directly with the public (like housing or public works) regionally accessible. Citizens are encouraged to stop by for information on taxation, evaluations, fines, infractions, and licenses, and to use the service as a one-stop access point to the municipal administration. Citizens are urged in various ways to consult their local BAM to find a variety of documents, from city reports on sale to the general public and documents relating to current consultations, to information about and for local DAC meetings. Incidentally, availability of English documents is somewhat limited. The city is required to publish all by-laws, minutes and official documents in both French and English. This does not necessarily apply to reports and general information. For instance, the 10-volume urban plan the City released in 1992 was entirely in French, except for the background document and the report on Notre-Dame-de-Grace/Côte-des-Neiges. Even if a report has been printed in English, if you live in a French-speaking neighbourhood, supply may be limited.

Residents may have had trouble reaching City Hall before the introduction of this new level of administration, but the current situation seems to mystify as much as it clarifies. BAMs are not always up-to-date on current debates. They receive material long after it has been deposited in city archives. Because BAMs are supposed to be the only access point, citizens are rarely told that documents will appear in the city archives or at the downtown city library at 1210 Sherbrooke East

(5923) long before they get to BAMs. It is crucial to call in advance as the availability of material is often not properly coordinated. It would be ideal to be able to visit a neighbourhood centre for this type of information, but the system is far from efficient

Calling ahead is an exercise in itself, as phones remain busy for hours at a time. In 1991 alone, the phone lines handled 552 993 calls, up nearly 200 000 from the previous year. Even when you get through, you may be told a document is "technically" available, only to discover that it hasn't actually arrived once you make the trip. Worse, if you call with an unusual question like the average salary of a city Councillor, or what the role of a specific department is, you're more than likely to end up with no information at all, or instructions for what turns out to be a lengthy game of telephone tag, being passed from office to office.

Perhaps the main problem with the system is that it is very much geared to what the city wants you to know. If your request fits in with the city's idea of what citizen participation should be, it will be handled efficiently, if not, Access-Montréal can be as frustrating as any other level of government.

Villeray: 7217 Saint-Denis, 6381/82
Rosemont: 3304 Rosemont, 6386/87
Mercier: 6070 Sherbrooke, 6716/25
Centre: 275 Notre-Dame East, 6395/96
Notre-Dame-de-Grâce: 5814 Sherbrooke West, 6731/32
Pointe-aux-Trembles: 13068 Sherbrooke East, 6618/6703
Côte-des-Neiges: 5885 ch. de la Côte-des-Neiges, 6403/32
Hochelaga-Maisonneuve: 4295 Ontario East, 6391/93
Saint-Michel: 7960, boul. Saint-Michel, 6375/76.
Plateau Mont-Royal: 1374, Mont-Royal East, 6752/53
Rivière-des-Prairies: 8910 Maurice-Duplessis, 6755/57
Ahuntsic: 545 Fleury East, 6742/44
Sud-Ouest: 3177 St-Jacques West, 6458/6519

NOTES

1. Herland, Karen, "Breaking Rank," *The Montreal Mirror,* September 26-October 3, 1991, p. 9.
2. Boskey, Sam, city Councillor, Democratic Coalition, private conversations 1990-9
3. Herland, Karen, "Hiring Targets are Shot Down," *The Montreal Mirror,* December 12-December 19, 1991, p.
4. Herland, Karen, "House Bound," *The Montreal Mirror,* March 12-March 9, 1992, p.
5. Lamarche, Robert, "La Famille Slomo," *Voir,* March 21-27, 1991, p. 5.
6. Krakow, Eve, "The Killing Fields," *The Montreal Mirror,* April 23-April 30, 1992, p.

7. Herland, Karen, "Dumping Responsibility," *The Montreal Mirror,*, April 9-April 16, 1992, p. 6.
8. Raboy, Marc, "The Future of Montréal and the MCM," in *The City and Radical Social Change*, D. Roussopoulos, ed., Black Rose Books, Montréal, 1982.
9. Roy, Jean-Hugues and Brendan Weston, eds., *Montréal: A Citizen's Guide to politics*, Black Rose Books Ltd., Montréal, 1990.
10. Herland, Karen, "Lost in the Paper Shuffle," *The Montreal Mirror,* Nov. 21-28, 1991, p. 7.
11. Montréal Citizen's Movement, *La Ville que nous voulons*, Party Program, 1990.

REFERENCES

Baccigalupo, Alain avec Luc Rhéaume, *Les Administration municipales québécoises des origines à nos jours, Tome I Les Municipalités*, Editions ARC, Ottawa, 1984.
Boskey, Sam, City Councillor, Democratic Coalition, private conversations 1990-92.
Bourrassa, Guy and Jacques Léveillée eds.,*Système Politique de Montréal*, L'Association Canadienne-Française pour l'avancement des sciences, L'ACFAS, #43, 1986.
Brown, Eleanor, "Meetings Still Secret," *The Montreal Mirror,* April 18-April 25, 1991, p. 9.
By-law 7261, *By-law respecting the Standing Committees of the Conseil de la Ville*, 01/26/87.
By-law 7988, *Amendment to the By-law respecting the District Advisory Councils,*1/23/91.
By-law 8079, *By-law on the remuneration of members of Council,*, and amendment, By-law 8349, Ville de Montréal, 03/30/89.
By-law 8640, *By-law respecting the Standing Committee on Ethics for the members of the Council*, 09/19/90.
Herland, Karen, "Breaking Rank," *The Montreal Mirror,*, September 26-October 3, 1991, p. 9.
Herland, Karen, "Dumping Responsibility," *The Montreal Mirror,*, April 9-April 16, 1992, p. 6.
Herland, Karen, "Green Report has Gray Areas," *The Montreal Mirror,* November 28-December 5, 1991, p. 10.
Herland, Karen, "Hiring Targets are Shot Down," *The Montreal Mirror,* December 12-December 19, 1991, p. 8.
Herland, Karen, "House Bound," *The Montreal Mirror,* March 12-March 9, 1992, p. 8.
Herland, Karen, "Lost in the Paper Shuffle," *The Montreal Mirror,* Nov. 21-28, 1991, p. 7.
Kemp, Johanne, Chef de Division commissions et comités du conseil, private conversation, 1990.
Krakow, Eve, "The Killing Fields," *The Montreal Mirror,* April 23-April 30, 1992, p. 7.
Kumar, Nantha, "Diluted Policy," *The Mirror,* April 16-April 23, 1992, p. 8.
Laberge, Léon, City Clerk, private conversation, 1990.
Lamarche, Robert, "La Famille Slomo," *Voir,* March 21-27, 1991, p. 5.
Ministère des Affairs Municipales, *Guide de l'élu/e Municipal*, Les publications du Gouvernement du Québec, 1990.
Montréal Citizen's Movement, *1986 Program*, 1986.
Montréal Citizen's Movement, *La Ville que nous voulons*, Party Program, 1990.
Roussopoulos, D., ed.,*The City and Radical Social Change*, Black Rose Books, Montréal, 1982.
Roy, Jean-Hugues and Brendan Weston, eds., *Montréal: A Citizen's Guide to politics*, Black Rose Books Ltd., Montréal, 1990.
Thompson, Elizabeth, "Beef city's minority-hiring program: panel," *The Gazette,* August 12, 1992, p. A1.
Thompson, Elizabeth, "Doré faces a palace revolt tomorrow," *The Gazette,* September 19, 1992, p. B1.

Ville de Montréal, *Annual Report 1991*, Secrétariat général, Service de la planification et de la concertation, Module des communications, 2nd Quarter, 1992.

Ville de Montréal, *Bilan des Activités 1991-1992 et Plan de Travail 1992-1993*, Standing Committee on Administration and Quality of Services, May 11, 1992.

Ville de Montréal, *Bilan des Activités 1991-1992 et Plan de Travail 1992-1993*, Standing Committee on Culture and Community Development, May 11, 1992.

Ville de Montréal, *Bilan des Activités 1991-1992 et Plan de Travail 1992-1993*, Standing Committee on Economic Development, May 11, 1992.

Ville de Montréal, *Bilan des Activités 1991-1992 et Plan de Travail 1992-1993*, Standing Committee on Environment and Public Works, May 11, 1992.

Ville de Montréal, *Bilan des Activités 1991-1992 et Plan de Travail 1992-1993*, Standing Committee on Planning and Housing, May 11, 1992.

Ville de Montréal, *Cahier d'information économique et budgétaire 1992*, Service de la planification et de la concertation, Module des communications, 4e trimestre, 1991.

Ville de Montréal, *Étude de la proposition de reglement modifiant le reglement sur les comités-conseil d'arrondissement*, Administration and Quality of Services, Standing Committee, March 4, 1991.

Ville de Montréal, *Guide du Commerçant*, Commission d'initiative et de développement économiques de Montréal, Service de la planification et de la concertation, 4th Quarter, 1991.

Ville de Montréal, *Montréal et son Gouvernement, précis d'organisation politique et administrative*, Bureau de Recherches Economiques, 1970.

Ville de Montréal, *Montréal et son Gouvernement, précis d'organisation politique et administrative*, Bureau de Relations publiques, November, 1972.

Ville de Montréal, "Plan d'action pour une gestion intégrée des déchets solides et des matières récupérables à la Ville de Montréal, décembre 1991.

Ville de Montréal, *Programme annuels des travaux des commission permanantes du Conseil Avril 1991*, April 8, 1991.

Ville de Montréal, *Répertoire des interventions de la Ville de Montréal en matière d'environnement*, décembre 1991.

Weston, Brendan, "Citizens mount legal challenge," *The Montreal Mirror*, August 9-August 16, 1990, p. 7.

Weston, Brendan, "Hegemony," *The Montreal Mirror*, November 29-December 6, 1990, p. 8.

2.2 HOW MANY CIVIL SERVANTS DOES IT TAKE TO DO ANYTHING?

Besides the political side of municipal government, 13,000 civil servants work in 14 city departments occupying 400 different offices. Only half of those departments actually handle concrete needs of citizens (like housing or public works), the others exist merely to support and coordinate themselves and Montréal's "image."

Although political decision-making and policy writing is a necessary part of a responsible city government's tasks, much of the day-to-day work involves snow removal, garbage disposal, maintenance of parks and roads, and other blue collar jobs. Yet the city budget shows that white collar positions outnumber blue collar ones by two to one. Fully 40% of the city's expenses go towards salaries and benefits for employees. Montréal has yet to prove itself as light-years ahead of other municipalities in terms of long-range planning and policy-making, as such a large civil service would imply.

In an excellent series of articles demystifying where the City of Montréal spends its money, that appeared in *The Gazette,* in 1991, William Marsden, Andrew McIntosh and Rod Macdonell wrote, "But while property taxes rise and municipal services are reduced, the one thing in local municipal administrations that appears to be untouchable — almost sacred — is the bureaucracy."[1] Certainly, while Montréal's administrative budget and white collar staff remains steady, budget cuts over the course of 1992 were in the areas of fire prevention and some community projects. Meanwhile, the city's 73 top managers all earn over $70,000/year. Thirty-two of them make over $90,000 annually.[2]

Another MCM initiative meant that even those services that do deal with the public have greatly expanded. The entire network of Access-Montréal offices and DACs were originally supposed to bring Montréal's government closer to its citizens. The former were conceived as local centres where permits, information and referrals could be handled. While this is essentially true, constantly occupied phones and a lack of coordination in getting material produced at City Hall into the offices has meant that it's often more efficient to go downtown. This calls into question the existence of the thirteen fully staffed offices. The DACs represent the same type of duplication of services (and of costs) since decision-making is severely restricted in these offices and most of the issues raised at meetings have to go on to the Executive Committee or department involved. Much of the real work still takes place in the corridors of City Hall, although it has passed through more hands. In other words, extra layers of bureaucracy have been added without necessarily being cost-efficient in the long run.

When MCM internal discontent spread through the party's own Councillors over the summer of 1992, the power and expense of the city's padded bureaucracy was a major sticking point. Many Councillors were concerned that the growing coordination and liaison staff in Access-Montréal offices were actually cutting into their jobs. Others wanted to see key figures like Pierre Le françois and Doré's Chief of Staff, Jean-Robert Choquet, gone altogether, blaming their decisions, without adequate supervision, for some of the city's embarrassing and expensive gaffs.[3]

In a press release issued upon his resignation from the MCM in October 1992, Michel Prescott said (among other things) that he could no longer support the "maintenance of an already slow and unproductive bureaucracy, whose sheer weight makes it hard to substantially reduce costs." Prescott charged that civil servants dithered endlessly over negotiations on basic services while Montréalers suffered from their lack. He said that radical reforms were needed, not the "improved productivity" promised by the Mayor which "would only serve to demotivate the staff."[4]

General Secretariat- Secrétariat général
275 Notre-Dame East, Offices 1,5,7,9, H2Y 1C6
Secretary General: Pierre Le françois (2996)
Public Affairs: Pierre Labrie (3417)
This office acts as a liaison between the municipal government and the departments listed below. All information transferred between the two branches of government must be relayed through this office. Much of the work done here is support and organisation to ensure that the Executive Committee has the tools and background material necessary to make decisions. This means that in 1990, the office staff produced 7,000 background reports for the Secretary General and the Executive Committee.[5]

The General Secretariat was created by the MCM. The MCM named a Secretary General at $133,000/yr. This is 15% more than the mayor's income. The office was originally created in 1987 with a budget of $4.5 million. Within five years, that figure had almost tripled. The Secretary General's three assistants each make about $110,000/year and the office pays about 125 other employees.

Office of Public Consultations — Bureau du Consultation de Montréal
(BCM)
300 St-Paul East, 3rd floor, H2Y 1H2
President: Luc Ouimet (0297)

Public Relations: Claude Krynski (0764)
Information: (7807)
This office coordinates all large-scale public consultations ordered by the Executive Committee. They tend to include issues with far-reaching public consequences, like the future of Mount Royal. Although the BCM can only take on mandates determined by the Executive Committee, the office has the freedom to decide which of three types of consultation will be held on a given issue (the differences are around length and depth of consultation). The president of the BCM produces a list of 21 local experts in the field. The Executive Committee then chooses anywhere between two to four (depending on the size of the consultation) of the candidates and names them as Commissioners for the consultation. The Commissioners oversee the hearings. The process can range from 10 weeks to 6 months. Generally, the BCM ensures that all relevant documentation is available for consultation through Access-Montréal offices, that people who wish to speak during the process can do so, etc. The BCM then reports back to the Executive Committee within 90 days. The City government is under no obligation to abide by the recommendations made by the office.

The budget jumped from $400,000 to $700,000 in 1991 almost exclusively because of administrative costs. There were no major consultations held during that year. At the time, BCM spokesperson Claude Krynski said, "We don't want to do that many [consultations]. We're more concerned with the quality of consultations, preparation takes a lot of work." [6] During that year, preparations were made for a city-wide consultation on solid waste disposal that began in fall of 1991. The city's preferred plan involved incineration as a major component, disappointing many environmental groups. Yet the BCM recommended a two-year freeze on increased incineration and further study of the options available. It also suggested that the Miron Quarry remain open until a suitable alternative is in place. Finally, it suggested that the government had been unrealistic in many of its projections and that a far more comprehensive, long-term plan was needed. The Executive Committee has yet to respond to these recommendations. A final decision will be made in early 1993.

Front Line Departments

Housing and Urban Development — Service de l'Habitation et du developpment Urbaine
276 St-Jacques West, H2Y 1A6
Director: Pierre Ouellet (4523)
These issues are clearly key to both the MCM and MUC governments. Both levels of government have Standing Committees to handle policy-

making, a coordination office between the two bureaucracies, and Montréal alone employs over 550 people in this department. The department handles all aspects of urban planning, development and housing regulations. Approves any permits related to construction and renovation as well as inspection and enforcement of these regulations. This department's annual budget has hovered around $41 million for the last three years.

The Zoning and Regulation office (2622) is responsible for all questions and complaints around potential zoning infractions.

The Permits Office at 810 Saint-Antoine East, H2Y 1A6 (3181) grants permits, inspects and levies fines for construction, building and noise, to parking, pests and animals.

Housing at 330, rue St-Paul East, H2Y 1H2 (3888) regulates and provides affordable housing by managing new developments and overseeing renovation work. Housing also handles complaints and enforces the housing code. There are only 17 inspectors for the entire city. Their mandate is to intervene only when there is a clear danger to public safety. They can be useful in cases of landlord harassment (water or electrical shutdowns for non-payment of rent, lock changes, etc.) If any immediate work needs to be done, they can do it at the landlord's cost, although most inspectors operate on the assumption that a warning to the landlord is enough to get things fixed. [7]

This office determines land usage in terms of parking spaces, traffic routes and road extensions. The specific technical aspects of carrying these decisions out are handled through public works. Demands for parking lots or parking meters must be made in writing to 810, rue Saint-Antoine East., Bureau S.100, Montréal, H2Y 1A6. If you're the victim of a broken parking meter, you can be reimbursed through Access-Montréal.

A special section on technical environmental counselling ensures that plans are environmentally responsible and comply with current regulations (3112).

The City's newly unveiled master urban plan was produced by this department. The urban planning division at 8203 is useful for current maps, territorial studies and topographical information about the city.

Recreation and Community Development — Service des loisirs et du developpement communautaire (LDC)
7400 Saint-Michel Boulevard, Rm. 219, H2A 2Z8
Director: Jean-Vianney Jutras (4553)
Welfare Administration: Marcel Lemoine (4940)
The over 2,000 civil servants employed in this department design, operate and promote everything from heritage sites, public museums and parks to libraries and the city's network of municipal cultural

centres (Maisons de la culture). The department also monitors provincial programs for low-income residents (welfare, daycare, shelters, the homeless, etc.) by allocating funds for those purposes. Although welfare payments themselves are furnished by the Province, the City has been steadily increasing this department's budget to $113 million for 1992.

Social Assistance at 1125, rue Ontario East. H2C 1R2 (4940) is specifically responsible for handling provincial welfare for Montréal recipients. Through this program, the City also manages workfare programs for people on welfare like PAIE and Extra. In the spring of 1992, the city announced the creation of 1000 temporary municipal positions through three different levels of such workfare programs. These programs have been criticized for creating an underclass of workers who are not covered by minimum wage or basic labour code guidelines. Several welfare advocacy groups, formed a common front to force the Province to amend Bill 37, the welfare reform bill that introduced the workfare programs. They had been lobbying the municipal government to join in the fight, because of their role in administering such programs. The City's decision to exploit the program put it squarely in opposition to the common front.[8]

This office is also responsible for a special Bureau d'aide aux nouveaux arrivants which helps new immigrants apply for refugee status and provides them with emergency income through welfare. The office is equipped to deal with requests in several languages. It is located at 3910 Ste-Catherine East, (8838).

Parks, Horticulture and Science at 4101, rue Sherbrooke East., H1X 2B2 (1452) manages green spaces, bike paths, outdoor recreational equipment, and large parks projects. The recent creation of a new paramunicipal corporation to manage scientific/ecological parks and museums changed this office's responsibilities on 1992. Refer to the chapter of paramunicipals for more information.

In terms of cultural development, the office helps to run the city's network of cultural facilities, providing space and resources for community activities and projects. One existing project is the Strathearn Intercultural Centre, just off the Pine/Park interchange. The city helped turn the abandoned school into a community/art space, but in the summer of 1989, tensions flared when the LDC tried to take too active a role in controlling the direction of the centre. Organizations that had been involved from the beginning accused bureaucrats of trying to establish a satellite to its Maison de la culture, instead of allowing the community to determine its own needs and programs.[9] By fall of 1992, the Centre's management was waiting for word from the Executive Committee on whether they could retain autonomy altogether, or would have to work within the civil service's parameters.

Fire Prevention — Service de prevention des incendies de Montréal
4040 Park Ave., H2W 1S8
Director: Raymond Therrien (3761)
This department includes separate divisions for actual fire-fighting (divided into 23 locations) and for fire prevention. The department's annual budget is currently just under $125 million. Statistical information on the number of emergency calls is also collected through this department. Firefighters are concerned about lay-offs as cost-cutting measures by the City have meant the loss of 175 jobs between 1991 and 1992.

Public Works — Service des travaux publics
700 Saint-Antoine East., H2Y 1A6
Director: René Morency (3945)
This department handles both the planning and maintenance of systems for water, sewage, streets, lights, roads and garbage and snow removal with a staff of over 3,300 people and a budget of nearly $300 million. Actual pollution controls for clean air and water are the domain of the MUC, and are not addressed by this office.

For emergency situations like broken traffic lights, flooding, streets blocked due to accidents, problems with street lights, etc., the City advises contacting Access-Montréal, either locally or through the general number at 3434. This emergency line is open from 7 am to 11 pm Monday-Friday. Be warned that the line is usually busy and patience is necessary.

Environmental Engineering — Module Genie de l'environnement (3870) — handles the provision of drinking water and waste management on all levels, while ensuring that appropriate environmental controls are maintained. In an internal report, the city's environmental engineer, Jean-Pierre Panet named "reasonable cost" as an environmental priority of the city.[10]

The 1991 budget for curbside recycling jumped $1 million to $2.6 million this year, ostensibly because the number of participating households will double. Nonetheless, there were only 70,000 households involved by the end of 1991. Currently there are also 120 sites throughout the city where recyclables can be dropped off. Information about the one closest to you, and what exactly can be dropped off there (some spots take only paper and glass, others metals and plastics as well) is available through your Access-Montréal office. Although a plan is in the works for handling toxic or dangerous domestic waste (for example, photographic chemicals) it won't be operable until the fall of 1992.

Environmental Management (5760) employs technical experts for landfill sites. Incineration falls under the supervision of Henri Bonneilh (1496). Both of these means of waste disposal have been severely criticized by the DCM in council. Safety in and around the landfill site, due to potentially toxic emissions has been called into question repeatedly by DCM councillor Marvin Rotrand, and usually dismissed by the government.

This office is also responsible for various types of traffic management. Call 1683 for information around installing special ramps or handrails, or reserved parking for wheelchair access. A demand to shut down a street for a festival must also be made at this number.

If you're concerned about sidewalk circulation, either because of excavation or restaurant/bar terrasses, call 3803.

If your car or bike has disappeared because of work going on where you last parked it, call the city pound at 5219, 5223 or 5232 to arrange to reclaim it. The city also runs an annual auction of bikes that are not reclaimed, usually at amazing prices, call to find out when the next one is.

CIDEM — Commission d'initiative et de développement économiques de Montréal
770 Sherbrooke Street West, 11th floor, H3A 1G1
Director: Pierre Ypperciel (5628)
Creates and promotes economic development projects with public and private, local and international interests — specifically high tech, aerospace, tourism, textiles, bioresearch and communications. In its original incarnation, its mandate included arts promotion as well. Much of what the department's 85 employees do revolves around private consultation and policy development. The department's budget is over $13 million, but it also manages several funds that are listed separately in the city's overall budget.

The department is responsible for a variety of programs involving development of different economic sectors, like the Sociétés d'initiative et de développement des artères commerciales (SIDAC) — which helps revitalize individual commercial streets. This program's budget was upped by 66% in 1991. Opération Commerce, another special project, runs a fund of $12 million to help merchants and tenants of buildings with businesses gain tax credits or renovate their buildings. It also has a special office to support and communicate with SODIM, a related paramunicipal corporation which promotes industry (and works out of the same office).

The office cooperates with both federal and provincial representatives to run a network of Corporations de développement économique communautaire (CDEC) which were designed to encourage local business and employment. These corporations are mandated to create links between the community and the business world and often end up being geared more towards established commerce, not community initiatives. A special report produced with the aid of this department in 1990 dictated that what, until then, had been an autonomous, community-directed loose network of such corporations, with similar names and funding sources, should become completely government regulated.

This kind of government control was felt by the CDEC's that existed in Plateau Mont-Royal and Centre-Sud. In 1990, the city announced that the CDECs, both of which had existed for several years, would have to work together, since they were both in the same City-defined district, or lose their funding. The groups had very different philosophies and clientèles, with the Plateau's favouring community development, small "micro-businesses," and an approach encouraging cooperation and resource-sharing, while the Centre-Sud project worked along more traditional lines. At that time, the Plateau's project broke away from the network, taking the name Centre d'innovation en développement économique local de Grand-Plateau (CIDEL-GP). In spring 1992, with days before funding was to be renewed, the city announced that funding to the CIDEL-GP would be cut off unless they worked with the CDEC. Although $150,000 had been budgeted for the CIDEL-GP, the money was frozen and the centre eventually had to close.[11]

Meanwhile, the Corporation développement de l'est (CDEST) was ordered to stop serving the entire east of the island, including Pôinte-aux-Trembles, Ville D'Anjou and Montréal-est, and to concentrate on the confines of the district as the city defined them, or lose its financial support. Danielle Avaline, director of CDEST said in an interview in November, 1991, "It's a shame that artificial geographic boundaries are being used to stifle community initiative." For her, trying to meet such differing needs is difficult, "Mercier has more environmental, basically middle-class concerns, but Hochelaga-Maisonneuve has a better network of advocacy groups, eventually the neighbourhoods may be able to learn from each other."[12]

The CIDEM's mandate is huge and it is often difficult to obtain information about specific projects. It is very geared towards the high tech industries the MCM seems to favour.

CIDEC — Commission d'initiative et de développement culturels
425 Place Jacques-Cartier, 3rd floor, H2Y 3B1
Director: Janine Beaulieu (1149)
Information (4629)
The department's staff of about 30 people fund and promote cultural activities in the areas of communications, film, design, heritage, creative arts and science. It is a relatively new department, created in 1987. In the year between 1991 and 1992, the budget jumped nearly 20% to almost $5 million.

The office determines cultural policy. One of the policies they are responsible for concerns the issuing of permits for street vendors in the city. During the summer of 1992, a vendor came forward after having secretly taped a meeting of the committee determining whether or not his work could be sold on Montréal streets. His tape revealed that the committee spent more time discussing their feelings about him, not his work.[13]

Various divisions handle support in ways ranging from technical advice to international relations, to events promotion and coordination for established artist's groups. Most events are sponsored in tandem with other public, private or community interests.

Resource and Support Services

Finances — Service des finances
155 Notre-Dame East, H2Y 1B5
Director: Roger Galipeau (6630)
This department spent over $30.5 million in 1992 to monitor funds for all levels of municipal government: administration, services and paramunicipal corporations. Handles taxes directly paid to the city (school taxes are now collected by the school boards). Also responsible for maintaining the city accounts. Produces the annual budget based on the decisions and direction of the Executive Committee. Since financial management regulations come from the provincial government, this department ensures that changes in these regulations are passed on to other departments. A staff of over 400 employees is needed to do this internal bookkeeping. In the last two years, the department's budget has gone up by $3.5 million, even though twenty positions were eliminated during that time.

Copies of city budgets and information are available by calling 4822. Annual financial reports that combine economic and budget information from the city are available every summer, for the previous year, by calling 8989, or through Access-Montréal.

Supplies and Property
Service de l'approvisionnement et immeubles
9515, rue Saint-Hubert, H2M 1Z4
Director: André Murphy (5380)
This department requires 2,200 people to manage the city's material resources. Separate divisions handle maintenance, acquisition, rental and planning for the use of space and buildings owned by the city. Similar work done for the city's supply of rolling-stock. The department's budget of just under $200 million, an increase of $20 million in the last two years, makes it the most costly of the City's internal departments.

Corporate Affairs — Service des affaires Corporatives
500 Place d'Armes, 15th floor, H2Y 3W9
Director: Ginette St-Germain (4475)
Responsible for the city's legal concerns. There are also a series of divisions responsible for legal matters: Civil Affairs offers legal advice to the city. Criminal and Penal Affairs runs the municipal court system. Also responsible for representing the city in court. The department employs nearly 500 people and a current budget of just under $38.5 million.

Municipal court handles traffic and parking violations in the city. It is also where you go for any contravention of municipal by-laws (i.e. noise, loitering, demonstration-related charges, etc.) If you find yourself unable to pay a fine call 1849 to make suitable arrangements. The court is across from city hall at 775 Gosford.

The Gazette's investigative reporting team blew the whistle on the municipal court system in a series that appeared in July, 1992. They charged that municipal court judges earned more than $100,000/year working only half days and increasing the current backlog of cases to 750,000. They were also critical of other unnecessary delays because of negligence on the part of court staff and lawyers.[14] The head of the Québec Bar Association immediately responded asking the province to open an official inquiry, while Doré denied any need for an investigation and claimed the reports were "exaggerations." [15]

The Civil Service Commission at 1453 Beaubien East, B 300 (4269), is a semi-autonomous commission made up of community representatives. Responsible for monitoring the fairness and legality of hiring practices.

Recently the range of services linked to managing human resources was switched to this office. Thus work agreements and contracts are produced here, as well as staff policies and guidelines for retraining programs. These policies do not necessarily affect unionized staff. In May of 1992, Montréal became the first municipality to offer same-sex spousal insurance benefits to its professional staff and elected officials.

Liaison Services

City Clerk — Bureau de Greffe
275 Notre-Dame East, B. 15, H2Y 1C6
Clerk: Me Léon Laberge (3142)
Archives (2678)
Responsible for providing technical support for all meetings held by city government including publicity, preparation of supporting documents, etc. Prepares and registers all official documents/decisions of the municipal government (minutes, resolutions, announcements, etc). It

runs city elections and by-elections. This is one of the few city departments where both the staff and the budget has grown, instead of a shrinking staff and ballooning budget. In 1992, the department employed 90 people with a budget of $10.2 million.

Requests made through the Access to Information Act are handled here. If any information is refused you by any department of the city, an application, in writing, can be made to the City Clerk who must respond within 20 days. If an application is refused, the request can be taken to the provincial Access Appeal Committee. This committee does have the right to "protect" certain information.

The Office of Commissions and Committees of Council (3770) supports Standing Committees and DACs (2858). It provides schedules, agendas and information on how to register questions for upcoming meetings. It also keeps all reports from these bodies available to the public for up to two years, at which point they become archive material.

Archives (2615), located in the basement of City Hall, keeps all official documents including all by-laws, maps, minutes of council meetings, etc. Available for consultation only — photocopying is 25¢ a page and you will not be allowed to take anything upstairs to the 10¢ machine. You need to arrive here with the exact title of the document you want, otherwise you'll probably leave empty handed. There is no general or thematic catalogue of material produced by the city so a general question like "can I see the minutes of the meeting when City Council approved City Hall renovation costs" won't be answered here, unless you already know the date of the meeting in question.

Planning and Coordination — Service de la Planification et de la Concertation
275 Notre-Dame East. Rm. 05, H2Y 1C6
Director (and Assistant Secretary General): Pierre Beaudet (2996)
Citizen Relations: Stella Guy (1887)
Access-Montréal Superintendent: Denise Bibeault (5350)
This is mainly the city's public relations department. It was established in 1988 and is run by the Assistant Secretary General as part of his/her duties. The office aids the government in communications and accessibility. It is also responsible for the city's image in relation to other levels of government and other cities. Between 1990 and 1992, it's staff remained relatively stable and currently stands at 500 employees. Meanwhile, the department's budget has increased by $5 million to a total of $53 million.

The Protocol and Welcome office is technically responsible for ensuring that flags of visiting dignitaries are flying when they arrive and that related receptions don't offend their customs. In this very public 350th anniversary year, this office's budget has leapt by 83%, to over $1 million to help finance all the wining and dining. This amount is not considered part of the official spending for the party.

Planning and Research at 333 Saint-Antoine East, 4th floor (6465), has one section for Socio-Economic Research, which compiles the city's socio-economic statistics by district. The most recent documentation is based on the 1986 census and updated versions using the 1991 statistics are not expected out before 1993. Ivan Féherdy at 5903 is responsible for overseeing this work.

Most city documents designed for the general public (guides, annual reports, budgets, etc.) are produced by the communications sector of this office. If you're trying to find out if an updated version is available, or when it will be, call 4037. An internal phone book to the city's government is also available here for $10. You may be asked to pay by cheque.

Citizen Relations (1887) develops and manages city-wide programs and measures to ensure accessibility and responsibility to citizens. Works in areas like decentralization of services. The network of 13 Access-Montréal offices are also part of this department. Complaints about these services or other city departments should be made at 1111.

The Intercultural Office of Montréal (known by its French acronym, BIM) at 6133, was established in 1988 to ensure that the particular needs of Montréal's many cultural communities are understood and served by city employees. Mostly they translate general information pamphlets on the city into a host of languages. In May 1992, the city dismantled the office and decided to create a new committee made up of representatives from each of the city's services who would work from within to achieve the same ends under the title Intercultural Affairs Division. Representatives of cultural communities are waiting to see what the new approach will bring, but are sceptical of the political will behind the project.[16]

Auditor's Office — Bureau du Verificateur
276 Saint-Jacques, Rm. 605, H2Y 1N3
Auditor: Guy Lefebvre (2208)
Handles an independent audit of all city departments and paramunicipal corporations. Apparently it does practice what it preaches because although staff has remained constant at 42 civil servants, the budget for the department has only gone up $500,000 to $3.8 million in the last two years.

The department organizes inquiries on the recommendation of the Executive Committee or Council as a whole. Responsible for overseeing the management of city funds and related issues. This is the only department of the whole city that answers directly to Council, not to the

Executive Committee or a Standing Committee. The auditor's reports tend to be fairly hard-hitting, especially in terms of the huge sums spent by the city's paramunicipal corporations. Over the last few years, it has made several recommendations to better monitor and control spending of these corporations, but the administration has been slow to respond. It has also challenged spending on some large ticket items. One example involved two hovercrafts the city purchased for emergencies, but have been unable to use because of difficulty getting them into operating condition. Similar concerns were raised about expensive computer equipment purchased without adequate training and background for workers who should use them.

NOTES

1. Marsden, William, Andrew McIntosh and Rod Macdonell, "Bloated bureaucracies drain money, services," *The Gazette,* November 16, 1991, p. B4.
2. *The Gazette,* Sidebar to op. cit. November 16, 1991, p. B5.
3. Thompson, Elizabeth, "Doré faces a palace revolt tomorrow," *The Gazette,* September 19, 1992, p. B1.
4. Prescott, Michel, Press Release issued upon his resignation, October 2, 1992.
5. McIntosh, Andrew, "A buffer of highly paid bureaucrats," *The Gazette,* November 16, 1991, p. B5.
6. Herland, Karen, "An Expensive Silence," *The Montreal Mirror,* August 29-September 5, 1991, p. 8.
7. Herland, Karen, "State of Disrepair," *The Montreal Mirror,* February 13-February 20, 1992, p. 7.
8. Herland, Karen, "Make Work, Not Jobs," *The Montreal Mirror,* May 28-June 4, 1992, p. 7.
9. Herland, Karen, "Squeezing them out," *The Montreal Mirror,* July 18-July 25, p. 6.
10. Panet, Jean-Pierre, *Le Plan de gestion integré de la Ville de Montréal,* Service des Travaux Publiques, Module Genie de l'environnement, Section du Plan de Gestion des dechets, September, 1989.
11. Herland, Karen, "Community Cuts," *The Montréal Mirror,,* March 26-April 2, 1992, p.8.
12. Herland, Karen, "Lost in the Paper Shuffle,"*The Montreal Mirror,* November 21-November 28, 1991, p. 7.
13. Thompson, Elizabeth "City plays favourites: street vendors," *The Gazette,* June 23, 1992, p. A3.
14. Marsden, William, Andrew McIntosh and Rod Macdonell, series of articles on municipal court in *The Gazette,* July 18, 19 and 20, 1992.
15. McIntosh, Andrew, "No need to probe Montréal municipal court Doré tells city council, *The Gazette,* August 11, 1992, p. A5
16. Harvey, Marie-Claude, "La Ville a discrètement aboli le Bureau Interculturel de Montréal," *La Presse,,* July 7, 1992, p. A5.

REFERENCES

Baccigalupo, Alain avec Luc Rhéaume, *Les Administration municipales québécoises des origines à nos jours, Tome I Les Municipalités,* Editions ARC, Ottawa, 1984.

The Gazette, Sidebar to op. cit. November 16, 1991, p. B5.

Herland, Karen, "An Expensive Silence," *The Montreal Mirror,* August 29-September 5, 1991, p. 8.

Herland, Karen, "Community Cuts," *The Montréal Mirror,,* March 26-April 2, 1992, p.8.

Herland, Karen, "Lost in the Paper Shuffle," *The Montreal Mirror,* November 21-November 28, 1991, p. 7.

Herland, Karen, "Make Work, Not Jobs," *The Montreal Mirror,* May 28-June 4, 1992, p. 7.

Herland Karen, "Selling Garbage," *The Montreal Mirror,* December 12-December 19, 1991, p. 10.

Herland, Karen, "Squeezing them out," *The Montreal Mirror,* July 18-July 25, p. 6.

Herland, Karen, "State of Disrepair," *The Montreal Mirror,* February 13-February 20, 1992, p. 7.

Laberge, Léon, City Clerk, private conversation, September 4, 1992.

Marsden, William, Andrew McIntosh and Rod Macdonell, "Bloated bureaucracies drain money, services," *The Gazette,* November 16, 1991, p. B4.

Marsden, William, Andrew McIntosh and Rod Macdonell, series of articles on municipal court in *The Gazette,* July 18, 19 and 20, 1992.

McIntosh, Andrew, "Bar calls for action on court's problems" *The Gazette,* July 22, 1992, p. A1.

McIntosh, Andrew, "A buffer of highly paid bureaucrats," *The Gazette,* November 16, 1991, p. B5.

McIntosh, Andrew, "No need to probe Montréal municipal court Doré tells city council, *The Gazette,* August 11, 1992, p. A5

Panet, Jean-Pierre, *Le Plan de gestion integré de la Ville de Montréal,* Service des Travaux Publiques, Module Genie de l'environnement, Section du Plan de Gestion des dechets, September 28, 1989.

Prescott, Michel, Press Release issued upon his resignation, October 2, 1992.

Roy, Jean, "L'évolution des pouvoirs du Comité exécutif de la ville de Montréal (1954-1983)" in *Le Système Politique de Montréal,* Guy Bourrassa and Jacques Léveillée eds., L'Association Canadienne-Française pour l'avancement des sciences, L'ACFAS, #43, 1986.

Thompson, Elizabeth, "Doré faces a palace revolt tomorrow," *The Gazette,* September 19, 1992, p. B1.

Ville de Montréal, *Budget 1992,* Service des finances, Module du budget, November 29, 1991.

Ville de Montréal, *Budget 1991,* Service des finances, Module du budget, December 4,1990.

Ville de Montréal, *Guide du Commerçant,* Commission d'initiative et de développement économiques de Montréal, Service de la planification et de la concertation, 4th Quarter, 1991.

Ville de Montréal, *Montréal et son Gouvernement, précis d'organisation politique et administrative,*1970.

Ville de Montréal, *Montréal et son Gouvernement, précis d'organisation politique et administrative,* Bureau des relations publiques, November, 1972.

Ville de Montréal, *Réorganisation des services municipaux Phase III,* Service de la planification et de la concertation, 2 volumes, June,1988.

2.3 TAKING CARE OF BUSINESS —
   PARAMUNICIPAL CORPORATIONS

The city operates 10 paramunicipal corporations (similar to federal crown corporations) involved in profit-making ventures, like the acquisition of buildings for housing, or the running of public facilities such as La Ronde. The city itself can not act in a profit-making capacity, but it can apply to the Province for permission to set up a profit-making corporation. For the most part these corporations rely on municipal subsidies to do their work.

The city can also operate non-profit corporations for specific kinds of projects. A recent example is the corporation running the 350th birthday party. In these cases, the City must apply to the Province for non-profit status, as any other group may do. The City also maintains some form of representation on the boards of directors.

These bodies are a relatively new phenomenon — very few of them are over 10 years old. When the MCM came into power in 1986, it began work on "protocols" (letters of agreement) between these organizations and the city, in an effort to standardize practices. The next year, the city auditor reported that none of the corporations were complying with these directives.[1] The auditor still remains critical of the operations of these bodies.

The amount of money these corporations receive from the city is not always clear. Direct subsidies are listed in the city budget (and are therefore approved through council), but indirect subsidies can account for up to millions more. For example, SOPAC (see below) runs the Palais de Civilisation. The 1991 budget listed almost $2.5 million in direct subsidies to that corporation. The city also picks up the tab for the general maintenance and infrastructure of the building. But, in the spring of 1991, Executive Committee member Joseph Biello announced an additional $8.4 million city grant to renovate the building, over and above the budgeted grant to the corporation.[2]

In 1990, Brendan Weston, in a *Mirror* editorial, stated that the paramunicipals represent "[a]bout $200 million in hidden subsidies, and acquisitions...[which] will never get much scrutiny by most city councillors."[3]

The city's role in profit-making activities like real estate development is also questionable. Because they are backed by the city, bank financing is far easier to get than it is for private companies. Most of these corporations were founded on seed money that has ballooned over the years due to city support.[4] SODIM, responsible for industrial development, has seen its administrative costs grow by 232% since the

MCM got to city hall in 1986. SHDM, which is now one of Montréal's biggest real estate companies, has had a 548% leap in municipal subsidies in the same time period. This was revealed as part of a report on municipal spending produced by *The Gazette's* investigative team during November, 1991. The article also reported that the SHDM, SODIM and SIMPA, which manages land in Old Montréal, of $407 million with a combined property holdings of only $383.5 million. Four-fifths of these corporation's current holdings were bought after the MCM came into power in 1986. All three of these corporations have also seen their staff's increase dramatically over the last few years.[5]

The city's arm's length presence may help the financial health of these corporations, but there are few control mechanisms in place. In 1989, the Standing Committee on Administration and Finance undertook a series of consultations exploring ways to make the corporations more accountable to City Council. The committee produced about 11 recommendations, suggesting that major spending and policy decisions be brought to Council, and that paramunicipals be expected to comply with municipal policies concerning South African and companies involved in the nuclear industry. The Executive Committee took the teeth out of these recommendations, stating simply that paramunicipal organizations had to deposit certain kinds of information with the secretary general, and in some instances be monitored by the Executive Committee (never council as a whole). The audit for 1990, which took place after these new rules were established, remained critical of how these corporations are run. Council does approve their budgets but, this is generally a rubber stamp affair after a brief 20 minute presentation by the Executive Committee. The media have reported several instances where ex-board members of both SODIM and SHDM, or their relatives, have been involved in lucrative deals with the corporations after their resignations.

The creation of a new paramunicipal in 1992, the Société des musées des sciences naturelles de Montréal highlights some of the contradictions inherent in financial vs. political priorities for these corporations. Rumours of a new paramunicipal that would 'manage' the Botanical Gardens, Insectarium, Planetarium and Biodome and been circulating for a few years. The 1992 budget listed a special 'scientific fund' that jumped 44% from the previous year to $28.8 million. By January, the amount of money the new paramunicipal was to receive in start-up costs happened to be the same sum.[6]

By the time the paramunicipal became official, in the summer of 1992, the Botanical Gardens and Insectarium were no longer to be managed by the corporation, due to scientific and public pressure. However, a scandal still brewed when it was announced that Pierre Bourque a civil servant who had revitalized the Botanical Gardens, and developed the idea for the Biodome in 1988, would be offered a seat on the board of the corporation, but that the board's chair and the Biodome's general director would both be occupied by outsiders named by the city. Sources close to Bourque charged that the Biodome was about to become a tourist operation, while the original scientific aims of the project would be lost. They also were concerned about the amount of public accountability and responsiveness which would be lost with the shift to paramunicipal status. Since the Biodome relies on plants from the Botanical Gardens, it is also unclear how the two bodies will interact if one is run as a corporation and the other remains a city project.[7]

While we wait to see what the future brings in terms of these fears, the city has already applied for a patent for a paramunicipal to run parking lots, and is considering another one for the operation of municipal libraries. According to the city's latest *Annual Report*, the administration collected $14.3 million from its 96 parking lots in 1991, excluding profits made from selling licenses for another 270 commercial lots. Where this money will go if it becomes the property of an external corporation remains a question.

What follows is a general list of existing paramunicipals and their roles.

Association Montréalaise d'action récréative et culturelle - AMARC
Pavillon d'administration,
Ile Notre-Dame,
Montréal, QC
H3C 1A9
Director General: Jean Émond (5574)
General Information: (6222)
An official paramunicipal established in 1983 to supervise Man and His World and La Ronde (the fair grounds originally built for Expo '67 by Drapeau's government) with the goal of making them self-sufficient. As such, AMARC is no longer directly subsidized by the city. However, the city grants it all property it uses free of charge, and did give it $7.5 million loans in both 1990 and 1991. The rest of AMARC's budget of $20 million comes from private industry, provincial sources and admission prices. The seven member board is named by the Executive Committee. There were some legal problems in 1989 when an employee was brought up on civil charges. Concerns about conflict of interest within the society's board, and possible inside information around certain contract bidding were raised during the ensuing inquiry. AMARC hires up to 800 employees, almost 90% of whom are students looking for summertime work. Extra funding from other levels of government has been obtained for special sites on the islands, including a biosphere (not to be confused

with the city's Biodome) which is expected to be unveiled in 1993, at a cost of $17.5 million.

Corporation d'habitations Jeanne-Mance — CHJM
150 Ontario East
Montréal, QC
H2X 1H1
General Information: (1221)
Manages 796 dwellings in Centre-Sud, just west of Saint-Laurent Boulevard on Ontario Street, housing some 2,300 residents. The project was established by the city and the CMHC in 1959 as a slum clearance program. The whole project was a precursor to the kinds of subsidized housing established through existing housing departments at the municipal level and through the HLM program. Its seven member board consists of four members named by the Executive Committee and three by residents. It received a direct municipal subsidy of $645 900 in 1992 (or about 12% of the CHJM's total budget). The organization has a separate tenants' group (845-6394) very active in FRAPRU. According to the 1992 city budget the CHJM retains its own distinct character although it shares the same management as the OMHM (see below).

Corporation "Montréal, les fêtes de 1992"
329 rue de la Commune West
Montréal, QC
H2Y 2E1
General Information: (1992)
Established in 1988 as a temporary non-profit corporation to promote, coordinate and manage the events of the 1992 350th anniversary party. It is autonomous in terms of management and decision-making, but the 25-member board is named by the City and it's entire operating budget is a direct city subsidy, some $14.5 million in total. According to the *Mirror* this paramunicipal is "a new breed...not legally responsible to City Council or the city auditor." The article went on to say that although the city's own Finance and Administration Committee recommended that the corporation be made more accountable, the Executive Committee was only prepared to allow the corporation to go through an audit.[8] In 1991, the auditor's report charged that the board never made its financial statements available to City Council.

This organization has been plagued by bad publicity. Problems started at the end of 1990 amid accusations that it was spending far too much money and was relatively short on concrete decisions or programs for the festival. Around that time, several key administrators resigned from the corporation in disgust. One of them,

Marcel Tremblay, turned up as a CPM candidate in NDG's November 1991 by-election.

Months (and in some cases weeks) before the party kicked off on May 15th, 1992, large gaps remained in the information available about the summer-long festivities. The official calendar for the party included many regular Montréal summer festivals (like the fireworks competition, world film festival, jazz festival, NDG's Sunday in the Park and Carifête to name but a few) under the billing, 'special for the 350th', which roughly translates into extra cash being thrown their way to enable the city to profit from well-established tourist attractions and community events.

The grandiose project was heartily endorsed by the MCM. Detractors were dismissed with the official response that 'now more than ever, Montréalers need a party,' or variations on that theme. When asked during the presentation of the 1992 budget just how much money was earmarked for the celebration, Executive Committee Chair Léa Cousineau responded, "I don't really know what to count as part of the 350th," and went on to explain that many related costs (like clean-up or cultural promotions) are considered part of city service budgets and will never be attributed to the corporation's financial statements.[9]

The party's costs were not limited to extra maintenance staff. Huge sums were spent by the city on other projects in order to prepare Montréal for the party. Large-scale schemes, like the $58 million Biodome, were conceived as part of the summer's tourist attractions and rushed through for 1992. The city also earmarked several million dollars to upgrade and construct several museums to be unveiled over the summer. The $23 million renovations to City Hall could probably also be considered spending for the city's facelift. Tourism became such a strong theme for the summer that an unofficial 'clean-up' of the city extended beyond property maintenance. Organizations working on behalf of the city's homeless population demonstrated to protest what they saw as an increase in police harassment and arrests in an attempt to sweep 'undesirables' off of Montréal's fresh face.

The MCM's approach to the party amounted to a rather cynical public relations exercise during a time of economic recession. The point was underlined when Mayor Doré appeared in a television commercial for Coke, one of the party's corporate sponsors.

Office municipal d'habitation de Montréal — OMHM
152 Notre-Dame East,
7th Floor
Montréal, QC
H2Y 3R4
Director General: Normand Daoust (2103)

General Information: (6442)
Established in 1969 to acquire, build and manage low-income housing, referred to by the French acronym, HLM. Eligibility is determined by Provincial norms. There are over 15,000 applicants waiting
for subsidized housing, although the OMHM already runs 18,455
rental units, housing 27,000 people. The board is made up of nine
members, some named by Executive Committee, two senior residents, two residents of family dwellings and two from the provincial
government. The city is usually expected to pay for the land allocated
for new projects (though this is not generally considered a direct
subsidy). Subsidies for debt are divided between the provincial
(Société d'habitation du Québec) and Montréal governments. Because the subsidies and composition of the board are split among so
many levels of government, this is not considered strictly a
paramunicipal corporation, although it is often listed as such. The
city provided a direct $8,396,300 subsidy in 1992, representing just
under 7% of the Office's total budget. In return, OMHM is required
to pay housing taxes back to the city for all its buildings.

Société de développement industriel de Montréal — SODIM
1200 McGill College Ave.
Suite 1500
Montréal, QC
H3B 4G7
Director General: Gaëtan Rainville (2155)
Allows the city to be involved in industry through the purchase, sale
and administration of industrial properties. The corporation, established in 1981, can also fund the renovation or relocation of existing
industries. It has a nine member board made up of city officials and local
businesspeople, all named by the Executive Committee. SODIM
received $2,935,000 in direct subsidies from the city in 1992, nearly twice
the subsidy it received in 1991. On top of that, after the budget was
passed, another $3 million was approved by Council, and several mil-
lions more were approved to reimburse specific programs run through
the corporation. Its mandate allows it to have up to $500 million in
property or active investments at any one time.

   Current projects include obtaining land to revitalize an industrial
park along the Lachine Canal and another in NDG. Both parks are
expected to be operational in 1996. The land along the Canal is heavily
polluted and the corporation is waiting for money from the province to
help clean it up.

   The city's 1990 audit report, released in April 1991 criticized
Montréal for inadequately monitoring its business dealings when it was
revealed that one of SODIM's private partners in a $330-million project

in Pointe Saint-Charles was a convicted international drug dealer.[11] Several recommendations on how to avoid future scandals were included in the report. The city's track record of ignoring any recommendations around direct financial controls on paramunicipals indicate that the advice probably won't be followed. The last few years have seen the auditor make similar recommendations time and again with little substantial change in the corporation's operations.

Runs a variety of programs including:

Programme de cooperation industrielles de Montréal — PROCIM — to help owners of industrial buildings to improve their property.

Programme de rénovation des aires industrielles de Montréal — PRAIMONT — same goals as above but may work on its own, acquiring and improving properties. 2178.

A new program, Operation Commerce, has been established to extend the mandate of REVICENTRE that ran out in 1991 after five years. It helps to improve the quality of commercial areas.

Société de Gestion de l'Ile Notre-Dame
7400 Saint-Michel Boul.
Office 201
Montréal, QC
H3A 2Z8
General Director: Marc Campagne (6089)
General Information: (6093)
Eleven member board. It was set up as a temporary non-profit venture to oversee the management of Ile Nôtre-Dame. It is not clear how this society's mandate differed from that of AMARC and SOPAC (see below), both of which already work on the island. Opposition councillors protested in February 1991 when council approved some $865,000 to improve the island, without any way to monitor decisions. By 1992, its budget was $1,243,600. It is no longer considered a paramunicipal, but part of the Recreation and Community Development department. It is interesting that a temporary body has found a permanent niche within an office.

Société de l'habitation et de développement de Montréal — SHDM
1055 Réné-Lévesque Boul., East
8th floor
Montréal, QC
H2L 4S5
Director General: Robert Cohen (8500)
General Information: (2040)
The result of the merger in 1988 of two former paramunicipals, the Société municipal d'habitation de Montréal (SOMHAM) and the Société

de développement de Montréal (SODEMONT). As a non-profit corporation it acquires, renovates and manages buildings, and also
provides loans for this purpose, mainly for residential units. Officially
considered a paramunicipal, it is headed by a six member board.
Received $4,518,600 in direct subsidies from city (8% of its total budget)
in 1992. It also received loans totalling nearly $20 million over the last
few years.

Unlike the OMHM, the housing purchased by the SHDM, isn't
necessarily destined for low-income residents. It also establishes co-ops,
non-profit spaces (with community groups), and sometimes condos.
The SHDM is involved in the purchase and renovation of rooming
houses. The corporation also manages some special funds to help
private owners improve their buildings. Along with housing projects, it
manages 15 buildings which house community, cultural and recreational facilities.

For the last couple of years, the SHDM has concentrated on purchasing buildings falling into disrepair, bringing the buildings up to
code and then offering the units back to the original tenants with an eye
towards encouraging them to turn the property in co-ops. They have
managed to convert some 12,000 units.

Its main function is to improve housing stock but some housing
activists have charged that the project is actually promoting low-level
gentrification. Once buildings are improved, some former tenants can
no longer afford the rents and are pushed out of the neighbourhood,
while the buildings attract a higher class of occupant. Although the
work is necessary, architect Michael Fish, long active in municipal
politics, has suggested that renovations are sometimes more elaborate
than is required, and that contractors are paid 20-25% more than they
receive in the private sector, costs that are all passed on the taxpayers.
Other activists charge that bureaucrats at the SHDM hide behind more
expensive, flashy projects to protect their jobs. The SHDM defends its
pay scale as more in keeping with the worth of the work.[12]

Funding cutbacks to housing subsidies on the federal and provincial levels have caused the City government to curtail the SHDM's
initiative in renovating substandard housing stock. Instead of going to
bat for the SHDM, and encouraging other levels of government to
continue to support such projects, the City seems to be proposing a new
direction. A report in the 1992 budget suggests that the SHDM should
improve and strengthen ties with the private sector in its operations (like
certain "large European and American cities"). Private partnerships are
being considered for building on vacant territories purchased along the
river, east of Old Montréal (the Faubourg Québec), six million square
feet purchased near Blue Bonnets and in certain downtown projects.
The likelihood that these projects will be accessible to average-income

residents, and in the case of Blue Bonnets, residents of the existing neighbourhood, is slim.

The Blue Bonnets purchase, in 1991, included the track itself. In the fall of 1992 a series of reports in local media pointed out that revenues brought to the City through the track fell far short of projected revenues quoted when the track was first purchased. As well, although the full property was taxable when the site was privately owned, only land occupied by buildings is currently taxed, bringing $400,000 less to the City annually. Opposition and independent Councillors have been clamouring for full financial records.[13] The 1992 audit report barely mentions SHDM, or the racetrack purchase at all, mainly because the paramunicipal's board was four months late turning papers over to the auditors.[14]

Société immobilière du patrimoine architectural de Montréal — SIMPA
164 Nôtre-Dame East
Montréal, QC
H2Y 1C2
Director General: Clément Demers (6215)
General Information: (8702)
Formed in partnership with the Québec government in 1981. Non-profit organization created to restore, promote and manage heritage buildings (both residential and commercial) in Old Montréal. Its seven member board includes one director-general, two members from Québec's civil service, two from Montréal's, one from a City Committee. The Executive Committee names five officers, two others are named by the provincial government. The director-general is the only permanent employee of the society.

The 1992 subsidy from the city is $800,000, but it received a $13 million loan in 1991. It pays the city a token sum for the use of properties valued at over three million dollars. It also works with several city departments, and it is possible that it indirectly receives resources from them that never appear on the books. Its total interests in 1991 were over $150,000,000, according to the city's 1991 budget.

Société du Palais de la civilisation — SOPAC
Post Office, 275 Notre-Dame Rd., East
Montréal, QC
H2Y 1C6
Director General: Louise Beaudoin (4560)
General Information: (4560)
Created in 1986, one year after the start of a special exhibition held in an abandoned pavilion at Man and His World. Runs the Palais, and has expanded to include other sites on Ile Notre-Dame and Ile Sainte-

Hélène. Coordinates international events and exhibits. Half its $4.8 million budget is a direct subsidy from the city; the rest of the budget comes from ticket sales, private sponsors and corporate partnerships. Extra costs run into the millions as mentioned above. The city handles the rent, heating and maintenance of the site in addition to the subsidy. In 1991, the Gulf War made it impossible to bring a Roman exhibit to the Palais, and with the exhibit postponed to 1992, the city took advantage of the lack of activity to devote extra money to renovations.

Opposition councillors have criticized the amount of money spent by SOPAC on international art in comparison to the $2.55 million given to CIDEC to promote local artists. The 15 member board is named by the city.

Société des terrains Angus — SOTAN
4230 Moîse-Picard Rd.
Montréal, QC
H1X 9Z7
Director General: Pierre Ducharme (6969)
General Information: (6969)
The corporation was established in 1983 to work with the Québec government (Ministry of Municipal Affairs) to convert the area bounded by Saint Joseph, Boubonnière, Rachel, Hogan and Iberville into housing stock. Seven member board, three members named by the Executive Committee, three by the provincial government and a chair co-named by both governments. Both governments also share all costs. This official paramunicipal has specific quotas in terms of the number and type of housing units to be created (i.e. low income, vs. rental, vs. condo). In 1992, *La Presse* revealed that much of the soil in the area might have been contaminated during its past use as a railway yard. There are now calls to do a complete soil evaluation, and potential clean up.[15] The 1991 auditor's report of the city questioned the existence of the corporation itself. Since the sale of the contaminated land is the only reason SOTAN exists, the auditor suggests that the entire structure be dismantled.

NOTES

1. Macdonell, Rod and Elizabeth Thompson, "Take a close look at future business partners, city urged," *The Gazette*, Tuesday April 9, 1991, p. A 3.
2. Brown, Eleanor, "Sink Hole" *The Montreal Mirror*, February 28-March 7, 1991, p. 10.
3. Weston, Brendan, "City Limits," *The Montreal Mirror*, December 6-December 13, 1990, p. 10.
4. Boskey, Sam, private conversation, July 3, 1992.

5. Macdonell, Rod and William Marsden, "Paramunicipals fail to pay their way," *The Gazette*, November 16, 1991, p. B4.
6. Herland, Karen, "Creating Another Monster," *The Montreal Mirror*, January 23-January 30, 1992, p. 10.
7. Lacroix, Liliane, "Le 'père' évincé du Biodôme et son équipe continuent de défier la Ville," *La Presse*, July 3, 1992, p. A1. and Trottier, Éric, "Pierre Bourque est écart de la direction du Biodôme," *La Presse*, June 30, 1992, p. A1.
8. Lalonde, Michelle, "Privatizing Government," *The Montreal Mirror*, April 4, 1991, p. 7.
9. Herland, Karen, "Budget Won't Budge," *The Montreal Mirror*, December 5-December 12, 1991, p. 8.
10. Favreau, Marianne, "Montréal renonce au refuge pour inénérants rue Saint-Hubert," *La Presse*, January 25, 1991, p. A3.
11. Macdonell, Rod and Elizabeth Thompson op. cit.
12. Roslin, Alex, "Waste Efficient," *The Montreal Mirror*, July 16-July 23, 1992, p. 8.
13. Delean, Paul "Deal with city gives racetrack big property-tax break," *The Gazette*, September 19, 1992.
14. Roslin, Alex, "City Mugged at the Track," *The Montreal Mirror*, July 9-July 16, 1992, p. 7.
15. *La Presse*, "Terrains Angus à analyser," July 3, 1992, p. A2.

REFERENCES

Baccigalupo, Alain avec Luc Rhéaume, *Les Administration municipales québécoises des origines à nos jours, Tome I Les Municipalités*, Editions ARC, Ottawa, 1984.
Boskey, Sam, private conversation, July 3, 1992.
Brown, Eleanor, "Opaque Island" *The Montreal Mirror*, February 7-February 14, 1991, p. 7.
Brown, Eleanor, "Paving Rome" *The Montreal Mirror*, February 14-February 21, 1991, p. 9.
Brown, Eleanor, "Sink Hole" *The Montreal Mirror*, February 28-March 7,1991, p. 10.
Delean, Paul "Deal with city gives racetrack big property-tax break," *The Gazette*, September 19, 1992, p. A3
Favreau, Marianne, "Montréal renonce au refuge pour inténérants rue Saint-Hubert," *La Presse*, January 25, 1991, p. A3.
Herland, Karen, "Budget Won't Budge," *The Montreal Mirror*, December 5-December 12, 1991, p. 8.
Herland, Karen, "Creating Another Monster," *The Montreal Mirror*, January 23-January 30, 1992, p. 10.
Herland, Karen, "Expanding to fill the space,"*The Montreal Mirror*, December 26-January 9, 1992, p. 7.
Kuitenbrouwer, Peter "Homeless Shelter fired employee for organizing workers, union says," *The Gazette*, Saturday February 16, 1991, p. A4.
Lacroix, Liliane, "Le 'père' évincé du Biodôme et son équipe continuent de défier la Ville," *La Presse*, July 3, 1992, p. A1.
Lalonde, Michelle, "Privatizing Government," *The Montreal Mirror*, April 4, 1991, p. 7.
Macdonell, Rod and Elizabeth Thompson, "Take a close look at future business partners, city urged," *The Gazette*, Tuesday April 9, 1991,p. A 3.
Macdonell, Rod and William Marsden, "Paramunicipals fail to pay their way," *The Gazette*, November 16, 1991, p. B4.
La Presse, "Terrains Angus à analyser," July 3, 1992, p. A2.
Roslin, Alex, "City Mugged at the Track," *The Montreal Mirror*, July 9-July 16, 1992, p. 7.
Roslin, Alex, "Waste Efficient," *The Montreal Mirror*, July 16-July 23, 1992, p. 8.

Roy, Jean, "L'évolution des pouvoirs du Comité exécutif de la ville de Montréal (1954-1983)" in *Le Système Politique de Montréal*, Guy Bourrassa and Jacques Léveillée eds., L'Association Canadienne-Française pour l'avancement des sciences, L'ACFAS, #43, 1986.

Trottier, Éric, "Pierre Bourque est écart de la direction du Biodôme," *La Presse*, June 30, 1992, p. A1.

Ville de Montréal, *Annual Report 1991*, Secrétariat Général, Service de la planification et de la concertation, Bureau des communications, 2nd Quarter, 1992.

Ville de Montréal, *Budget 1992*, Service des Finances, Module du budget, November 29 1991.

Ville de Montréal, *Budget 1991*, Service des Finances, Module du budget, December 4, 1990.

Ville de Montréal, *Les Protocoles d'entente spécifiques entre la Ville de Montréal et les sociétés paramunicipales SIMPA - OMHM et CHJM*, Commission permanente de l'Administration et des Finances, June 18, 1990.

Ville de Montréal, *Les Protocoles d'entente spécifiques entre la Ville de Montréal et les sociétés paramunicipales AMARC-SODIM-SOPAC-SHDM et SARTM*, Commission permanante de l'Administration et des Finances, August 13 1990.

Ville de Montréal, *Rapport financier annuel 1989*, Service des Finances, Module de la comptabilité, arch 30, 1990.

Ville de Montréal, *Report of the City Auditor to the Conseil Municipal: for the year ending December 31, 1991*, 2nd Quarter, 1992.

Ville de Montréal, *Sommaire des Réalisations, Novembre 1986 à Décembre 1989*, Cabinet du Comité Executif., First Quarter, 1990.

Weston, Brendan, "City Budget Boosters" (p. 8) and "City Limits" (p. 10), *The Montreal Mirror*, December 6-December 13, 1990.

Section III

Beyond the City

Organizational Chart of the Montréal Urban Community

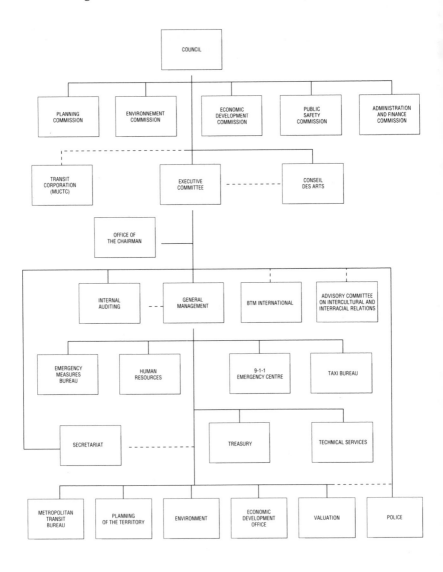

From Communauté urbaine de Montréal, Annual Report 1990, General Management, Communications, 2nd Quarter, 1991. p. 8.

3.1 MONTRÉAL URBAN COMMUNITY GOVERNMENT

The MUC was incorporated in January 1970 by a provincial regulation. It replaced the Metropolitan Montréal Corporation, which had existed since 1959.

The MUC covers 494 km², 76% of which is already developed. The bureaucracy employs just over 7,000 people, about 60% of whom are part of the police force. The Montréal Urban Community Transit Corporation (MUCTC) employs another 8,000 people.[1] Although the MUC's 1992 budget rose less than one percent from the previous year, the overall costs of the MUC bureaucracy have been increasing steadily to $28 million, double what it was in 1975.[2] However, Montréal's Secretary General earns an astronomical salary, MUC's Director General is the highest paid municipal director in Canada with an annual salary of $134,413. The MUC's current debt is $2.1 billion. It is becoming increasingly clear that the bureaucracy is growing almost despite the MUC government. Westmount Mayor, Peter Trent, a member of the MUC Council and long-time critic of MUC spending was quoted in a *Gazette* report as saying, "If you blew up the MUC administration, all those (MUC) agencies would still function."[3]

The shared responsibilities of the MUC fall into a few general categories. On a financial level, the MUC is in charge of evaluating property values in each municipality, based on a provincial formula. It also looks at economic promotion and development for the island.

The MUC is responsible for urban planning issues that affect its whole territory. This extends to joint coordination for the creation of regional parks and drafting of plans of areas that are shared by municipalities.

The MUC is concerned with environmental issues that affect all residents of its territory. This means monitoring air and water pollution. Joint waste management and recycling projects are also within its jurisdiction. As well, the MUC handles food inspection of all produce delivered to or served on the island. Public security, including the police force and emergency measures, is also an MUC concern.

Finally, public transit is shared by the MUC. This includes the Metro system and buses, as well as taxi permits.

The MUC is financed by proportional contributions from member municipalities (Montréal earmarked $484 million in its 1992 budget) and by provincial subsidies.

Political Structure

Council

The MUC Council is made up of 79 members including a representative (mayor or designate) from each municipality, all members of the Montréal city Council (including the mayor), and the chair of the MUC's Executive Committee. The Island of Dorval (population 3) is represented by the City of Dorval.

In Council, as in all formal aspects of the MUC government, special regulations ensure that neither the suburbs nor Montréal can control voting. All proposals must be passed by a double majority: over 50% of Councillors representing the city of Montréal and over 50% of all other representatives. Each member has one vote per 1,000 people in their constituency (in the case of the city of Montréal those votes are equally divided equally among all Councillors.)

This Council votes on all matters except those legally declared to be the domain of its Executive Committee. Generally speaking, any item under the jurisdiction of the Council is brought to the Executive Committee which then reports back to Council. Council can either reject, accept, amend or re-submit items to the Executive Committee for further review. The Council can establish Committees, Special or Standing, to study any issue and report back to Council.

Executive Committee

The MUC Executive Committee has 13 members, including a chair and two vice-chairs. The chair is elected by the entire Council and must resign her/his municipal affiliation before accepting the position. The other 12 members of the Executive Committee are the chairs and vice-chairs of the MUC Council and of each of its five Standing Committees: Administration and Finance, Planning, Economic Development, Environment and Public Safety. The Executive Committee is responsible for the administrative side of the Council. Decisions are made by a simple majority vote.

Standing Committees

Each of the current Committees was established through a law passed at the provincial level. Plans are underway to coordinate the work of these Committees with those at the municipal level to ensure that work is not duplicated.

Each Committee (except Public Security) can have up to seven members, including a chair and a vice-chair. In all cases, responsibility is divided between Montréal and the other municipalities (i.e., if a Committee is chaired by a suburban mayor, the vice-chair will be a Montréal Councillor). At least two members must be Councillors from the city of

Montréal and two must be from other municipalities. Council votes on all members.

The Public Security Committee is made up of seven members, including a chair and vice-chair. One member is named by the provincial government, the other six are named by the Council, three from the city of Montréal, three from other municipalities.

All Committees can receive mandates to study or report on a particular issue through the Council or the Executive Committee. All reports of the Public Security Committee must go through the Executive Committee first, and some of its reports are considered confidential. It is also the only Committee to hold private meetings, all others are public. Each Committee must hold at least four meetings per calendar year. The Public Security Committee must ensure that at least two of these are public. Meetings must be advertised in advance in local newspapers and must have an open question period.

All decisions are made by a simple majority. In the case of a tie, the decision does not carry. All decisions must be written up and submitted to both Council and the Executive Committee. (Except confidential reports of the Public Security Committee which go only to the latter). Decisions must then be endorsed either by Council or by the Executive Committee.

Arts Council

Incorporated by the provincial government in 1980, this body is chosen by the MUC Council and made up of 22 volunteer citizens who sit for four year terms. The MUC Council also names the chair and two vice-chairs, on recommendation of the Executive Committee. Members of the Arts Council are not paid, but they can apply for a secretary and small support staff through the MUC. Vice-chairs cannot be directors or consultants of any group receiving funding.

The Council maintains a complete list of all artistic and cultural associations, societies, corporations, individuals and groups in the MUC. It also manages a fund that supports artistic endeavours by recommendation to the MUC Council. Funding is provided in four main areas: visual arts and literature, dance, cinema and multimedia, music and theatre. The fund is made up of donations, special monies and a small percentage of the MUC budget. There is current pressure by some municipalities that this fund consist of an automatic 1% of the MUC's total budget.

Besides direct donations to MUC-based artistic associations, the Council also purchases art for display in public buildings and parks.

Advisory Committee on Intercultural and Interracial Relations

This special Committee was established in 1985 to improve representation of visible minorities within the bureaucracy, as well as to improve relations between the MUC and area minority groups. The 13 members of the Committee are chosen representatives of a variety of cultural community groups. Until the summer of 1992, four MUC Council members were also involved, but new policy then determined that there would be no political representation on the Committee. The Committee has no budget and staff of its own.

The Committee monitors hiring policies and community relations for the MUCTC and police force, as well as the MUC government. The Committee produced a declaration in 1990 encouraging the elimination of all forms of racial discrimination in MUC operations. Less than 8% of the MUC's civil service are members of minority groups, with fewer than half of those belonging to visible minorities. Meanwhile, fewer than 1% of the police force's officers and 2.2% of the MUCTC's staff belong to visible minorities.[4]

Bureaucracy

Office of the Chair: This office provides general technical support for the Executive Committee and, by extension, for Council as a whole, by researching and preparing dossiers on items for discussion. Its staff is also involved in public relations, by helping to coordinate high profile conferences and events, economic cooperation and relationships with other levels of government.

Secretariat: This office provides support to the political side of the MUC government by maintaining all documentation and archives, handling legal issues ranging from contracts to complaints. Printing of all MUC material is also coordinated through this office.

Director General: The Director General administers MUC affairs under supervision of the Executive Committee. This position retains authority over directors of all MUC services with the exception of the Secretariat and the Police Department. She/He acts as liaison with these directors and with the Executive Committee, ensuring that the latter's plans are distributed and followed up on. Various services of the MUC are monitored through this office.

Communications: All general MUC documentation is approved through this office.

Taxi Bureau: This office is regulated by a special by-law controlling taxi operations. Is responsible for the issuing and renewal of all taxi and limousine permits within the MUC. Sets standards with taxi inspections.

911 Emergency Centre: After five years of operation, just over 100 operators handle the 2 million calls received annually by the service.

Human Resources: Hiring and retraining for all MUC staff.

Internal Auditing: This division reports to the Executive Committee through an intermediary Committee made up of Council members.

Standing Committees: The work of the various Committees of Council is supported through this office.

Treasury Department: This office presents all service budgets to the Executive Committee, ensuring that all MUC finances are handled according to regulations and that all MUC accounts are paid. Responsible for keeping the accounts and overseeing all financial matters. Provides monthly financial updates to the Executive Committee. Ensures that budgets are adhered to and MUC employees are paid.

Technical Services: Established in 1990, this office coordinates phone and data management systems. It also handles real estate management and purchasing.

Planning: Coordinates territorial use and development of land and common areas. Holds consultations on these issues. Developed one global development plan in 1986. General parameters are to improve quality of life, ensure the equitable sharing of communal resources, encourage development, and preserve and enhance communal green space/ water/heritage. All municipalities are responsible for their own local plans but they must submit them here for review. Thus, Montréal's current master urban plan must meet with the standards of these plans.

Evaluations ensure that current property values and regulations are available and up-to-date to help municipalities determine property taxes. Provides an updated triennial record of property values.

Economic Development Office: In charge of maintaining all current facts and data making them available to those who are interested in investing in projects within the MUC. Other responsibilities include maintaining ties with business interests in other cities, promoting economic expansion through conferences.

Metropolitan Transit Bureau: Established in 1980, it researches needs and standards in the area of metro construction. MTB International has worked as an international consultant.

Emergency Measures Bureau: Coordinates emergency plans for the region including routes for transporting hazardous materials across the island, and establishing a code for warning symbols. Established in 1988.

Environment Department: Responsible for monitoring air and water pollution, quality of food throughout the MUC, and the construction and use of waste water networks. Monitors food, regulates distributors and fines for infractions. It has been involved in the construction of a waste water treatment plant for the east end of the island. The work is long overdue, and many east end plants continue to pollute the St-Lawrence while waiting for the treatment plant to clean up their effluent.

Police

Since 1972, the police service for the island has been consolidated under the jurisdiction of the MUC. The resolution of a labour dispute between Montréal and the police force was partially responsible for the creation of the MUC. The director of the police force reports directly to the Executive Committee. As of 1990, the budget for the force was $353,585,000. Administration costs alone have risen $130% since 1985.[5] Its crime solving rate has remained steady at about 29% over the last five years.

In the last several years, charges of racism levelled against the police force have multiplied. Young Black men in areas like Little Burgundy, Côte-des-Neiges and NDG have all reported being regularly stopped by police without provocation. Since 1988, the deaths of five Black men in incidents involving the police have been reported. In nearly every instance, the men were unarmed.

In the case of Marcellus François' shooting during the summer of 1991, the public was outraged when transcripts of the inquest into his death revealed that police officers had only a photocopy of a photograph to identify the suspect, that they referred to the suspect as a "nigger" on police radio, and the only relationship between the man they were looking for, Kirt Haywood, and François was that they were both Black. Sgt. Michel Tremblay was not fired or jailed for the fatal shooting of François, although police director Alain St-Germain decided to remove Tremblay from the MUC SWAT team, and did admit that mistakes were made in the operation that killed François. This was the most serious reprimand ever received by any of the officers involved in the suspicious shootings over the last few years. Members of the police brotherhood were so outraged by the slap on the wrist, that they marched 2 000 strong, in full uniforms to protest the decision in February 1992. Four months later, lawyers filed papers against the MUC in a lawsuit claiming over $5 million in exemplary damages for François' four children.

Relations between the Black community and police in Little Burgundy are particularly strained. Station 24 Lieutenant Pablo Palacios may currently be involved in an internal investigation (spokespeople consistently refuse to confirm this) for his unorthodox tactics. CBC-TV Newswatch cameras recorded Palacios entering apartments of Black residents by claiming to be a pizza delivery man and by using keys to public housing units furnished by the OMHM. (At the time, OMHM officials said they had furnished keys to empty apartments, suspected of being crack houses, long before the report aired. They claimed to be unaware that the police still had copies of the keys). More serious charges levelled by members of the Black community suggest that

Palacios had dubious links to François, Haywood (who later was found murdered) and Osmond Fletcher, another Black man killed during a police chase in Little Burgundy in November 1991.

Less serious charges against the police force include harassment, extreme police presence at Black events, rallies and demonstrations, and several cases of false arrest. The Black community has responded by establishing a phone hotline for Blacks with complaints against the police (957-9609). In its first three months of operation, it received 200 calls. And the Black community is not the only one with complaints.

In the summer of 1990, police used excessive force to raid a gay and lesbian party held after-hours in a loft in a business district. Those present charge that the police herded, taunted and beat them. Eight arrests were made that night. Two days later, during a peaceful sit-in to protest the arrests and refusal of police to negotiate, police in riot gear beat 200 protesters, arresting 48 of them. Many involved reported sexist and anti-gay remarks made by officers. Several required hospital attention and one man was forced to stay overnight after having his testicles severely bashed by a nightstick. He also filed charged against the MUC. A similar action at a party for Black teenagers held in north Montréal in the summer of 1992 was also botched by over-zealous officers. Tensions led to a riot in the area that night.

Police have responded to these and similar charges on two fronts. On the one hand they have instituted an Intercultural Initiatives Program in 1989, in which police officers at various stations pick ethnic or cultural communities to deal with and to exchange perspectives with. A series of meetings are then arranged between officers and members of one community group. The resource manual for the program hardly takes a hardline approach, "the course designers started with the premise — so simple yet apparently so difficult to accept — that police officers are not particularly racist, or at least not any more racist than anyone else."[6] The project has led the police force to announce funding for four representatives of the Black community to work with them as liaison officers. The officers will be hired jointly by the police and specific community organizations. Critics fear that the officers may end up being apologists for the police.[7]

At the same time, the MUC announced quotas for an equal access hiring program for the police force in 1991.

MUCTC

Although the MUCTC is a separate corporation, it maintains legal and financial ties with the MUC. Responsible for the operations of the bus and metro system, the MUCTC must have its budget and triennial reports approved by the MUC. The MUC must also approve decisions around the MUCTC's fares and borrowing. In 1988, the MUCTC cut its senior staff by two-thirds, but added another 100 employees in an effort to "decentralize" services. Although the number of busdrivers has been cut by 600 in the last five years, administrative costs have been rising steadily, by 114% between 1980 and 1990.[8]

Costs are climbing still higher. The operating deficit of the MUCTC is assumed proportionally by all member municipalities. The MUCTC was also partially subsidized by the provincial government. In 1991, the Province announced changes in the funding formula, and, with Bill 145, they abolished $75 million in subsidies to Montréal alone, as part of an omnibus bill to transfer more of the tax burden unto municipalities.

Although the management of the MUCTC is like that of any private corporation, the board of directors is made up of seven members of the MUC Council and two private citizens. The corporation also has a Complaints Committee, made up of representatives of users of the system, and MUCTC administrators. The Committee only has the power to make recommendations, and usually reviews the MUCTC's handling of any incident. In 1990, the Committee examined 133 complaints, or 6% of those launched.

Charges of racism have also been made against employees of the MUCTC. In the last year, several Black and Hispanic men and women have made charges against MUCTC employees ranging from racist language to use of violence.[9] In a few instances, passengers claimed that MUCTC officers called police during arguments and police officers immediately arrested non-white passengers without investigating the situation. At least one lawsuit against both the MUC and the MUCTC over such a situation is currently underway.

Meanwhile, despite a three-year old affirmative action hiring policy, only 8% of all MUCTC drivers are members of visible minorities.

Régie intermunicipale de gestion des déchets sur l'Ile de Montréal

This is a special body charged with determining a plan for the disposal of solid waste for all municipalities except Montréal, which is working on its own plan. LaSalle mayor Michel Leduc heads the Régie. Established in 1985, the régie has worked mostly in secret, only revealing its support research to the hand-picked consultation Committee it created in 1991. By the time the "consultation" was called, the régie had already signed a deal with Les Chaudières Foster Wheeler to operate an incinerator and sorting site. Although the corporation was originally supposed to assume construction costs as well, at the last minute those costs were transferred to the régie. Foster Wheeler is a US-based multi-national corporation that had been involved in pollution infractions and cost overruns with similar projects across North America. The corporation also builds nuclear reactors. Three mayors refused to sign the deal, which must still receive provincial approval.

Environmentalists are also concerned by potential conflicts of interest, since the régie is essentially made up of MUC Council members and it is the MUC that is responsible for monitoring air pollution on its territory.[10]

NOTES

1. All statistics found in this chapter are compiled through the *Annual Report 1990*, Communauté urbaine de Montréal, General Management-Communications, 2nd quarter, 1991, occasionally in comparison with *Cahier d'information économique et budgétaire, 1991*, Ville de Montréal, Service de planification et de la concertation, Module des communications, 1990.
2. Marsden, William, Andrew McIntosh and Rod Macdonell, "Bloated bureaucracies drain money, services," *The Gazette,* November 16, 1991, p. B4.
3. Idem.
4. *The Gazette,,* "Dismal track record on minorities," part of Marsden et. al. op. cit., November 16, 1991, p. B5
5. Marsden, William et. al., "Bloated bureaucracies drain money, services," op. cit.
6. Herland, Karen, "Watching the Detectives," *The Montreal Mirror,*January 16-January 23, 1992, p. 8.
7. Roslin, Alex, "Cops Lurking About, *The Montreal Mirror,* July 16-July 23, 1992, p. 9
8. Marsden, William et. al., "Bloated bureaucracies drain money, services," op. cit.
9. Herland, Karen, "Taken for a Ride" *The Montreal Mirror,*December 19-December 26, 1991, p. 7.
10. Herland, Karen, "Secret Contracts" *The Montreal Mirror,*October 3-October 10, 1991, p. 7.

REFERENCES

Baccigalupo, Alain avec Luc Rhéaume, *Les Administration municipales québécoises des origines à nos jours, Tome I Les Municipalités*, Editions ARC, Ottawa, 1984.

Bellemare, Pierre, "Querelle avec un chauffeur d'autobus: un joueur de football noir poursuit la CUM et la STCUM," *La Presse,* July 7, 1992, p. A5.

Communauté urbaine de Montréal, *Annual Report 1990*, General Management, Communications, 2nd Quarter, 1991.

The Gazette,, "Dismal track record on minorities," part of Marsden et. al. op. cit., November 16,

GIUM, *Dossier Urbain: Arrondissement Rosemont/Petite-Patrie*, Prepared for the Service de l'habitation et du développement urbain, Ville de Montréal, June 1989.

Herland, Karen, "Community Bruised by Report" *The Montreal Mirror,*January 30-February 6, 1992, p. 7.

Herland, Karen, "Secret Contracts" *The Montreal Mirror,*October 3-October 10, 1991, p. 7.

Herland, Karen, "Taken for a Ride" *The Montreal Mirror,*December 19-December 26, 1991, p. 7.

Herland, Karen, "Urban Shuffle," *The Montreal Mirror,* April 2-April 9, 1992, p. 8.

Herland, Karen, "Watching the Detectives," *The Montreal Mirror,*January 16-January 23, 1992, p. 8.

Marsden, William, Andrew McIntosh and Rod Macdonell, "Bloated bureaucracies drain money, services," *The Gazette,* November 16, 1991, p. B4.Ministère des Affairs Municipales, *Guide de l'élu/e Municipal,* Les publications du Gouvernement du Québec, 1990.

Orsini, Michael, "François heirs sue for $5.4 million,: *The Gazette,,* June 20, 1992, p. A3.

Roslin, Alex, "Consultation Matters, *The Montreal Mirror,* July 16-July 23, 1992, p. 9

Roslin, Alex, "Cops Lurking About, *The Montreal Mirror,* July 16-July 23, 1992, p. 9

Roy, Jean, "L'évolution des pouvoirs du Comité exécutif de la ville de Montréal (1954-1983)" in *Le Système Politique de Montréal,* Guy Bourrassa and Jacques Léveillée eds., L'Association Canadienne-Française pour l'avancement des sciences, L'ACFAS, #43, 1986.

Roy, Jean-Hugues, "Noir et Flics: L'Impasse," *Voir,* July 30-August 5, 1992, p. 6.

Société de transport de la Communauté Urbaine de Montréal, *Rapport Annuel 1990,* 3rd Quarter, 1991.

SODEM, *Dossier Urbain Arrondissement Mercier/Hochelaga-Maisonneuve, Rapport Final,,* Ville de Montréal, July, 1991.

Ville de Montréal, *Budget 1992,* Service de planification et de la concertation, Module des communications, 4th Quarter, 1991.

Ville de Montréal, *Cahier d'information économique et budgétaire, 1991,* Service de planification et de la concertation, Module des communications, 1990.

Ville de Montréal, *Les orientations et les stratégies du Plan d'urbanisme de Montréal* Service de l'habitation et du développement urbain, Bureau du plan d'urbanisme, 2nd Quarter,1992.

Section IV

Montréal in pieces

4.1 DIVIDE AND CONQUER

What follows are profiles of the city and each of the nine districts. These boundaries were defined by the MCM in 1988. These districts were originally conceived as part of a network of "neighbourhoods" that would have their own mini-Councils to address political issues locally. This concept was distorted over the years (see District Advisory Councils in the section on Montréal government).

Instead of naturally created neighbourhoods that share similar socio-economic or cultural backgrounds and concerns, the city instead chose to divide and conquer. "According to a document released by the city, the overriding divisional concerns were geographic, with boundaries determined by railways, autoroutes and bridges, not economic needs or traditionally defined neighbourhoods."[1] The resulting 'districts' often spread over kilometres, encompassing a variety of different kinds of neighbourhoods with vastly different priorities. The districts now serve more as a tool for city planners, rather than as a basis for community grass-roots organizing or a level of neighbourhood self-government.

In fact, as a tool for city planners, the districts' size make them remarkably useful. Major discrepancies can be glossed over within a district, and statistical analysis can provide much more positive, homogeneous representations of areas. Each district has at least one smaller section in which factors like physical isolation, the quality of available housing, proximity to industrial zones, lack of green space and community centres, and general poor planning all feed off each other to create relative ghettos.

The standard of living has been dropping steadily in Montréal, "Almost every neighbourhood on the island of Montréal has poor people. And I'm talking Rosemont, St-Michel, Rivière-des-Prairies, Pierrefonds and many others," said Réal Tremblay, a community activist who participated in a forum on Montréal poverty in May, 1991.[2] The proximity of "haves" and "have-nots" will become a larger problem in the next few years as the more well-to-do residents in various pockets of the city will resent the resources, services, and shelters needed by the city's growing underclass in or near their neighbourhoods. Furthermore, a single DAC is responsible for the needs of its whole constituency, and it's usually easier, quicker and more within their mandates to handle requests for beautifying a city park than addressing inadequate housing or overwhelming poverty. Requests for new park benches are more likely to be approved than requests for increased popular education support services.

Urban Planning

For the last five years, the MCM administration has concentrated on creating a Master urban plan for the city, with the stated intention of examining each and every district and defining problems and priorities. From 1987 to 1990, the focus was put on the downtown Ville-Marie district. A lengthy series of reports, counter-reports and public consultations involving the DAC, the Executive Committee and public and private urban planners resulted in a plan that was released during the summer of 1990. If the outcry around that proposal was any indication, the other eight may cause a city-wide revolt.

The downtown master urban plan was ostensibly the result of years of consultation and decision-making. Admittedly, trying to harmonize the needs of various developers, residents, workers, and visitors to the city's hub would be a difficult task at best. However the city committed a grave error when, at the last possible minute, it decided to push through over 300 (mostly developer-backed) additional amendments within three days over the summer. Opposition Councillors within the Democratic Coalition, Heritage Montréal and other community groups were furious. The plan was passed by the MCM-ruled Council but the example does not bode well for the rest of the districts.

While this was going on, background research on the other eight districts was commissioned. Independent urban planners produced reports in 1989. The city then responded with their own mini-versions of planning priorities in a series of eight documents entitled *Synthèse des enjeux d'aménagement et de développement* which were presented to the public through their DACs in 1990. The city unveiled its final versions of planning and priorities in eight volumes, along with *Les orientations et les stratégies de Plan d'urbanisme de Montréal*, 114 page back-up document, in June 1992. The work required to consult Montréalers and produce the plan cost $2.5 million, according to André Lavallée, Executive Committee member responsible for it.[3]

These versions are expected to be approved by December 1992 in City Council, after a public consultation process. Consultations are to be held through DACs and as coordinated by a special committee of City Council constituted to study the whole package. Given that the Ville-Marie plan had a six-month consultation period, the four months allotted for the eight other plans are hardly sufficient.[4]

Zoning laws are slated to change to comply with the new strategies by 1994 (an election year), pending examination of the needs of some key areas, although the general outlines of the plan are to be respected in all decision-making processes until then. Interestingly, during the period of consultation, city-financed projects are going ahead, in keeping with the promises made in the plan. At the same time, new commercial endeavours that would be allowed once the plan was passed, are not being granted permits.[5] Planners are expected to produce annual reports and to revise or amend the plan if necessary, based on these reports and a special five year review.

The Plan

The city's project is far-reaching and ambitious, its full implementation could easily run into billions of dollars. Each district has been studied, nearly block by block, and the plans are presented in glossy 60 page packages with full colour maps and all the best of intentions. Details on everything from existing housing stock, to shopping areas are provided, along with complete demographic information on each district. Potential problem areas are analysed and solutions offered.

Some of the methods of measuring lifestyles in different districts are questionable. Economic analyses of each district concentrate on the number and kind of jobs available within the territory, and relate them to the education and training of residents. Yet, there is no reason to presume that jobs offered in an area are directly related to the employment patterns of residents. The presumption that people work in the same neighbourhood that they live is never backed up nor even explained. Thus, knowing the type of employment, or number of jobs available in any area gives us no real clues as to the level of employment or employment needs of residents. It is useful for gauging the general health of local commerce, some traffic patterns and problems, and in some cases, potential for gentrification — for instance where cafés and boutiques spring up to serve the people employed in an area, and not its residents.

The size of the project, and potential for changes between now and its passage make any kind of specific analysis of the plan useless. Each plan has a series of recommendations for everything from suggestions for street by street guidelines as to building heights and densities, to proposals for parking lots and changes in traffic circulation. This analysis will only interpret the general priorities of the administration for each district. Every plan details the areas where housing stock and quality of life need work, where traffic circulation needs improvement through the extension of roads, and those where clearer distinctions need to be made between industrial/commercial and residential areas through the creation of 'buffer zones' etc.

There are some solutions that apply to the city as a whole. The government has pledged to make public transit a priority, working to extend metro lines and provide express bus lanes on key routes. Special reserved parking on residential streets (SRRR) is to be increased, particularly in areas where residents have to battle for parking with nearby commercial districts. Speed limits in residential areas are to be reduced from 50 to 30 km/hour. Trucks will be limited to certain main arteries, and kept off side streets.

The city's bike paths, parks and community/recreation centres will be improved, particularly in neighbourhoods where such resources are scarce. Culture and tourism are also priorities for the city, with attention being paid to existing and potential attractions, be they museums, institutions, churches, potential heritage sites, parks or waterways.

Housing stock will be improved and care will be taken to ensure that neither industry nor commerce adversely affects residential neighbourhoods, either through their operations or by the increased traffic they attract. Each district will have designated commercial streets, with business being curtailed on other roads. On what little developable land remains, new projects will be built on a human scale, all the while maintaining the tone and scale of existing buildings.

What it Means

Sounds beautiful. The problems behind the plans (however much they're changed or amended) probably won't be obvious for years. There is no real time frame for these improvements, although the documents suggest that they will be dealt with within the next ten years. These kinds of vague promises are suspect, the MCM promised the creation of a network of bicycle paths in 1986. By the end of their first term, they had completed only nine km of lanes.[6]

In fact several of the proposals scattered throughout all eight plans are actually promises that were made in the MCM's 1986 party program, or announced at various points since then and never finalized. Naturally, they are still relevant and should be included, but the repetition of old promises without necessarily having the means to finally enact them is no more encouraging within the plan than it was outside of it.

Much of what is discussed in the plan implies partnership with a variety of sources. Extensions on metro lines need the approval (and financial support) of the MUCTC. Some of them are, again, old promises or decisions that have already been made at other levels of government, and are simply being repeated by the city government. Many of the express bus lanes mentioned in the plan have been in the works for years. Four were announced just before the last general election in 1990, only to meet with disapproval from local merchants who were afraid that parking and drop-by shopping would decrease as a result. Both local residents and merchants organized together against the Park Avenue express, but their arguments were ignored.

Many of the development plans (particularly in areas that the city has recently purchased, like the land around Blue Bonnets) or in underdeveloped areas like Rivière-des-Prairies, rely on interest from private developers as well. Plans to create business districts along Sherbrooke east of Viau, around Vendôme metro and at the Décarie/Jean-Talon intersection will require finding tenants for newly developed office towers. The abundance of empty office space in the newly-revitalized downtown core doesn't bode well for these satellite business districts. During 1991, vacancy rates in downtown towers jumped from 10.6% to 16.9%.⁷ Decisions around 'heritage sites' as defined by the city need provincial approval and protection. Many road extensions and modifications will need either money, approval, or both from other levels of government and other potentially effected municipalities.

As well, some of the planning is so vague that while contradictions are not obvious now, they may well be by the implementation stage. The idea of park-like buffer zones between industry and residential sectors is fine in theory, but recreation in the shadow of smokestacks seems hardly inviting. This is particularly true of the four districts that some-how touch the CP line curving through the centre of the city. Since 1986, the MCM has promised to consolidate industry along this strip, while also creating green space and improving residential stock. Negotiations with CP over the use of the land have yielded few results, to date.

The city's recommendations on waste management carry unrealis-tic expectations for garbage disposal. The potential need for other landfill sites once both quarries are closed within the next two years is never really addressed. Plans to improve tourism in some districts which are not currently considered tourist attractions (like along the Lachine Canal or Gouin Boulevard), devote little attention to how to incorporate that kind of potential activity and nuisance into neighbourhoods.

Any interpretation of the plan must be done with an under-standing of the concept of 'acquired rights' for zoning. Municipal by-laws around zoning tend to include specific regulations around acquired rights which state, in effect, that existing establishments will not be touched. Thus, if a mixed residential and commercial neighbour-hood is rezoned entirely residential, businesses won't be forced to leave the next day. Existing businesses are restricted from expanding and no new businesses will be given permits to open up. It may be years after the zoning change is enacted before businesses in the neighbourhood find themselves so constrained by the inability to expand that they chose to move away altogether, in the interim, the neighbourhood remains mixed.

Also glaring in the plan is what it leaves out. No mention is made anywhere of improving wheelchair access to public buildings or instal-lations. In addition, the MCM made several promises in its 1986 party program to improve safety, lighting and resources for women on Montréal streets. The plan for Plateau Mont-Royal/Centre-Sud is the only one that even refers to street safety for women, and that is just in passing.

As well, although each district has been studied in detail, many of the key areas highlighted for changes are vaguely addressed. Follow-up documents with specifics for these areas in each district are not expected until up to two years after the plans are passed. Once a new development approach has been agreed to in theory, its practical application will be left in the hands of the bureaucracy.[8]

The introduction to the support document for the plan states, *"Ce document, malgré un contenu largement technique, a un caractère politique et doit donc être approuvé officiellement par les élus municipaux."*[9] Besides the obvious politics involved in defining what any given district's role should be within the larger context of the city (industrial support, tourist attraction, etc.), decisions around which aspects of planning become priorities and which are continually shelved will also reveal the political intentions of the administration.

There is something a little unsettling about a municipal government deciding to remake the whole city in its image. Admittedly, coordinated planning has never been implemented in Montréal, but the control and paternalism suggested in the document is problematic. Cameron Charlebois, president of the Urban Development Institute of Québec was quoted as saying, "There are so many doors out, so many traps, so many coinciding obligations that there's nothing you can do on your own without having to sit down with the (city) planning department and make them almost a partner in your design."[10]

About This Section

Each district is profiled, including facts that may help you organize local residents and/or give you an idea of what some of their key concerns are. In most cases, issues are discussed for a given region only if they vary considerably from the city's norm, or in relation to the rest of the district. Pertinent highlights from the city's master urban plan are included as a measure of how the city intends to handle local problems. An overall profile of Montréal as a whole is included for easier comparison.

The number of health, educational, social and recreational services offered within an area has a direct bearing on quality of life for residents. The amount and quality of green space is also relevant. This includes recreational space and bike paths, trees, parks and other urban necessities.

The socio-economic information provided for each region gives us several clues for local action. Linguistic and cultural information is important for those who want to reach local residents. The type of household also plays a role (organizing where mothers are alone raising young children is very different from organizing seniors or nuclear families).

Education, income and unemployment levels are barometers for the needs and concerns of residents. If lower income families are losing their homes to condo buyers (as in parts of the Sud-Ouest district), measures need to be taken to ensure that housing options remain available. Increasing high tech industry in an area of town where residents have education levels and experience in keeping with a manufacture-based economy does nothing for local residents, unless appropriate retraining programs and resources are created along with the industries. In fact, it could encourage gentrification if professionals attracted to the jobs decide to move nearby and force property values (and prices) up.

Commerce and industry play a major role in the life of a community. Commerce is important for neighbourhoods in terms of the well-being of residents. If basic necessities (grocery stores, pharmacies) are not available in neighbourhoods with older residents, their autonomy becomes extremely limited. If the small local businesses serving a particular cultural community (say kosher bakeries) are being crowded out by boutiques designed for an upscale crowd drawn by gentrification, the community will suffer.

Huge industrial zones located near residences, or that isolate communities, need to be addressed. Industrial activity has contaminated land and water in many parts of the city. Areas with increased industrial activity suffer not only from the pollution of the factories themselves, but also from problems associated with heavier truck traffic. Neighbourhoods located next to train tracks and major arteries are also affected by the noise and pollution. Equally important are abandoned or under used industrial sectors that outlived their usefulness decades ago. Many of these left behind soil pollution that still affects neighbourhoods built years later. Environmental concerns are noted separately, where they are a major influence in district life.

Housing stock is important for several reasons. It usually follows that lower income neighbourhoods have poorer available housing, higher renter (vs. owner) rates, more crowded conditions and suffer from proximity to industrial or heavy traffic zones. Older real estate is not necessarily a problem in and of itself, but absentee landlords and poor maintenance adversely effect some of these areas as well. Statistics on vacancy rates (rates here are from October 1990 CMHC figures) indicate whether rents are determined by tenants or owners. Higher vacancy rates mean that tenants can be more choosy. Finally, the percentage of income spent on rents is an indication of the economic status of residents. Most housing rights activists suggest that no more than

30% of household income should be spent on rent. Many pockets of the city have residents paying an average of 40-50%.

The Voter Profile section is included to provide a sense of the political orientation of the districts. There are a few norms to keep in mind. Montréalers (like most voters) tend to go with the incumbent unless they want to express extreme dissatisfaction with the current administration. The 1990 MCM sweep is no big surprise. The voter turnout hovered at around 35%, on average. This may be due to either satisfaction or apathy, but the latter is more likely. Even in Drapeau's heyday, after four consecutive terms in office, he still managed to draw 50% of eligible voters to the polls.

Results reflect the existence of five major municipal parties at the time of the 1990 election and the 1991 by-election. The subsequent merger of the Civic and Municipal parties should be taken into account. When most polls re-elected the MCM (or the few opposition incumbents), second choices and upsets should be given a lot of weight. That enough people would be so dissatisfied to oust an incumbent (even by a slim margin) is noteworthy. The runners up indicate whether or not a riding is leaning towards the more right wing (Municipal or Civic Party) or left wing (Democratic Coalition or Ecology Montréal) candidate. The idea of second place is fairly nebulous; in some cases, second place may mean 30% points behind, in other cases 10%. I've noted specific instances only when the margin was fairly close, or considerably above the average. For instance, a DCM vote of 9% is noteworthy in the east end, where they rarely gained more than 3% of the vote. Complete election results are noted in Appendix B.

Local community advocacy groups and community media are listed for districts where such information was available. Unfortunately, ethno-cultural groups are underrepresented because of a lack of time and resources to distinguish between social and advocacy organizations. More complete listings are available in *The Guide to Ethnic Montréal* (by Barry Lazar and Tamsin Douglas, Véhicule Press, Montréal, 1992). If no groups are mentioned, or if you can't find one that shares your concerns, refer to other districts or the general listing in the Montréal profile for city-wide groups that may be able to refer you to local activity.

All socio-economic data is from the 1986 census, as the 1991 figures won't be compiled and analysed until 1993. Information around housing stock may be more recent and employment figures were taken from a 1988 report. Although information is presented in the present tense for easier reading, keep in mind that, since then, the recession, GST, TPS and dozens of bankruptcies and plant closings mean that the current economic situation is probably much worse than the one depicted here.

NOTES

1. Herland, Karen, "Lost in the Paper Shuffle," *The Montreal Mirror*, Nov.21-Nov. 28, 1991, p. 7.
2. McLaughlin, Ann, "Face facts: city is poor, group says," *The Gazette*, May 21, 1991, p. A 3.
3. Thompson, Elizabeth, "It's all there — piled high in a corner closet," *The Gazette*, August 29, 1992, p. B2.
4. Roslin, Alex, "Incomprehensible," *The Montreal Mirror*, July 2-July 9, 1992, p. 10.
5. Thompson, Elizabeth, op. cit.
6. Claire Morissette in Jean-Hugues Roy and Brendan Weston, eds., *Montréal: A Citizen's Guide to Politics*, Black Rose Books, Ltd., Montréal, 1990.
7. Ville de Montréal, *Annual Report 1991*, Secrétariat Général, Office de la planification et de la concertation, Module des communications, 2nd Quarter, 1992.
8. Thompson, Elizabeth, op. cit.
9. Ville de Montréal, *Les orientations et les stratégies du Plan d'urbanisme de Montréal*, Service de l'habitation et du développement urbain, Bureau du plan d'urbanisme, 2nd Quarter, 1992.
10. Thompson, Elizabeth, op. cit.

REFERENCES

McLaughlin, Ann, "Face facts: city is poor, group says," *The Gazette*, May 21, 1991, p. A 3.

Herland, Karen, "Lost in the Paper Shuffle," *The Montreal Mirror*, Nov.21-Nov. 28, 1991, p. 1.

Montréal Citizen's Movement, *1986 Program,*, 1986.

Roslin, Alex, "Incomprehensible," *The Montreal Mirror*, July 2-July 9, 1992, p. 10.

Roy, Jean-Hugues and Brendan Weston, eds., *Montréal: A Citizen's Guide to Politics*, Black Rose Books, Ltd., Montréal, 1990.

Thompson, Elizabeth, "It's all there — piled high in a corner closet," *The Gazette*, August 29, 1992, p. B2.

Ville de Montréal, *Annual Report 1991*, Secrétariat Général, Office de la planification et de la concertation, Module des communications, 2nd Quarter, 1992.

Ville de Montréal, *Les orientations et les stratégies du Plan d'urbanisme de Montréal*, Service de l'habitation et du développement urbain, Bureau du plan d'urbanisme, 2nd Quarter, 1992.

Ville de Montréal, *Plan directeur de l'arrondissement Plateau Mont-Royal/Centre-Sud*, Service de l'habitation et du développement urbain, Bureau du plan d'urbanisme, 2nd Quarter, 1992.

Weston, Brendan, "Citizens mount legal challenge," *The Montreal Mirror*, August 9-August 16, 1990, p. 7.

Montréal

Map from Ville de Montréal, Pour mieux vivre Montréal, 1991-1992, 4th Quarter, 1991, pp.36

101

4.2 MONTRÉAL

Area

The 175 km² of the city of Montréal stretches through the centre of the island of Montréal, along with a large part of the eastern tip. The actual territory of the city is split up by the existence of several other municipalities, four between the bulk of the city and the eastern section. Within the central part, Hampstead, Outremont, Westmount and St-Laurent divide different sections.

The city has gone through rapid economic, social and demographic changes in the last fifty years. As is the case with most urban centres, the biggest reason for this has been residents, industry, and business moving to the suburbs. Although Montréal's population is steady at just over one million residents, the Montréal Metropolitan region (including all island municipalities and nearby suburbs on the north and south shores) is three times that. Montréal proper has lost about 200,000 residents in the last 25 years, while Metropolitan Montréal has gained some 500,000.

Topography/Institutions

In the first four years of the MCM's administration, they created a total of 66 new parks, and one beach. This still puts Montréal's total of land devoted to green space at just 6%, or half of Toronto's.[1] The city plans to develop another 134 hectares of green space (primarily on undeveloped land in Rivière-des-Prairies and along the northern shore of the island). Adding that to the 2,000 ha already existing won't considerably improve the quality of green space. Nearly a third of the existing green space consists of small lots in neighbourhoods, which the city concedes need major replanning and improvement. The real problem remains that areas with the greatest need for green space, like Centre-Sud, Park Extension, Mile End, Côte-des-Neiges and Hochelaga-Maisonneuve are also the most developed, with little available land to turn into parks.

The city has some 500 cultural centres, including public and private galleries, museums, theatres, etc. The vast majority of these installations are located within the downtown core, Old Montréal and along St-Laurent and St-Denis. The city runs 12 Maisons de la culture and 23 community libraries, as well as three central libraries for books, records and films. The government has pledged to improve the distribution of similar centres throughout the city. The city has been involved in one way or another in the construction, renovation, revitalisation or development of 17 major cultural centres (museums, theatres, scientific centres) since 1989. Nine of those opened in the summer of 1992, in time for the 350th birthday party.

Demographics

Less than two-thirds of Montréal's 1,014,945 residents are French speaking. The proportions of English and "other" who consider neither English nor French their mother tongue are almost equally divided at 15 and 16% respectively. These figures do not accurately represent whether those who don't identify as English or French are recent immigrants, or second or third generation European.

About a third of Montréal's families are headed by a single parent and about half of the city's married couples are childless. Just under a quarter of Montréal families are headed by two parents, compared to 44% for the greater Montréal are. Nearly half of all Montréal households are single people or people living as roommates, twice as many as the percentage of such households for the province as a whole.

Average household revenues in Montréal are about $26,000, $7,000 below that of the Metropolitan region. Clearly, a city the size of Montréal includes major disparities in terms of income. Averages mask the fact that almost one-third of the city's population lives below the poverty line and one-quarter of all residents were dependent on either UIC or welfare by May 1991.[2] The poorest of all Montréalers are single mothers, with an annual income of just over $10,000. The city of Montréal's annual report for 1991 states that an average 88,882 welfare cheques were processed every month. Unemployment hits roughly 14% of the population. A quarter of Montréal's adult population never finished grade 9.

Housing

The City finally put a long-awaited housing policy into effect in 1991. The policy earmarks specific funding to subsidize renovations and construction of new housing. Most of these projects are managed through the SHDM.

There are about 444,000 homes in the city of Montréal. Naturally, housing within the city is on average far older than the more recently developed suburbs. Housing in the Sud-Ouest, Centre-Sud, Plateau Mont-Royal and Petite-Patrie is by far the oldest, most of it having been built at the turn of the century. Only a third of the city's homes are less that 30 years old. Although age isn't necessarily a sign of deteriorating housing, in many pockets of the city, absentee landlords and older buildings combine to create unsafe housing. A 1991 study commissioned by the city established that about 15% of available housing needed work, and a third of those were in seriously poor condition. Another 15% needed general maintenance and upkeep.[3]

The city proposes building some 60,000 new units on land that is available. More than half of those projects are slated for downtown (where the city is trying to attract upscale residents) and in Rivère-des-Prairies (where undeveloped land is readily available). Some land is also developable in Villeray and Pointe-aux-Trembles.

New projects don't necessarily mean affordable housing. As of 1986, 14% of households spent 50% of their income on rent alone. There are 15,719 households on waiting lists for subsidized housing.[4] The city has set Petite-Patrie, Park Extension and Côte-des-Neiges as priority targets for such measures. From 1987 to 1992, the city had established 4,500 units of low cost housing. The government is looking towards reconditioning existing housing stock into subsidized housing, but recent cuts to the program at the federal level make it harder for the city to meet its targets.

The MCM recently lifted the freeze on condo conversions it imposed early in its reign. The city hopes this will allow more middle-income residents to be able to afford their own homes. Tenants' rights groups are concerned that this will limit the amount of affordable housing available in the city and lead to gentrification, pushing out current tenants.[5]

Commerce/Industry

Two thirds of all available office space is in the downtown Ville-Marie district. The city's new plan proposes three satellite business centres along Sherbrooke St. East, Décarie and Jean-Talon and near the Vendôme metro.

In terms of commerce, the city wants to revitalize Ste-Catherine St., which has become a major embarrassment as stores flock to shopping malls in town, and in the suburbs, or to downtown's impressive "underground city," with miles of below ground malls. In fact, growth in the underground city is also being curtailed by the new master urban plan. For the rest of the commercial streets in the city, the plan defines which ones should be revitalized and which should be phased out.

Industry is a major priority for the city. Improving the quality of industrial parks in the Sud-Ouest, Mercier-Ouest, along the CP line, in Rivère-des-Prairies and other pockets of the city are part of the administration's plan to improve Montréal's economy. After the 1992 budget was passed, the city announced that it would inject several million dollars into industrial development, mostly via its paramunicipal corporations involved in related activities.[6] At around the same time, the province promised $415 million to revitalize Montréal industry.

The city's background document for its urban plan explains that in the last two generations, Montréal has shifted from an industrial to a service-based economy, with 80% of Montréal's jobs available in the service sector.[7] It remains to be seen whether injecting money into industry will be able to stem the tide, or whether the administration should focus on shifting its priorities to providing training for the new types of jobs that are emerging.

Transportation

In 1986, the MCM's program promised a move away from the private automobile for both health and security reasons. Fewer cars and wider walkways, especially downtown, were part of the party's vision.[8] Yet, the city has come to rely more and more on income generated through leasing parking lots, as well as taxing them. Urban plans call for parking space requirements for new developments, not alternatives to automobiles.

At the same time, the city's new plan suggests that bicycle paths are a priority, as are increased accessibility and improvement of the public transit system. Since public transit is the domain of the MUCTC, all the city can really do is establish priorities for its involvement in that corporation.

Several pockets of the city, especially Saint-Michel, parts of the Sud-Ouest and the areas bordering downtown and off-island bridges suffer from the problems associated with excessive traffic. The city plans to try to extend some roads, reroute others and keep truck traffic off residential roads.

Environment

Environmental responsibilities are shared by all levels of govern-ment and the role of a city is to ensure "public health." The definition imprecisely includes public health campaigns (like the city's vague "use condom" signs in bathrooms to prevent the spread of AIDS), hygiene (for instance controlling animal waste in parks), noise pollution (limits on when and how loudly public work can take place in residential neighbourhoods), and green spaces and trees within the city's territory.

The divided jurisdictions allow for a lot of buck passing. Montréal's long industrial history has left many parts of the city's territory pol-luted, particularly in the Sud-Ouest, Mercier, along parts of the CP track, the east end and, of course, the rivers. Clean up costs for each spot will run into the millions. The city is waiting on funding promises from the province.

Montréal's government found itself running public consultations on incineration and waste disposal parallel to a similar consultation on behalf of the suburban mayors' Régie intermunicipale de gestion des déchets sur l'Ile de Montréal. Comparatively speaking, the city's consultation was more open than the Régie's. The city offered three different possible plans, the Régie only one, involving a $500 million incinerator promoted by Foster-Wheeler, an American-based corporation. In fact, the Régie had already signed an agreement with Foster Wheeler before the consultation even began. Although Montréal's consultation was not quite that predetermined, the city's ad campaign for the consultation read, "various possibilities will be discussed, including those favoured by the city."[9]

Yet, the BCM recommended that no incineration plants should be constructed for the next two years, pending further study. It also concluded that the Miron Quarry should remain open past 1994, until a satisfactory solution to landfilling can be found. The report is now in the hands of the Executive Committee, who will make a decision by early 1993.[10] Neither of these recommendations are likely to prove too popular. The first flies in the face of suburban municipalities' plans to construct a new incinerator in the east of the island, in addition to Montréal's Des Carrières plant. The second contradicts the MCM's oft-postponed plan to shut the quarry. The province's jurisdiction in this area has led it to demand that all municipalities reduce waste by 50% by the year 2000. This reduced reliance on incineration and landfill sites may be necessary.

Meanwhile, a more aggressive campaign promoting recycling, waste reduction and encouragement of recycling industries in both the public and private sector is urgently needed. The city has also commissioned several studies on better disposal of snow after its removal from streets. Currently, most snow is dumped, untreated, into the St. Lawrence river.[11] Alternatives, not more studies, are now needed.

Community Advocacy Groups

Although most community groups work locally, there are several umbrella organisations or resources that work on behalf of the whole city. The following are some of the most active:

Action Rébuts
3620 University Ave.
Eaton Building, rm. 505
Montréal, QC
H3A 2V2
398-7457
Anti-incineration lobby group.

AKAX
4175A Décarie Boulevard
Montréal, QC
H4A 3J8
369-2529
Action group on behalf of Black
youth.

*Alliance des communautés
culturelles pour l'égalité dans la
santé et services sociaux
Strathearn Intercultural Centre*
3680 Jeanne-Mance, Suite 331
Montréal, QC
H2X 2K5
842-6891

*Association pour la défense des
droits des assistés-sociaux*
2735 Notre-Dame West
Montréal, QC
H2J 1N9
932-3926

Au bas de l'echelle
6839-A Drolet, suite 305
Montréal, QC
H2S 2T1
270-7878
Lobby group on behalf of non-
unionized women workers.

Black Community Council of Québec
2121 Old Orchard
Montréal, QC
H4A 3A7
482-8802

*Centre for Research Action on Race
Relations*
3465 Côte-des-Neiges, Suite 801
Montréal, QC
H3H 1T7
271-8207

*Coalition for the Rights of Welfare
recipients*
2365 Grand Trunk Street
Montréal, QC
H3K 1M8
932-5916

*Fédération des cooperatives
d'habitation de l'Ile de Montréal*
3680 Jeanne-Mance, #317
Montréal, QC
H2X 2K5
843-6929

*Fédération des groupes ethniques du
Québec*
3500 Fullum Street
Montréal, QC
H2K 3P6
523-8889

*Le Front d'action populaire en
réaménagement urbain (FRAPRU)*
1212 Panet
Montréal, QC
H2L 2V7
522-1010
City-wide, very active, tenant's
rights lobby group

Heritage Montréal
406 Nôtre-Dame East,
Montréal, QC
H2V 1C8
842-8678
Lobby group for the preservation
of city heritage sites and buildings

Institut de formation en développement économique communautaire
420 St-Paul East, 2nd floor
Montréal, QC
H4J 2H2
281-2081
economic development

Le Monde à bicyclette
Strathearn Intercultural Centre
3680 Jeanne-Mance, Suite 341
Montréal, QC
H2X 2K5
844-2713
Pro-bicycle lobby group

Montréal Harvest
9015 Meilleur Street
Montréal, QC
H2N 2A3
381-6641
Collects and redistributes food from stores and restaurants.

Mouvement Action-Chômage de Montréal
6839-A Drolet
Montréal, QC
H2S 2T1
271-4099
Information and lobby group for people receiving unemployment insurance.

Native Friendship Centre
3730 Côte-des-Neiges Rd.
Montréal, QC
H3H 1V6
937-5378

Nous nous intégrons en commun, inc.
1951 de Maisonneuve East, #102
Montréal, QC

H2K 4M2
598-7677
Lobby group for disabled people.

Régroupement des comités logements et associations des locataires
1331-A Ste-Catherine, East
Montréal, QC
H2L 2H4
521-7141
Complete listings of all active tenant's rights groups throughout the city

Régroupement des organismes du Montréal ethnique pour le logement
6655 Côte-des-Neiges, #270
Montréal, QC
H3S 2B4
341-1057
Tenants rights group specifically concerned with discrimination around housing issues

Reseau d'aide aux personnes seules et itinérantes de Montréal
94 Ste-Catherine East
Montréal, QC
H2X 1K7
879-1949
Lobby group on behalf of homeless people

Service d'aide aux Néo-Québecois et aux immigrants
Strathearn Intercultural Centre
3680 Jeanne-Mance, Suite 317
Montréal, QC
H2X 2K5
842-6929
Helps new immigrants deal with various levels of government and lobbies on their behalf.

Société pour vaincre la pollution
445 Saint-François-Xavier, rm. 20
Montréal, QC
H2Y 2T1
844-5477

Transport 2000 Québec
3865 St-Denis
Montréal, QC
H2W 2M4
844-4024
Lobby group for public transit users

STOP
716 rue St-Ferdinand,
Montréal, QC
H4C 2T2
932-7267
Anti-pollution lobby and public education group

Community Media

CINQ-FM (Radio Centreville)
5212 Saint-Laurent
Montréal, QC
H2T 1S1
495-2597

CKUT (Radio McGill)
3480 McTavish
Suite B15
Montréal, QC
H3A 1X9
398-6787

The Montreal Mirror
400 McGill, 2nd floor
Montréal, QC
H2Y 2G1
393-1010

Voir
4130 Saint-Denis
Montréal, QC
H2W 2M5
848-0805

NOTES

1. Roy, Jean-Hugues and Brendan Weston, eds., *Montréal: A Citizen's Guide to Politics*, Black Rose Books, Ltd., Montréal, 1990.
2. Johnston, David, "One-quarter of city is on welfare or UIC," *The Gazette*, May 13, 1991 p. A1.
3. Ville de Montréal, *Les orientations et les stratégies du Plan d'urbanisme de Montréal*, Service de l'habitation et du développement urbain, Bureau du plan d'urbanisme, 2nd Quarter, 1992.
4. Herland, Karen, "Playing House," *The Montreal Mirror*, March 26-April 2, 1992, p. 8.
5. Ibid.
6. Herland, Karen, "Expanding to fill the space," *The Montreal Mirror*, December 26-January 9, 1992, p. 7.
7. Ville de Montréal, *Les orientations et les stratégies du Plan d'urbanisme de Montréal*, Service de l'habitation et du développement urbain, Bureau du plan d'urbanisme, 2nd Quarter, 1992.
8. Morissette, Claire, "Streets that Breathe: Controlling Cars," in *Montréal: A Citizen's Guide to Politics*, Jean-Hugues Roy and Brendan Weston, eds., Black Rose Books, Ltd., Montréal, 1990. pp. 108-122.
9. Herland Karen, "Selling Garbage," *The Montreal Mirror*, December 12-December 19, 1991, p. 10.
10. Noël, André, "Montréal pourrait exploiter le dépotoir Miron au-delà de 1994," *La Presse*, July 4, 1992, p. A3
11. Ville de Montréal, *Répertoire des interventions de la Ville de Montréal en matière d'environnement*, December 1991.

REFERENCES

Bagnall, Janet, "Montreal home to fewer and fewer children, study finds," *The Gazette*, October 10, 1992, p. A3.
GIUM, *Dossier Urbain, Arrondissement Plateau Mont-Royal/Centre-Sud, Penser pour agir,*, Ville de Montréal, June, 1989.
Herland, Karen, "Expanding to fill the space," *The Montreal Mirror*, December 26-January 9, 1992, p. 7.
Herland, Karen, "Playing House," *The Montreal Mirror*, March 26-April 2, 1992, p. 8.
Johnston, David, "One-quarter of city is on welfare or UIC," *The Gazette*, May 13, 1991 p. A1.
Noël, André, "Montréal pourrait exploiter le dépotoir Miron au-delà de 1994," *La Presse*, July 4, 1992, p. A3
Roy, Jean-Hugues and Brendan Weston, eds., *Montréal: A Citizen's Guide to Politics*, Black Rose Books, Ltd., Montréal, 1990.
SODEM, *Dossier urbain arrondissement Mercier/Hochelaga-Maisonneuve, Rapport final*, Ville de Montréal, July, 1989.
Ville de Montréal, *Budget 1992*, Service de la planification et de la concertation, Module des Communications, 4th Quarter, 1991.
Ville de Montréal, *Les orientations et les stratégies du Plan d'urbanisme de Montréal*, Service de l'habitation et du développement urbain, Bureau du plan d'urbanisme, 2nd Quarter, 1992.
Ville de Montréal, *Répertoire des interventions de la Ville de Montréal en matière d'environnement*, December 1991.

Ahuntsic / Cartierville

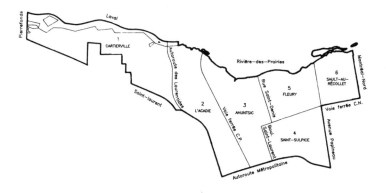

District I
Map from Ville de Montréal, Pour mieux vivre Montréal, 1991-1992 4th Quarter,
1991, pp. 38.

4.3 AHUNTSIC /CARTIERVILLE
District I

Area

This is the northernmost district of the city. It stretches for 12 kilometres along Rivère-des-Prairies, bounded to the west by Pierrefonds and Ville St-Laurent, to the east by Montréal-Nord, and to the south by Ville Mont-Royal and the Villeray/Saint-Michel/Park Extension district (separated by the Metropolitan Boulevard). At 24 km², it is the second largest district in Montréal.

Psychologically and physically, the district's isolation is underlined by the river to the north and the Metropolitan to the south, both rather imposing barriers. As well, the district is criss-crossed by CN and CP lines. Some parts of this district, like Rivière-des-Prairies/Pointe-aux-Trembles are more suburban than urban; its distance from the downtown core, more recent upscale development at the western and eastern boundaries of the district, and relative proximity to suburban communities contribute to this atmosphere.

The CP rail line bisects the area into Ahuntsic to the east, and Cartierville to the west. Even within Cartierville, there are huge discrepancies in the lifestyles of those living east and west of the Laurentian Autoroute. Those to the west tend to live in newer, single-family homes (like the residents of Pierrefonds across their western border) while those living in Cartierville east, are more similar to their southern neighbours in Park Extension in terms of cultural background and poorer available housing stock. The city's 1992 urban plan for the district described household incomes on the west as "two and even three times" that of the east.

The enormous discrepancies in terms of economics and age (a sizable and increasing elderly population can be found in some areas of Ahuntsic) have led to various tensions within the community. Pierre Gagnier, himself the Civic Party councillor in district 1 (Cartierville), the well-off western tip of the district, was part of a campaign in early 1992 to stop a proposed low-income housing unit from being built in the district because of the "undesirable" elements that it might attract. Meanwhile, there is an increased demand for social housing on the part of the older population.

Topography/institutions

Nearly 14% of the total district is green space, twice that of many other districts. In total, there are 80 parks, but many of them are tiny empty lots. The larger parks are concentrated in pockets along the river. A lot of the district's green space is not accessible park land but rather grounds for a large institutional presence in the area. Many of the regions institutions are on large plots of private land. They act as welcome visual green space, creating a sense of openness, but they cannot be readily utilized by the population as a whole. The district has nearly 30 public and private schools and colleges of various descriptions. There are seven hospitals and two CLSCs. The area also has two prisons (Bordeaux and Tanguay).

Besides the various schools and the recreational Centre Claude-Robillard, very little exists in the way of cultural/community centres. Ahuntsic has three libraries and one Maison de la culture. Cartierville is far poorer in community resources. Many of the community centres are located in various church basements throughout the district. The majority of community groups are golden age societies.

Demographics

Ahuntsic/Cartierville's total population is 122,410. This district's population has increased over the last 20 years, probably representing some of the drift from downtown as fewer people can afford to live in the city centre. The bulk of this increase has been in Cartierville and the southwest of Ahuntsic, where a lot of construction took place in the eighties.

The population is older than the city average; between 1981 and 1986, the over 65 population increased by 14%, compared to 6% for the city as a whole — the number of women over 65 doubled in that time period in Ahuntsic. Cartierville, west of the Laurentian autoroute, represents the highest concentration of "nuclear families," with the majority of single parent families living in the other half of Cartierville.

Nearly half of Cartierville's residents are neither anglophone nor francophone. The western part of the area has a large Italian population, while the eastern part tends to have more African or Asian immigrants. Pockets of Ahuntsic have a large proportion of European immigrants (mostly Italian). Seventy per cent of Ahuntsic's population is francophone.

Unemployment is not a major problem in the district, as unemployment figures are lower here than for the city as a whole. Average household incomes in the district, at $31,305, are far above the city's. Averages, in this case, hide problems. In Cartierville, one in five households has a combined annual income of $35,000. At the same time, one in three households lives on $10,000/year. The hidden poverty carries its own difficulties; at least one community worker was quoted as saying that a family in need had to go all the way to Plateau

Mont-Royal to find a food basket. The resources do not exist in the district.

More of the district's women have chosen to stay in the home full-time than enter the job market; the number of men with incomes of less than $10,000 is far less than the city average; the number of women is much greater, yet the low unemployment figures suggest that they are not actively looking for work.

Housing

Forty per cent of the district's land is used for housing, with 51,000 households in all. The bulk of the area, particularly south of the river, where the neighbourhood was originally established, is of relatively recent construction (post World War II). The majority of dwellings are in good structural shape.

Overall, the owner occupancy rate is 36%, but in Cartierville, west of the Laurentian, the rate jumps to 44%, representing more single dwellings. The northeast end of the district has the highest rate of renters, and housing stock east of the Laurentian in Cartierville is mostly smaller apartment buildings of six to 10 units. Most of these are rented and absentee landlords have led to the gradual depreciation of much of this housing. Dwellings on the other side of the CP tracks tend to be the standard duplex and triplex type. Overall, renters represent only two-thirds of all residents, considerably less than the three-quarter average for the city as a whole.

Subsidized housing is concentrated mainly in Ahuntsic, with about 1,300 units. Vacancy rates for Ahuntsic and Montréal-Nord combined are at 5.1%. Cartierville and Saint-Laurent have almost the highest vacancy rate in the MUC, 6.8%.

Commerce/Industry

The majority of commercial streets serve local needs. No commercial district offers city-wide appeal. The city established a CDEC in the district in 1991. Papineau, St-Laurent, Gouin, Henri-Bourassa, Fleury, Salaberry, and Crémazie are the main commercial routes. Small dépanneurs and local stores dominate the area and in many cases, residents must go to the nearby Place-Vértu, Rockland and Centre-Laval shopping centres to get name brands, clothes and shoes.

Only 5.6% of available land is devoted to industry. The Cité de la Mode, a concentration of textile factories, provides 32,000 jobs, and also attracts shoppers from across the city. Three other small industrial centres are located along parts of the railway lines and along the Metropolitan.

Transportation

The district is connected to Laval in the north by four bridges. Several main streets run both north/south and east/west. This area is a major access point; in the period between 1970 and 1987, bridge traffic increased by 142%. In 1987, 250,000 people used the bridges to commute, to the city. The traffic will increase as more and more people move to the suburbs. Parking becomes a problem, particularly around metro stations, and noise and air pollution rises.

Plans to expand the metro line all the way to Laval have yet to come to fruition. There are three metro stops within the district. In some cases, it is easier to take the commuter train in from the Deux-Montagnes line instead of relying on the metro or bus. The end of metro line 2 (Henri-Bourassa) is also problematic for the district because of the noise and safety problems created by the bus lines which converge on the site.

There are only two real bike paths in the area, along Christophe-Colomb and Gouin boulevards. Both of these are parts of main streets, making the paths less safe or attractive to cyclists than those that do not require battling car pollution, noise or stress.

Environment

The heavy traffic from the suburbs and the presence of the Metropolitan and other autoroutes through the district, create noise and air pollution problems, particularly during rush hours.

The central southern portion of the district is the only area where curbside recycling is available.

Rivière-des-Prairies is itself polluted by years of industrial dumping and should be cleaned up.

Voter Profile

This district has seen a fairly complex game of electoral musical chairs, although half of the six electoral districts voted MCM in 1990, only two remain, and there have been shifts in the other seats. Of the six electoral ridings, two of the winners, in 1990, were from the Municipal Party (representing two-thirds of all their seats in the city, with the last one belonging to Nick Auf Der Maur in the downtown core). Alain André won in district 3, which is not surprising as he was a mayoral candidate.

Pierre Gagnier won his seat in district 1 from MCM incumbent and former executive committee member Kathleen Verdon. This election seems to be as much a move to the right as an absolute rejection of Verdon. Verdon began to lose ground when she was pegged as an extravagant culture maven more interested in art than her constituency. She also never actually moved into the district, although she had promised to.

It is interesting that a third right-wing incumbent, Serge Sauvageau, lost the seat he'd won in district 6 in a 1988 by-election to MCM newcomer Sylvie Lantier. Lantier, a long-time MCM party member, won by a very small margin, but now sits as vice-president of the administration and quality of services committee. She and Pierre Lachapelle remain the only two MCM councillors in the district. Lachapelle's nearest contender was from the Civic Party.

The last election in district 4 was won by then MCM candidate Michel Benoit who left the party in March of 1992 to join the Civic Party. Gagnier also leapt to the CPM and by 1992, the merger of the two right-wing parties meant that André was a CPM Councillor as well.

Concerns

Both the number and kind of community organizations in Cartierville need to be improved. The invisible poor in the district require adequate services. Although the housing stock is in relatively good shape in the district, improvements are a priority for the east of Cartierville. More low-income housing is needed. As well, the aging population may soon need a particular kind of housing that does not currently exist.

Transportation is a basic problem, and improving both traffic and accessibility while reducing pollution is crucial. The city promises both improved circulation and extensions of the metro and suburban train network towards the north shore, although plans on both these projects have been in the works for years. The city also promises to improve parking and bus connections around the Henri-Bourassa metro, and to create reserved bus lanes and reserved parking programs for residents there.

The city plan for the district proposes that some of the land now owned by institutions should be redeveloped into accessible green space. The city also hopes to improve green space along the CP line, although the dirt and pollution associated with the tracks will certainly take away from the clean air/recreational aspects of parks. There are also promises to develop a beach once the river is cleaned up.

The city promises to consolidate and promote certain commercial and industrial sectors in the district, especially in the south of the district and along the Metropolitan.

Community Development

CDEC Ahuntsic/Cartierville
(no address as yet)
331-8738
Local economic development

Community Media

Journal Ahuntsic
1008, East Fleury
Montréal, QC
H2C 1B7
384-6161

REFERENCES

Bureau des élections, Service du greffe, *Election Montréal 1990,* (election results for councillors and mayor by district) November 6, 1990.
CONSAUR Inc.,*Dossier Urbain Arrondissement Ahuntsic/Cartierville,*Service de l'habitation et du développement urbain, Ville de Montréal, July,1989.
Durford, Nancy, "Good signs for tenants," *The Gazette,* March 14, 1991, C1.
Gilles Gauthier, "La Petite vie tranquille d'un quartier vert et bourgeois," *La Presse,* October 31, 1990.
Gilles Gauthier, "Un quartier où la fortune cotoie la misère...et le crack," *La Presse,* October 30, 1990, A13.
Thompson, Elizabeth, "The Master Plan" *The Gazette,* August 29, 1992, p. B2.
Ville de Montréal, *Arrondissement Ahuntsic/Cartierville: Synthèse des enjeux d'aménagement et de développment,* Service de l'habitation et du développement urbaine, Bureau du plan d'urbanisme, 1st Quarter,1990.
Ville de Montréal, *Les Loisirs au coeur de votre quartier,* Fall-Winter, 1990-91.
Ville de Montréal, *Plan directeur de l'arrondissement Ahuntsic/Cartierville,* Service de l'habitation et du développement urbain, Bureau du plan d'urbanisme, 2nd Quarter, 1992.
Ville de Montréal, *Profile Socio-Economique de l'Arrondissement Ahuntsic/Cartierville,* Service Planification et de concertation, Module recherche et planification, Division de la recherche, March 1989.
Wells, Paul, "Prosperous Cartierville is having its problems," *The Gazette,* October 22, 1990.

Villeray / Saint-Michel / Park Extension

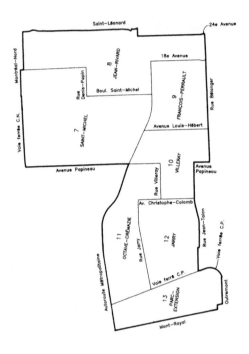

District II
Map from Ville de Montréal, Pour mieux vivre Montréal, 1991-1992, 4th Quarter, 1991, p. 46.

4.4 VILLERAY/SAINT-MICHEL/PARK EXTENSION
District II

Area

The district sits in the north centre of the city, between Ahuntsic/Cartierville to the extreme north. and Rosemont/Petite-Patrie to the south. On the west, the district is bounded by Town of Mount Royal and on the east by Saint-Léonard.

The district is subdivided into three main neighbourhoods. Park Extension is found on the far west, isolated to the east and south by the CP line. Villeray is located in the centre, between the tracks and Papineau, and the largest segment of the district is Saint-Michel. South Saint Michel is separated from the north by the Metropolitan autoroute. The northern sector is also fractured by the presence of both the Miron and Francon landfill dumps.

Park Extension is by far the most disadvantaged segment of the district, and in fact, one of the city's most troubled neighbourhoods. Socio-economic data reveal the area's serious problem with poverty and crime. When the city first defined the district, it did not even mention Park Extension in its name, but has added it in the last two years. Saint-Michel (east of the Francon quarry) experiences similar problems, but to a lesser degree.

The two quarries also create physical barriers within the district. Covering one fifth of the district's 1593 hectares of land, they isolate neighbourhoods. The truck loads of garbage delivered daily cause noise, smoke and a smell that can be intolerable. The 1986 MCM party program promised to close the quarry down by 1987, but deadlines have been regularly extended and the end of operations is now set for 1994. A recent public consultation suggested extending that deadline even further. The 192 hectares of space are to be used for some housing and a small industrial park, with nearly half of the land eventually turned into green space. The Democratic Coalition, in particular, has questioned the environmental safety of the quarry, especially in terms of the biogas emitted from the rotting garbage. The MCM has consistently downplayed the danger of the gas, and continues to suggest ways to turn it into energy or other means of conversion that won't eliminate it. No clear plans on how safe the site will eventually be, or how a clean-up will be financed are forthcoming. The Francon quarry is a dump for snow and no plans for shutting it down are being considered, although there are plans to improve the traffic and nuisance problems associated with the site.

In terms of the actual district determined by the city it is important to recognize that Villeray and Saint-Michel are separated from the

119

Rosemont/Petite-Patrie district by an artificial boundary along Jean-Talon. Historically, Villeray has been more closely connected to Petite-Patrie to the south than Saint-Michel, while Saint-Michel has felt more of an affinity with Rosemont. The city's determination of district boundaries forced local community groups to redefine the population's they serve.

Topography/Institutions

The largest park in the district is Jarry, located in the west of Villeray and cut off from Park Extension by the CP track. There are a few other large parks and some mini parks, but the district's overall percentage of green space is fairly low. Park Extension has only 10 neighbourhood parks, serving 30,000 residents. The highest proportion of green space is in central Villeray.

One hospital (in Saint-Michel) and three CLSCs are located in the area. The district has 20 schools, including one college, but no CEGEPs or other larger institutions that provide facilities for local residents.

There are three arenas in the district, one in Saint-Michel and two others in Villeray. Each sector (with the exception of Park Extension) has its own library. There are also seven community centres and two cultural centres. Overall, Park Extension suffers from a lack of community and cultural facilities.

Demographics

The district represents 14% of the total Montréal population, or 153,844 people. Like most other districts within the city, the population is decreasing. However, in this district the big population decline only began in the mid-seventies. Pockets of the district remain very densely populated. Park Extension and Saint-Michel North both house about 22,000 people/km^2, which is four times the city average.

The age distribution of the population has remained relatively constant due to a steady influx of new immigrants. The district experiences more migration than most, with some residents moving on after a few years and new immigrants taking their place.

Three-quarters of the district's families include children under 15, far more than the city's average.

Overall, one in three families is headed by a single parent.

On average, the district is only 6% anglophone. However, just under 40% of district residents consider themselves neither English nor French, a percentage that jumps to 93% in Park Extension. A quarter of Saint-Michel residents speak Italian as their first language. Nearly 40% of Park Extension residents speak Greek. The growing number of

Haitian, Sri Lankan and Latin American immigrants is redefining Park Extension's demographic composition.

Park Extension also faces the worst unemployment of the district, hovering at close to 20%. With a rate near 15%, the central area of Villeray is not much better off. Around 40% of the district's residents work in manufacturing. District residents make only about 80% of the average income for the city. In Park Extension, the average household income is $18,709. Four per cent of the district residents have an annual income above $35,000, compared with 12% in greater Montréal. The vast majority of residents are perhaps best described as working poor. The northwestern section of Villeray is in the best economic position.

Education levels are extremely low. Nearly 36% of district residents have less than a grade 9 education. This percentage climbs to 42% in Park Extension. Ten per cent fewer residents have a university degree than the municipal average.

Housing

Almost half of the district's housing was built in the period between 1946 and 1960; over 90% was constructed before 1971. Much of the housing built after 1960 was cheap, multi-unit dwellings with poor upkeep since then. Park Extension and the area of Saint-Michel east of the Francon Quarry are in the worst condition. The district was developed primarily as a rental community, and only 25% of residents own their own dwellings. The majority of home-owners live in northern Villeray, in veteran housing. The cheapest rents are in the district's west end. Vacancy rates are about 5%. Even so, a fifth of all municipal demands for social housing come from this district.

Commerce/Industry

Industry is located in the district's east and west extremes, south of Park Extension (built at the turn of the century), north in Villeray along the CP line, south below Jarry Park in the west, and around the quarries in the east. This latter area is badly planned and represents a mixture of residential, industrial and commercial uses. For example, just off the Metropolitan there is an industrial sector with textile and auto mechanic centres, warehouses and a senior citizens' home.

For the most part, commerce is localized, with small streets catering to the immediate needs of the local population. The only exceptions are some sections of Pie IX and Saint-Laurent. The commercial districts tend to be badly planned, with little control over building heights or use of previously residential space. Shoppers are attracted by the Jean-Talon Market and the nearby Rockland Centre.

Transportation

The district is fractured by both physical and psychological barriers in several ways. Park Extension is so thoroughly bounded by the autoroute, train tracks, and industrial parks that there are only five direct routes in or out of the neighbourhood. Since the quarries and the train tracks effectively cut off several east-west routes, traffic tends to run north-south. Jean-Talon and the Metropolitan are the only ways to enter the district from the west.

The Metropolitan autoroute crossing the district also creates a kind of "no-man's land" underneath it, unpleasant for pedestrians and used only sporadically for parking and enterprises like Christmas tree sales.

The sector of northern Saint-Michel located between the two quarries is isolated by the quarries as well as the CN line to the north and the Metropolitan to the south. Traffic from the 500 trucks a day that go to the quarries creates noise, safety and pollution hazards.

The area's bus network is adequate but restricted by the general traffic problems already outlined. The district is also served by Metro lines 2 and 5. Line 5 was badly planned and some stations are in such poorly lit, isolated areas that their use is limited. Overall, nearly half of the residents of the district do not own cars, so public transit, bike lanes and pedestrian walkways are a major priority.

Environment

Clearly the most pressing environmental problem is the Miron Quarry. Dangerous gases emitted from the site itself, as well as the nuisance of garbage trucks constantly driving to and from the dump create problems for nearby residents. The snow in the Francon Quarry does not produce similar gases, although truck traffic in the winter-time is equally unpleasant.

Saint-Michel is the only part of the district that benefits from curbside recycling.

Voter Profile

This district runs all over the political map. Although the electoral winners were predominantly MCM, there were a few surprises. In François-Perrault, district 9, Vittorio Capparelli, an MCM incumbent, beat Municipal Party incumbent, Frank Venneri. The MCM candidate apparently won because the Civic Party candidate helped to split the vote. In District 13 (Park Extension), a very close race between MCM and Municipal Party incumbents yielded a very slim victory for the MCM candidate, Konstantinos Georgoulis.

Finally, in Saint-Michel district 7, an unknown Civic Party candidate upset the MCM incumbent. Both were high profile Italian candidates in a predominantly Italian neighbourhood.

The mayoral race saw Doré slide to an easy victory. The two right-wing parties in the election divided second place between them.

Concerns

Park Extension needs major improvements in terms of access, public resources, education options, retraining and job development for residents to address the problems of isolation, poverty, crime, drugs, and safety. Improvements in housing stock both here and at the extreme east of the district are essential and must be kept affordable for current residents. The city has pledged to improve housing stock (turning some rental units into low-income housing), access to the area (including a footpath to nearby Jarry Park). The plan also promises to turn the Jean Talon railway station into a socio-cultural centre. The city also intends to exploit the industrial sector located along the south of Park Extension. Thus, even as it suggests improvements for east/west traffic, it will more than likely contribute to difficulties for residents who wish to travel south towards downtown.

The city has also promised to control traffic around Crémazie metro and extend metro line 5. These promises have been in the works for a while. Meanwhile, the reserved bus lane on Park was unveiled in September 1992, despite local protest.

The city's plans to redevelop the Miron Quarry include a provision for the creation of 4,000 housing units. Concrete plans on ensuring that the land is safe for residential and park use are needed. The city's urban plan refers to "rationalizing" biogas, which translates into using it to produce electricity, but not necessarily removing its potential to pollute the environment. The quarry site currently has a sorting site for recyclables; it's future if the landfill is closed remains a mystery, and alternate sites have yet to be determined.

The independent study commissioned in 1989 suggested that the Metropolitan should run underground, taking with it the psychological barrier, noise and air pollution. The city does not necessarily endorse this plan, although they will try to consolidate the use of the land around the autoroute, to ensure that it is primarily industrial.

The industrial sector in François-Perrault will be redefined as residential space, although the city plans to do that while maintaining the existing industry.

Community Advocacy Groups

Association des locataires de Villeray
7378 Lajeunesse #213
Montréal, QC
H2R 2H7
270-6703

Carrefour économique du Centre-Nord
1415 Jarry East, rm. 425
Montréal, QC
H2E 1A7
593-8458
Local economic development

Centre Donna
2348 Jean-Talon, east, Suite 205
Montréal, QC
H2E 1V7
727-7430
Italian women's centre

Service Mobile Communautaire du Moyen-Orient
7261 Henri-Julien
Montréal, QC
H2R 2A9
270-8510
Advocacy, information on behalf of Middle-Eastern communities

Community Media

Hebdos Métropolitaines
3750 Crémazie Boul. East,
Montréal, QC
H2A 1B6
374-9400

Journal Communautaire le petit monde
7950 2nd Ave.
Montréal, QC
H1Z 2S3
722-7708

Progrès de Villeray
7105 Saint-Hubert, #202
Montréal, QC
H2S 2N1
279-8419

REFERENCES

Bureau des élections, Service du greffe, Election Montréal 1990 (election results for councillors and mayor by district) November 6, 1990.

COPLANAM Ltée, *Dossier Urbain Arrondissement Villeray/Saint-Michel*, Service de l'habitation et du développement urbain, Ville de Montréal, June 1989.

Durford, Nancy, "Good signs for tenants," *The Gazette*, March 14, 1991, C1.

Hêtu, R., "Entre anciens et nouveaux immigrés, le choc," *La Presse*, October 23, 1990, p. A6.

Moore, Lynn, "Poverty, no jobs, cloud future for Villeray/Saint-Michel,"*The Gazette*, October 23, 1990, p. A5.

Roy, Jean-Hugues and Brendan Weston, eds., *Montréal: A Citizen's Guide to politics*, Black Rose Books Ltd., Montréal, 1990.

Thompson, Elizabeth, "The Master Plan" *The Gazette*, August 29, 1992, p. B3.

Ville de Montréal, *Arrondissement Villeray/Saint-Michel: Synthèse des enjeux d'aménagement et de développment*, Service de l'habitation et du développement urbaine, Bureau du plan d'urbanisme, 1st Quarter,1990.

Ville de Montréal, *Les Loisirs au coeur de votre quartier, Fall-Winter*, 1990-91.

Ville de Montréal, *Plan directeur de l'arrondissement Villeray/Saint-Michel/Parc Extension*, Service de l'habitation et du développement urbain, Bureau du plan d'urbanisme, 2nd Quarter, 1992.

Ville de Montréal, *Profile Socio-Economique de l'Arrondissement Villeray/Saint-Michel*, Service Planification et de concertation, Module recherche et planification, Division de la recherche, March 1989.

Ville de Montréal, *Rapport de la Concertation sur les enjeux d'aménagement et de développement Arrondissement Villeray/Saint-Michel*, June 1990.

Rosemont / Petite-Patrie

District III
Map from Ville de Montréal, Pour mieux vivre Montréal, 1991-1992 4th Quarter,
1991, p. 43.

4.5 ROSEMONT/PETITE-PATRIE
District III

Area

The district comprises only 9% of the city's territory at just under 15 km². However, its population represents 13% of the city's total, making it the city's third most densely populated area. This district lies between Villeray/Saint-Michel/Park Extension to the north and Plateau Mont-Royal/Centre-Sud and Mercier/Hochelaga-Maisonneuve to the south west and east respectively. It borders Outremont on the east and its north-west corner is bounded by Saint-Léonard.

Dividing the district twice lengthwise leaves Petite-Patrie on the west, Rosemont and Nouveau-Rosemont on the east. Demarcations are rue D'Iberville between the first two, and Pie IX Boulevard between the latter. As is the case for most of the districts running through the central part of the island, residents in the west are considerably poorer, with fewer community resources, than those in the east.

The western end of the district is bounded by the CP line, a major focus for the city's new urban plan, and an overall priority in the city's plan for this district. However, in Petite-Patrie, plans for the rail-line are doubly important because the city's Des Carrières garbage incinerator is located here. The Executive Committee won't establish its priorities in the wake of a lengthy public consultation on waste disposal until 1993. Of the three proposals offered for discussion (based on 16 different studies on what to do with the over one million tons of garbage we produce annually) the one requiring spending $200 million over the next 20 years (half of that on upgrading Des Carrières, only to close it by 2002) was promoted. Other scenarios involving increased reduction at source and recycling were dismissed by bureaucrats as "too radical," although the same reports quote polls suggesting that 90% of the population would more actively sort and recycle if the option was available to them. The plans offered no clear targets for recycling or reduction, although the province has passed a law asking each municipality to cut garbage in half by the year 2000. The city's proposals dodge the law by suggesting that burning garbage and creating energy is a form of "recycling," ignoring the pollution problems associated with the process. Reliance on incineration (the only part of the proposals with specific target amounts) is also a catch-22 situation, since the energy produced can only be maintained if the amount incinerated remains constant. Thus you can never reduce the amount of garbage you feed into the incinerator by encouraging reduction or increasing recycling options. The BCM pointed to some of these gaps in the pro-incineration perspective of the reports when it made its recommendations to the Executive Committee. The general tone of its report suggested a more rigorous study of options to incineration and a temporary freeze on improvements to Des Carrières until then.

As was mentioned in the section on district II, the city-defined boundaries have no relationship to traditional community divisions and many local community groups were forced to redefine their constituencies.

Topography/Institutions

Overall, the district is well served by health care, recreational and educational institutions. This is particularly true for the more recently developed Nouveau-Rosemont and least true for Petite-Patrie at the west of the district although the latter neighbourhood has nearly twice the residents living in a smaller area.

Petite-Patrie has the least green space overall, with five very small parks in it's western sector. Jarry Park, located a few blocks to the north of the district, is close, but hard to access because an industrial zone lies between them. The lack of green space, and scarcity of developable land, has made this neighbourhood one of the city's priority sectors for improving what little recreational space exists and finding alternatives. The city's recreation and community development office is working on these plans now. All other sectors have more accessible, larger parks within their boundaries. The more recently developed Nouveau-Rosemont has by far the largest amount of green space, including a large part of the Olympic Park.

There is one CEGEP and 35 other educational institutions in the district. The head office of the Catholic School Board is also located in the area. In terms of health care, Nouveau-Rosemont accounts for five of the nine hospital/CLSCs in the district. The other four are divided between the remaining three sectors. The institutions also control large chunks of land; in some cases the buildings occupy only 10 to 20% of the total area, leaving significant amounts of area green space inaccessible.

Petite-Patrie has no outdoor facilities, and only two indoor ones, compared with four interior and 12 exterior recreational centres in Nouveau-Rosemont. The west of Petite-Patrie counts only four socio-cultural centres, Nouveau-Rosemont has 21.

The very southern tip of the area is known as the Angus lots. Once a railway yard, it has become a residential sector, primarily established by the city through a paramunicipal organization (SOTAN). This area has few community resources, no green space and no recreational facilities. It is also the most densely populated area in the whole district, with a population density two and a half times higher than that of the city as a whole. About 50 hectares of this area remain to be developed. The city is trying to sell the last two pockets of this land it still owns, although both are heavily polluted from the industrial activity that when on there before.

Demographics

This district houses 133,295 residents, a reduction of 23% since 1971. Only 28% of all households in the district comprise more than three people, indicating a low percentage of traditional families. Nearly 40% of families in Petite-Patrie are single-parent.

The vast majority (84%) of residents are French-speaking and only 4% are anglophones. However, one in five of Petite-Patrie's residents speak neither English nor French as their first language, indicating that the other areas are far more homogeneous. Thirty-four per cent of the city's Ukranian population lives in Nouveau-Rosemont.

The population of the area is aging at a faster rate than that of the city as a whole. This is especially true in Nouveau-Rosemont where the over-65 population has nearly doubled since 1971.

In Petite-Patrie, the average household income is about $20,000, nearly $8,000 less than in Nouveau-Rosemont. Unemployment hovers at about 20% of the active population. Although unemployment is highest in western Petite-Patrie, it is also high (between 15 and 20%) along the district's western and southern borders. The north edge of the district fares considerably better while in Nouveau-Rosemont, it remains under 10%.

Education levels in the district are slightly lower than for the city. Almost one third of the district's residents have not completed grade 9.

Housing

The worst housing stock is located along the south-west boundary of the CP line that divides the district from Plateau Mont-Royal/Centre-Sud. This strip is far more industrial (indicating more air pollution, not the least of which comes from the Des Carrières incinerator), and the housing stock is generally older. Forty-one per cent of residents in this area spend more than 30% of their total income on rent, despite the fact that it has the lowest average rents in the district.

The vast majority of the housing is the typical duplex rowhouse, dating, in most sectors, from the turn of the century. With the exception of dwellings near the industrial sector along the western end of the district, stock is relatively well maintained for its age. West of Saint-Laurent, several blocks are occupied by a mix of industrial and residential buildings, causing serious problems of traffic, noise and pollution for those residents. There are more single family dwellings or semi-detached duplexes in Nouveau-Rosemont, reflecting its more recent development. Rosemount's vacancy rate is about 6.5%.

As the number of children in the district drops, some schools are being transformed into low-income housing. Approximately 500 low income units exist in the district, the result of different programs of various government levels, but 2 600 households remain on a waiting list for subsidized housing.

Commerce/Industry

There are 54,000 jobs in the district, largely due to the number of schools and hospitals in the area.

The district's western sector has the most commercial streets. Masson, running east-west through Rosemont, and part of Beaubien running in the same direction through Nouveau-Rosemont, are the only streets available in those areas.

Petite-Patrie has a far more varied commercial network, running both north-south and east-west. The Jean-Talon market (owned by the city) also attracts business from nearby districts. There are three municipally-sponsored commercial improvement programs (SIDACs) in the area, one on Masson and two within Saint-Édouard, along Saint-Laurent and Saint-Hubert.

In fact, those in Petite-Patrie who are employed, tend to be self-employed in a variety of family businesses. When the MCM significantly raised business taxes in their 1992 budget, local merchants reacted strongly. One merchant organized 300 other local residents to demonstrate at the April city council meeting, and to form the Anti-tax Movement.

Most industries are situated along the CP line in the most disadvantaged sector of the district. A large proportion of the industrial buildings are fast becoming unusable. Neighbouring residential areas must cope with air pollution, increased truck traffic, and in the area around the Des Carrières incinerator, carcinogenic emissions. The incinerator itself draws 400 trucks weekly.

Transportation

As outlined above, extensive truck traffic, particularly in the west of the district, causes problems for local residents. For the most part though, there are adequate north-south and east-west routes through the district.

Public transport in the area is fairly complete. The westernmost part of the district lacks sufficient bus lines but is best served by new metro routes. The metro is fairly accessible throughout the district. Line 2 runs just south of the southern boundary, line 3 runs along the west and the new line 5 runs north of the district.

The only existing bicycle path in the area is also the only one running north-south in the city, along Christophe-Colomb. This route is fairly dangerous, cutting across several main streets. There are plans underway to extend the Rachel path all the way to the Olympic Park, which would provide a needed east-west route.

Environment

The area's major environmental concern is the Des Carrières incinerator. Short term smoke and traffic problems as well as long term damage from toxic emissions must be addressed.

Petite-Patrie residents made repeated requests to the city for a curbside recycling program after it was introduced in 1988, and were finally included in the fall of 1991.

Voter Profile

This district holds one of the few electoral districts that re-elected a Democratic Coalition councillor, Pierre Goyer, in Saint-Éduoard district 14 (by a very narrow margin over the MCM), which made it the only Coalition seat outside of NDG. By June 1992, Goyer had left the party to sit as an independent because of disagreements over party structure. Otherwise, the district re-elected its MCM incumbents, including some big names like Executive Committee member André Lavallée in Bourbonnière district 19, and Executive Committee chair Léa Cousineau in Étienne-Desmarteau district 17.

The Civic Party placed second with about 20% fewer votes in every riding but one. In Rosemont district 20, the Municipal Party candidate actually placed a relatively respectable second against the MCM incumbent.

Reflecting some of the environmental concerns mentioned above, Ecology Montréal did slightly better than average in this district. Although the norm throughout the city was for the Civic Party and the Municipal Party to place second and third in districts where there were no obvious influences (i.e. incumbents from other parties, mayoral candidates, etc.), in Louis-Hébert district 16 (where the incinerator is located), the Ecology Montréal candidate came in ahead of the Municipal Party.

Concerns

The city has pledged to improve housing stock through much of Petite-Patrie and some pockets of Rosemont. The independent study, commissioned in 1988, suggested that besides improving existing housing stock, new residential areas could be created on unused land that now belong to certain institutions (hospitals/schools). The city has promised to increase public access to some land used by hospitals in Nouveau-Rosemont, but has no plans to turn any of it into residential property.

More green space and recreational facilities are essential for the west side of the district. The subsequent recreation and community development report should provide concrete solutions to the problem. Some of the undeveloped land in the Angus lots might be reserved for this purpose. However, the city's plans seem to indicate more concentration on the industrial than residential aspects of this area. Most of the concrete recommendations for this district concentrate on consolidating commerce and industry in certain neighbourhoods, but there is little mention of increased residential property or construction. The only new residential property will be built on the site of the Paul Sauvé sports complex, which the city intends to shut down.

Finally, action must be taken to shut down the incinerator located within the district.

Community Advocacy Groups

Canadian Italian Community Services of Québec
505 Jean-Talon, East
Montréal, QC
H2R 1T6
274-9461

Carrefour Latino-Américain
6837 Saint-Denis
Montréal, QC
H2S 2S3
271-8207

CDEC Rosemont/Petite-Patrie
2335 Beaubien East,
Montréal, QC
H2G 1N1
723-0030
Local economic development

Comité de logement de la Petite-Patrie
6747 St-Denis
Montréal, QC
H2S 2S3
272-9006

La Maisonnée
6865 Christophe-Colomb
Montréal, QC
H2S 2W4
271-3533
Multi-cultural centre.

Société populaire d'habitation de Rosemont
110 Jean-Talon East, 3rd floor
Montréal, QC
H2R 1V8
271-3339

Community Media

Courrier de l'Avenir
6519 Molson
Montréal, QC
H1Y 3C4
725-3385

REFERENCES

Adolph, Carolyn, "2 councillors exit Democratic Coalition, say party too rigid, too anglo," *The Gazette*, June 21, 1992, p. A3.

Bureau des élections, Service du greffe, Election Montréal 1990 (election results for councillors and mayor by district) November 6, 1990.

Durford, Nancy, "Good signs for tenants," *The Gazette*, March 14, 1991, C1.

Groupe d'intervention urbaine de Montréal, *Dossier Urbain Arrondissement Rosemont/Petite-Patrie*, Service de l'habitation et du développement urbain, Ville de Montréal, June 1989.

Herland, Karen "Enough is Enough," *The Montreal Mirror*, Nov.26-Dec. 5, 1991, p. 8

Herland, Karen "It's Not Easy Speaking Green," *The Montreal Mirror*, April 16-April 23, 1992, p. 11.

Thompson, Elizabeth,"Civic Party has high hopes to win seats," *The Gazette*, October 24, 1990 A6.

Thompson, Elizabeth, "The Master Plan," *The Gazette*, August 29, 1992, p. B2.

Ville de Montréal, *Arrondissement Rosemont/Petite-Patrie: Synthèse des enjeux d'aménagement et de développment*, Service de l'habitation et du développement urbaine, Bureau du plan d'urbanisme, 1st Quarter,1990.

Ville de Montréal, *Les Loisirs au coeur de votre quartier*, Fall-Winter,1990-91.

Ville de Montréal, "Plan d'action pour une gestion intégrée des déchets solides et des matières récupérables à la Ville de Montréal, December,1991.

Ville de Montréal, *Plan directeur de l'arrondissement Rosemont/Petite-Patrie*, Service de l'habitation et du développement urbaine, Bureau du plan d'urbanisme, 2nd Quarter,1992.

Ville de Montréal, *Profile Socio-Economique de l'Arrondissement Rosemont/Petite-Patrie*, Service de la Planification et de la concertation, Module recherche et planification, Division de la recherche, March 1989

Ville de Montréal *Rapport de la Concertation sur les enjeux d'aménagement et de développement Arrondissement Rosemont/Petite-Patrie*, June 1990.

Mercier / Hochelaga-Maisonneuve

District IV
Map from Ville de Montréal, Pour mieux vivre Montréal, 1991-1992 4th Quarter,
1991, p. 40.

4.6 MERCIER/HOCHELAGA-MAISONNEUVE
District IV

Area

This district takes up the southeastern extremity of the city proper, extending from the St-Laurent River in the south all the way to Sherbrooke street and the limits of Saint-Léonard, Ville d'Anjou and Rosemont/Petite-Patrie to the north. On the west, the district is bordered by the CP line, and on the east, the district of Montréal-East. Mercier/Hochelaga-Maisonneuve covers about 23.5 km².

The district is divided twice lengthwise into Hochelaga-Maisonneuve, Mercier-Ouest and Mercier-Est. The first two areas are separated by a large industrial park, the latter two by autoroute 25.

Hochelaga-Maisonneuve is the most disadvantaged area of this district. Isolated by the train tracks, the river, and a large industrial zone to the east, it is very insular. The usual problems associated with limited access, limited opportunity, rundown housing, and lack of facilities apply here as they do in other pockets of the city. However, the neighbourhood's manufacturing-based economy has been severely hit by plant closings and changing industry over the last few years, and there has been little recovery. In fact, in the winter of 1991, CBC television's W5 described the area as having the highest unemployment in North America, comparable to that of many developing nations.

Another major feature of this area is the huge industrial zone/Longue Pointe military base which stretches along the district's southern border by the river and occupies a vast amount of space through Mercier-Ouest. The concentration of so much industry, most of it built at the turn of the century, creates pollution, traffic, noise, physical and psychological boundaries. As much of this industrial zone was built at the turn of the century, many of the buildings are inadequate or in disrepair, making work less efficient and exacerbating the above concerns.

Topography/Institutions

Parks are fairly accessible and large, particularly in the east of the district. Hochelaga-Maisonneuve has fewer and smaller parks. Worse, the parks are badly planned in relation to each other and tend to be simply undefined green space instead of recreational areas.

The area boasts a large range of recreational centres of interest to all Montréalers: The Olympic Stadium, Botanical Gardens, Insectarium and Biodome take up a chunk of land in the north of Hochelaga-Maisonneuve, extending into Rosemont/Petite-Patrie.

There are two Maisons de la culture, a sprinkling of municipal libraries, some private recreation centres and at least one major theatre. There are also several undergraduate educational institutions, including one CEGEP. A number of clinics, CLSCs and hospitals are located in the district.

Hochelaga-Maisonneuve has a strong network of community groups, many focused on poverty, welfare-rights and popular education.

Demographics

The district houses 137,000 people, or about 13% of Montréal's total population. The population is fairly evenly divided between the three smaller sectors. This was not always the case; Hochelaga-Maisonneuve accounted for nearly 50% of all the districts' residents only 30 years ago. The average number of single-parent households is consistent with the city's, but fully 45% of families in Hochelaga-Maisonneuve are headed by one parent.

The district is predominantly francophone (almost 90%). The remaining 10% of the population contains very few self-identified anglophones. The rest of the population is primarily of European descent and concentrated in Mercier-Ouest.

Education levels drop significantly as you travel from east to west across the district. Almost 70% of residents in Hochelaga-Maisonneuve do not have a university degree and 43% are functionally illiterate. The W5 report put the drop-out rate at about 70%, mostly because students were too hungry to concentrate properly when in school. Local teachers have started to schedule exams earlier in the month, while cupboards are still full.

One third of Hochelaga-Maisonneuve's residents live below the poverty line and a quarter depend on some form of government income. The average revenue is just under $20,000/year. The average family revenue for the district as a whole is comparable to that of Montréal because Mercier-Est and Mercier-Ouest have considerably higher household revenues.

Housing

Reflecting the general economic differences between the three sectors, Hochelaga-Maisonneuve has a much higher proportion of renters (nearly nine-tenths of residents) than the other sectors. Dwellings there are also more densely packed. Two-thirds of these homes were built before the Second World War, and are now in poor condition. Currently there are some 1,100 households on waiting lists for low-income housing, yet only one project was built there in 1990, with another built in Mercier. Those two projects made that district the second to last beneficiary of municipal housing projects for that year, despite the obvious need. During the seventies, 12,000 homes were demolished to make way for an extension to the Ville-Marie expressway that never occurred. The devastated area has deteriorated into a wasteland and no real attempt has been made to fix the damage done.

Hochelaga-Maisonneuve compares poorly to Mercier, where housing density is lower and one or two story dwellings are the norm. Ninety per cent of the homes in Mercier were built within the last fifty years, a large proportion are occupied by their owners, implying better general upkeep. The rental rate in Mercier is only 60% and the vacancy rate 6.2%, compared with 5.2% in Hochelaga-Maisonneuve. Yet Mercier was accorded 52 renovated dwellings through the SHDM in 1990.

Commerce/Industry

The districts offers about 46,000 jobs, a quarter of those in commerce. There are four main commercial routes (Sherbrooke, Hochelaga, Ontario and Sainte-Catherine) and three shopping malls within the area. All of the commercial streets run east-west, reflecting the general orientation of the district. There are two SIDACs (along Ste-Catherine and Ontario) within Hochelaga-Maisonneuve, the only two in the entire district. There are plans to set up a SIDAC on Hochelaga in Mercier-Est.

Commerce is problematic for Hochelaga-Maisonneuve. There are no real supermarkets in the neighbourhood and the large elderly population relies on dépanneur delivery for food, especially during the winter. This creates an artificial inflation where everyone pays high dépanneur prices for food that could be much cheaper. Supermarkets are not attracted to areas with primarily low-income residents, so improvements are not forthcoming.

The district was built on industry, which still occupies 20% of the territory. The main sites include land along the port of Montréal stretching all across the south end of Mercier-Ouest and even further west. The central southern sector of the district is almost entirely industrial, isolating Hochelaga-Maisonneuve from Mercier and worsening living conditions in nearby residences. Hochelaga-Maisonneuve also has smaller pockets of industry, some quite close to residential sites.

Transportation

The district is often used by trucks travelling to and from existing industrial sites, as well as from industry located further east. Some of the main east-west thoroughfares suffer the associated noise, air pollution and general safety problem.

Although the area has the benefit of nine metro stops, the system is set up along east-west lines and provides relatively poor north-south service. Furthermore, with the end of the line located within the district, many people drive in from outside the area and leave their cars, making current parking facilities inadequate.

Environment

Along with the discrepancies in housing quality, environmental problems illustrate major divisions in terms of quality of life for residents. Although Hochelaga-Maisonneuve suffers from industry in the backyards of many residences, Mercier-Est benefits from a "Healthy City" pilot project established in 1988. The project was established by Montréal, in partnership with other levels of government as a model for environmentally sound and healthy residential planning and development. Since 1989, this area is one of a handful in the entire city with access to curbside recycling. When the city announced that 3,000 composters would be available to residents in the summer of 1990, one street in Mercier-Est was able to reserve 30 of them.[1]

Meanwhile, soil pollution due to current and shut-down industries remains a problem. Two different battery recycling plants around the Longue-Pointe military base in Mercier-Ouest have been found responsible for lead leaking into neighbouring yards and at least one school yard. SODIM, the city's paramunicipal corporation responsible for industrial development had pledged $2 million towards cleaning up the area before these leaks were discovered, and now claim they will need a further $3 million from the province to deal with the problem.

Voter Profile

The seven ridings in this district resoundingly re-elected MCM incumbents. The Municipal and Civic Party candidates placed very distant seconds.

The mayoral vote was highly in favour of Jean Doré, who garnered an average of about 70%. The Civic Party consistently came in second with about 25% of the vote, except for the eastern district 45, where the Municipal Party placed second.

Concerns

Both an outside report produced by SODEM and the city have established the revitalisation of the industrial sector as a priority for the district. In several areas where industry and residences are too close, the residences are to be phased out. Far more useful priorities would be retraining of existing residents and improvement of housing stock, particularly in the south of Hochelaga-Maisonneuve.

The city is also eager to establish a satellite business district along Sherbrooke east, between Viau and Autoroute 25. There are no guarantees that occupants will be found for the project.

Another priority for the city is to complete the Ville-Marie extension, as well as other major changes on roads through the district, this to improve traffic flow.

The stock of green space and many of the recreational/cultural resources should be improved. One solution put forward by SODEM is to open up the CEGEPs facilities to the general public.The city's plan calls for a new indoor pool in Mercier East.

The city has promised to revitalize the area's tourist attractions but the cost to local residents is not clear. The city claims it can harmonize industry with residences, but fails to explain how it will achieve this goal. Although many tourists are attracted to the Olympic Stadium (presuming it remains standing), the Botanical Gardens, and, now, the Biodome, the effects are not necessarily positive for local residents. In 1990, the city decided to charge a $2 fee for those who wished to visit the outside grounds of the Botanical Garden, essentially closing off one of the free benefits of the areas for Hochelaga-Maisonneuve residents.

A wide network of community groups in Hochelaga-Maisonneuve concentrate their experience and resources on pressuring provincial and federal governments around subsidized housing cuts, and reform of the welfare law through umbrella organizations.

Community Advocacy Groups

Association pour la défense des droits
des assistés sociaux du
Hochelaga-Maisonneuve
1519 rue D'Orléans
Montréal, QC
H1W 3R2
527-2369

CDEST
4435 Rouen
Montréal, QC
H1V 1H1
256-6825
Local economic development

Comité Chômage de l'est de Montréal
1691 Pie IX Boulevard
Montréal, QC
H1V 2C3
521-3283

Comité contre le racisme
d'Hochelaga-Maisonneuve
522-7597
This relatively new organisation had not yet rented permanent space at the time of publication. Call for the address.

*Coopérative d'action
communautaires des citoyennes de
Hochelaga-Maisonneuve
2048 Charlemagne
Montréal, QC
H1W 3S8
526-0159*
Provides popular education and
recreational resources for low-income families.

*Infologis Mercier
8987 Notre-Dame, East
Montréal, QC
H1L 3M4
354-7373*
Housing rights information

Community Media

*Nouvelles de l'est
3983 Sainte-Catherine, East.
Montréal, QC
H1W 2G4
524-1147*

NOTES

1. Herland, Karen, "Lost in the Paper Shuffle, "*The Montreal Mirror,* November 21-November 28, 1991, p. 7.

REFERENCES

Berger, François, "Une population en crise singulièrement aprouvé par le chômage, *La Presse,* October 25, 1990.

Bureau des élections, Service du greffe, Election Montréal 1990 (election results for councillors and mayor by district) November 6, 1990.

Durford, Nancy, "Good signs for tenants," *The Gazette,* March 14, 1991, C1.

Herland, Karen, "Expanding to fill the Space," *The Montreal Mirror,* December 26, 1991-January 9, 1992, p. 7.

Herland, Karen, "Lost in the Paper Shuffle," *The Montreal Mirror,* November 21-November 28, 1991, p. 7.

SODEM, *Dossier Urbain Arrondissement Mercier/Hochelaga-Maisonneuve,* Service de l'habitation et du développement urbain, Ville de Montréal, July 1989.

Thompson, Elizabeth, "The Master Plan," *The Gazette,* August 29, 1992, p. B3.

Ville de Montréal, *Arrondissement Mercier/Hochelaga-Maisonneuve: Synthèse des enjeux d'aménagement et de développment,* Service de l'habitation et du développement urbaine, Bureau du plan d'urbanisme,1st Quarter,1990.

Ville de Montréal, *Les Loisirs au couer de votre quartier,* Fall-Winter, 1990-91.

Ville de Montréal,*Plan directeur de l'arrondissement Mercier/Hochelaga-Maisonneuve,* Service de l'habitation et du développement urbaine, Bureau du plan d'urbanisme, 2nd Quarter,1992.

Ville de Montréal, *Profile Socio-Economique de l'Arrondissement Mercier/Hochelaga-Maisonneuve,* Service de la Planification et de la concertation, Module recherche et planification, Division de la recherche, March 1989.

Ville de Montréal, *Report of the City Auditor to the Conseil Municipal. For the year ending December 31, 1991,* 2nd Quarter, 1992.

Plateau Mont-Royal / Centre-Sud

District V
Map from Ville de Montréal, Pour mieux vivre Montréal, 1991-1992 4th Quarter, 1991, p. 41.

141

4.7 PLATEAU MONT-ROYAL/CENTRE-SUD
District V

Area

This is the smallest physical district in the city covering only 11 km². It is also the most densely populated, with 11,461 residents per square km. The area is bounded on the north and east sides by the CP rail line and extends to the St-Laurent river to the south. Along the west side, it is bounded by Amherst, further west along Sherbrooke to Parc and as far west as Hutchison above Mont-Royal.

The district is divided lengthwise through the middle by Sherbrooke Street, with very different populations above and below. Centre-Sud, to the south, is one of the city's poorest districts. Amherst is used as the dividing line, although traditionally, Centre-Sud has extended further west. The other district on the west is the downtown core, and the poor in the south of this district have been split off and added to the Ville-Marie district, where the majority of residents are condo-owners. This effectively muffled the voices of the disadvantaged. In the summer of 1990 local residents asked the executive committee to move this boundary west to St-Hubert (to include more of the poor of the Centre-Sud neighbourhood). They were flatly refused.

Topography/Institutions

The district has 90 hectares of green space. The vast majority of this space is big parks (Jeanne-Mance, Laurier and Lafontaine). Parc Lafontaine alone accounts for 40% of the district's green space. Beyond that, there is a lack of green space, particularly in Centre-Sud and Mile-End Plateau Mont-Royal west of Saint-Laurent boulevard). Rachel Street has a bicycle path, part of the city's long promised "green belt" project that links Lafontaine Park to Jeanne-Mance Park, and through it to Mount Royal. Because there is very little land left undeveloped in this district, it is unlikely any new large parks will be created.

Three CLSCs, four hospitals and several old-age homes are located here. The area also has eight high schools and 19 primary schools, although a declining younger population has meant that many schools in the district have been converted to other uses (low income housing, community centres). There are a number of speciality schools (i.e. the National Theatre School) as well.

On the municipal level, there are several cultural institutions, including two Maisons de la culture, the Central Municipal library and the only Phonothèque (music library) in the city. Other important institutions, like the International YMCA, Centre Saint-Pierre Apôtre and dozens of private galleries and theatres, are also scattered throughout the area. In fact, one-quarter of the city's cultural resources are in this district.

It is important to note that the bulk of the institutions are located in the centre and east of the district. Mile End and Centre-Sud lack public recreational facilities, green space and community centres.

Demographics

The population of the district, 125,730, comprises just over 12% of the total city population and over 100,000 fewer people than lived here in 1961. Centre-Sud alone has lost 45% of its residents over the last 20 years. This drop in population is in part due to a demographic shift away from young families and toward single people. Far more single resident, roommate households and childless couples live in this district than the city average. Just over half of the families in Centre-Sud have only one parent, compared to a third on average for the city. Even in the Plateau, single parent families are far above average at 40%.

Nearly 80% of area households are francophone. This is particularly true of regions east and south of St-Denis/Sherbrooke. In Mile End, one in two households does not consider French it's first language. Throughout the district, less than seven per cent of all residents are anglophone. It is worth noting that the western areas of the district which have a large European population also have a much larger anglophone population (roughly 17%).

The district's poverty and unemployment rates are higher than the city' average. The average household income is $20,880, nearly $6,000 below that of the city (and just barely above the $20,000 poverty line for families). But a new economic profile may be emerging. Young urban professionals who are underemployed or unemployed are concentrated in the central part of the district, either north near Laurier Park, or south of Sherbrooke St.

Housing

The district has 13% of the city's housing on only 6% of its land. Nearly two-thirds of all available housing in the district is over 50 years old; the average for the city is half that figure. Less than four per cent of housing was built between January 1981 and June 1986 (the time of the last census). The vacancy rate is roughly 5%.

Eighty-four per cent of residents rent their homes. Over 40% of renting households spend more than 30% of their total income on rent, a figure considered very high. This is particularly true in the Centre-

Sud district where available housing rarely conforms to standard codes.

There are wide discrepancies in housing statistics above and below Sherbrooke Street. Although a large network of co-op housing, some 1,000 homes, including several subsidized spaces both above and below Sherbrooke Street exists in the area, 2,000 families (living below Sherbrooke) sit on waiting lists for subsidized housing. Meanwhile, gentrification has hit Plateau Mont-Royal. Some 18,000 units have become co-propriétés in the last few years.

Commerce/Industry

The district offers 70,000 jobs, putting it, along with Notre-Dame-de-Grâce/Côte-des-Neiges as second only to the downtown core for employment opportunities. A third of those jobs are in commerce.The main north/south commercial arteries are Park Ave., St-Laurent, St-Denis and Papineau. East/West routes include Ontario, Ste-Catherine, de Maisonneuve, Prince-Arthur, Duluth, Rachel, Marie-Anne, Mount Royal as well as most streets that run between Park and St-Laurent above St-Joseph.

Centre-Sud, between Berri and Papineau, Réné-Levésque and Sherbrooke is Montréal's gay village. Not only do many gay men live in the area, a series of bars, restaurants and other businesses owned, operated or directed at a gay male clientèle can be found here. The MUC police also make their presence felt here, during the summer, 'inspections' for overcrowding or illegal alcohol sales are weekly, according to many managers.

Duluth and Prince-Arthur have undergone large-scale revitalization programmes. St-Laurent is becoming more upscale and bar oriented. Although recent legislation has curbed the opening of new bars, there are still dozens of licenses that have already been handed out and won't be affected by the cut-off date. Although the night life attracts its own kind of resident, the families and individuals who helped to create the neighbourhood are now dealing with the noise and debris of young bar patrons from all over the city, especially the nearby universities.

This sort of increased business also sends rents sky-rocketing so that the smaller family stores can no longer maintain their space. In short, while many neighbourhoods cannot always get their basic commercial needs met locally, residents in this district (partly because of spillover from nearby downtown) must deal with commercial spaces and rents far beyond the means of the immediate community.

The vast majority of industry is located along the length of the CP tracks that border the district's north and east edges. In the Maguire corridor to the north is the garment district. Along the far south, nearly at the river, are a large number of telecommunications centres (i.e. CBC studios) giving the area the name "Cité des Ondes." There are a few other pockets of industry along commercial streets, particularly north on St-Laurent and Park Ave, often within residential sectors. The area around the entrance to the Jacques-Cartier Bridge still has space for expansion/development.

Transportation

The large amount of traffic drawn by the area's commercial streets make parking difficult throughout the district. Traffic is also a problem, particularly at rush hours since the area comprises some of the main arteries leading to the downtown core.

The network of bicycle paths is improving; routes now exist in the south of the district and along Rachel for east-west traffic, as well as north-south along Christophe-Colomb. The safety of these routes is questionable. One cyclist was killed by a motorist while on the Rachel Street path in 1990.

Environment

Although residents in the area seem concerned with ecological issues (see voter profile), only the western part of Plateau Mont-Royal has curbside recycling. Some residents on the north-western sector are also active in trying to close down the Des Carrières incinerator, since much of its related pollution spills over into the north of this district.

Voter Profile

In the 1990 election, the four ridings in the east and south of the district the incumbent MCM candidates won with a clear majority. In all of these areas, the Civic Party placed a rather distant second (at least 40% of the vote behind the winner).

The real surprise occurred in the two western-most ridings (24 and 25). These electoral districts have the highest percentage of anglophones in the district, and a noteworthy number of European and new immigrants. Both elected MCM incumbents but neither won with a clear majority. The second choice was not the CPM, but Ecology Montréal. The MCM's Michel Prescott in Jeanne-Mance district 25 was only 11% of the vote ahead of the Ecology Montréal candidate. The good showing of Ecology Montréal Party here may be due in part to the presence of party spokesperson Dimitri Roussopoulos in district 25, the party's popularity with non-francophone voters and a heightened awareness of environmental issues. By September 1992, Prescott had left the MCM, after 10 years as a Councillor with the party, to sit as an independent. He cited slow pace and misplaced priorities of the MCM as his reasons for going solo.

Finally, in terms of the mayoral vote, the easy winner was Jean Doré right across the board. The Civic Party ran a very distant second throughout the district. The only surprise here is that in Mile End district 24 the DCM mayoral candidate, Pierre-Yves Melançon, did fairly well relative to the other runners up (though still far from the majority given to the MCM).

Concerns

According to an independent study that GIUM did in 1989, concentrations of poor neighbourhoods, lack of subsidized, quality housing and the poor condition of much of the housing present a serious problem area for this district. Public recreational facilities and green spaces are also lacking, particularly in the district's west and south sectors. Very little land remains available for development, and much of it is expensive. More public parking is also essential. The city has promised to work on these areas, particularly in relation to Mile End and Centre-Sud. The city's plan calls for the development of underused centres in both these neighbourhoods as community recreational spaces. It also suggests creating more residential development around the Jacques Cartier bridge.

However, the bulk of the city's recommendations concern the industrial base along the CP line and commercial development.[1] Some commercial streets have been over- or inappropriately developed (i.e. industry located in what are essentially residential areas to the north and concentrations of expensive boutiques in areas that can not really support them). This causes traffic problems and lowers the quality of life for near-by residents. Industry needs to be redeveloped away from residential neighbourhoods. The city has promised to put a brake on commercial development, especially in the northwest of the district.

At the same time, the city wants to promote the cultural character of the district, by encouraging cultural production, supporting the Cité des Ondes and redeveloping some of the abandoned, underused industrial space along the CP line into rehearsal, studio or distribution space for artists.

Community Advocacy Groups

ACT-UP
3600 Hôtel-de-Ville
Montréal, QC
H2X 3B6
527-2423
AIDS activist group

Association des locataires des habitations Jeanne-Mance
1530 Sanguinet, #2
Montréal, QC
H2X 3G1
845-6394

Association pour la défense des droits des assistés-sociaux
770 Rachel Street East
Montréal, QC
H2J 2H5
521-1602
Lobby group for welfare recipients

CDEC du Centre-Sud/Plateau Mont-Royal
1800 Parthenais, rm. 300
Montréal, QC
H2K 3S3
Local economic development

Centre Africa
1644 Saint-Hubert
Montréal, QC
H2L 2W4
843-4019
Community organization for residents originally from Africa

Centre des femmes de Montréal
3585 St-Urbain
Montréal, QC
H2X 2N6
842-2780/81

Centre des femmes du Plateau
5148 Berri
Montréal, QC
H2J 2S3
273-7412

Centre des gais et lesbiennes de Montréal
1355 Ste-Catherine East,
Montréal, QC
H2L 2H9
528-8424

Chinese Neighbourhood Society of Montréal
5615A Park
Montréal, QC
H2V 4H2
273-6441

Coalition des personnes atteintes du VIH
3600 Hôtel-de-Ville
Montréal, QC
H2X 3B6
282-6673
Advocacy group on behalf of people with HIV

Comité de récupération et recyclage Plateau/Mile End
5014 rue Mentana,
Montréal, QC
H2J 3C3
387-7751
Environmental lobby group

Comité logement de Centre-Sud
2083 Beaudry, suite 90
Montréal, QC
H2L 3G4
521-5992
Tenant's rights

Comité logement Saint-Louis
2165 Mont-Royal East
Montréal, QC
H2H 1K2
527-3495
Tenant's rights

Comité sida aide Montréal
3600 Hôtel-de-Ville
Montréal, QC
H2X 3B6
282-9888
Advocacy, support and education on
AIDS-related issues

Cooperative d'éducation populaire
des citoyens d'Olier
772 Rachel East
Montréal, QC
H2J 2H5
525-1829
Tenant's rights, popular education, retraining programs for
women

Info-Ressource femmes et logement
Inc.
1200 Laurier est #212
Montréal, QC
H2J 1G9
272-9304
Tenant's rights group focusing on
issues affecting women

The Intercultural Institute of
Montréal
4917 Saint-Urbain
Montréal, QC
H2T 2W1
288-7229
Information, referral and
documentation on various cultural communities

L'Hirondelle
4652 Jeanne-Mance
Montréal, QC
H2V 4J4
272-0680
Support and education for immigrants

Communauté Milton-Parc
Strathearn Intercultural Centre
3680 Jeanne-Mance, Suite 314
Montréal, QC
H2X 2K5
289-9646
The land trust of neighbourhood
housing coops

Organisation populaire des droits
sociaux
1651 Logan Ave.,
Montréal, QC
H2L 1V1
521-3283
Welfare rights lobby group

South Asia Community Centre
3600 Hôtel-de-Ville
Montréal, QC
H2X 3B6
842-2330

3rd Avenue Resource Centre
3609 St-Laurent,
Montréal, QC
H2X 2V5
849-3271
Social action group concerned
with issues affecting immigrants
and racism

Milton-Parc Citizens' Committee
P.O. Box 1258
Succ. Place du Parc
Montréal, Québec
H2W2R3
844-6029
Local citizens' group founded in 1968

Community Media

Fugues
1212 St-Hubert
Montréal, QC
H2L 3Y7
848-1854
Local gay magazine

Journal St-Louis et Mile-End
4181 St-Dominique
Montréal, QC
H2W 2A7
844-0388

RG
P.O.B. 5245
Succ. C.
Montréal, QC
H2L 4K1
523-9463
Local gay magazine

NOTES

1. Groupe d'intervention urbaine de Montréal, *Dossier Urbain Arrondissement Plateau Mont-Royal/Centre-Sud: Penser pour agir,* Service de l'habitation et du développement urbain, Ville de Montréal, June 1989.

REFERENCES

Berger, François, "Une quartier voie de passer aux mains de la 'petite bourgeouisie' décapante," *La Presse,* October 26, 1990, p. A8.
Bureau des élections, Service du greffe, Election Montréal 1990 (election results for councillors and mayor by district) November 6, 1990.

Durford, Nancy, "Good signs for tenants," *The Gazette*, March 14, 1991, C1.

Groupe d'intervention urbaine de Montréal, *Dossier Urbain Arrondissement Plateau Mont-Royal/Centre-Sud: Penser pour agir*, Service de l'habitation et du développement urbain, Ville de Montréal, June 1989.

Herland, Karen, "Community Cuts," *The Mirror,*, March 26-April 2, 1992, p.8.

Herland, Karen, "Squeezing them out," *The Montreal Mirror*, July 18-July 25, p. 6.

Thompson, Elizabeth, "The Master Plan," *The Gazette*, August 29, 1992, p. B2.

Ville de Montréal, *Arrondissement Plateau Mont-Royal/Centre-Sud: Synthèse des enjeux d'aménagement et de développment*, Service de l'habitation et du développement urbaine, Bureau du plan d'urbanisme, 1st Quarter,1990.

Ville de Montréal, *Les Loisirs au coeur de votre quartier, Fall-Winter*, 1990-91.

Ville de Montréal, *Plan directeur de l'arrondissement Plateau Mont-Royal/Centre-Sud*, Service de l'habitation et du développement urbaine, Bureau du plan d'urbanisme, 2nd Quarter,1992.

Ville de Montréal, *Profile Socio-Economique de l'Arrondissement Plateau Mont-Royal/Centre-Sud*, Service de la planification et de la concertation, Module recherche et planification, Division de la recherche, March 1989.

Ville de Montréal, *Rapport de la Concertation sur les enjeux d'aménagement et de développement Arrondissement Plateau Mont-Royal/Centre-Sud*, June 1990.

Ville de Montréal, *Réponse du Comité éxécutif aux recommandations du Comité-conseil sur les enjeux d'aménagement et de développement Arrondissement Plateau, Mont-Royal/Centre-Sud, September, 1990*.

Ville Maria

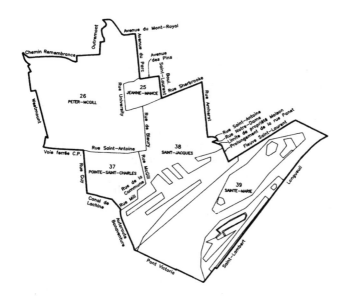

District VI
Map from Ville de Montréal, Pour mieux vivre Montréal, 1991-1992 4th Quarter, 1991, p. 45.

4.8 VILLE-MARIE
District VI

Introduction

The central area of Montréal has experienced massive changes over the last 25 years. Under the Drapeau regime, Montréal began to move away from dependence on industrial production (centred around the Old Port and the Lachine Canal) to finance and commerce, a shift reflected in the development of the office district centred around Place Ville-Marie. The process has continued under the MCM; from transport and housing to skyscraper design, the Ville-Marie master plan seeks to rationalize the diverse elements which make up the core of a "world-class" financial and commercial metropolis. Resistance to this process is long-standing as well; from historic preservation activists in the sixties and seventies to community groups in the eighties, many organizations have challenged the proposed landscape in the district. The following is a short outline of the state of affairs in the downtown core, as well as a profile of the area.

Area

Ville-Marie covers 12.09 square kilometres, stretching roughly from Atwater Street and the border with Westmount in the west to Amherst in the east, and from Mount Royal park and the border with Outremont in the north to the Lachine Canal and the St-Laurent River in the south. While it does not have a very large population compared to other areas, it is undoubtedly the most important centre of activity, and has a complex and diverse character.

The city has divided the Ville-Marie district into 17 sectors for planning; each sector has a distinct set of characteristics indicating the wide discrepancies within the small district. These characteristics are in many cases matters of controversy, inasmuch as they illustrate different effects of the dramatic transformation Montréal's downtown core has undergone: the widening gulf between rich and poor; the conflict between development and heritage; the tension over pollution and public open space.

The diverse and unique characteristics of the Ville-Marie district are highlighted by its neighbours. Bounding communities include the incredible wealth of Westmount and Outremont and low-income communities like Centre-Sud, Pointe Saint-Charles, and Saint Henri. Election ridings manage to include parts of these poorer sections with the comparatively well-to-do residents of downtown proper to homogenize the needs and economic problems of the district as a whole.

Topography/Institutions

Aside from commercial and industrial activity, Ville-Marie is also a major pole for users of public and semi-public institutions. Not only do these institutions employ a significant number of people, they act as valued community resources, offering services to users from the local to the international level. Three universities (Université du Québec à Montréal, Concordia, and McGill) and three CEGEPs attract some 100,000 students to the district every day. There are also more than ten hospitals and other organizations involved in medical services and research.

A number of other activities take place in the district. Several international organizations are located there; for example, Montréal is the civil aviation capital of the world, with five major regulatory agencies in the downtown area. The downtown core is also home to a number of United Nations offices. Facilities such as the Palais de Congrès, the World Trade Centre, and Place Bonaventure attract conventions from around the world.

Ville-Marie is also home to the largest concentration of cultural activities in the region, and forms one of the most important centres of cultural activity in the country. Cultural activities are concentrated into four areas: numerous small art galleries, as well as the Musée des Beaux Arts, the McGill School of Music, and the McCord Museum of Canadian History are located on Sherbrooke St. West; Place des Arts and the recently moved Musée d'art contemperain on Ste. Catherine St. West form an important point. Old Montréal features a number of street activities in the summer and has several theatres, numerous galleries, and a significant community of artists and musicians.

Demographics

The social structure of the central area is evolving to reflect the changes which have transformed it. As of 1986, 50,160 people lived in the district. This represents a small increase from 1981, but even more importantly, it indicates a turnaround from the flight of residents from the inner city over the last thirty years. For example, in the 10 years between 1971 and 1981, the central area lost nearly a quarter of its population to other districts and municipalities. The development of white-collar jobs and services has brought residents back downtown to live (including yuppies), but a social profile shows an area still in flux.

Statistics reveal some of the changes. Compared with the city as a whole, Ville-Marie has a large concentration of singles and "non-family households" (together, these make up about 75% of the population). These statistics do not show important factors such as age and ethnicity. The district has been and continues to be attractive to older people (65+) — they make up almost one fifth of the district's population, although their number has been diminishing over the last decade. In the eighties there was a rapid growth of the 35-44 year age group — they now make up over one quarter of the population and represent the part of the office workforce which has moved back to a gentrified and redeveloped downtown core.

The central area is quite ethnically diverse; 30% of the population are immigrants, including a sizeable Asian population in Chinatown in the southeast of the district. Notable is the continued status of the central area as an enclave for anglophones. Thirty per cent of the district's population claim English as their first language, compared with 11% of the city's population.

The economic gaps noted above are striking when revenue figures for downtown proper are compared to Centre-Sud (parts of which are in this district). The average household revenue is $62,000 in downtown, whereas in Centre-Sud fully half of the adult population is not active at all (either on welfare, UIC or too discouraged to even try to look for work).

Housing

There are about 30,000 residences in the district. Along the north-eastern and northwestern edges, housing is predominantly typical triplexes. In the northeast, many of those homes are part of a large network of housing co-ops established there in the last few decades.

However, both of these parts of the district, are dotted with 12-20 storey apartment buildings. These types of high-rises are more concentrated towards the centre of the district. Nearly 60% of the housing in the district is made up of small apartments of three rooms or less.

The kinds of apartments vary dramatically. Upscale homes and condos are available along Sherbrooke and Dr. Penfield. Meanwhile, some apartment blocks and social housing units along the outskirts of the district house a mix of new immigrants, students, welfare recipients and some professionals. Many of these are run by agencies and maintenance is often low.

Ville-Marie is also the site of one of the MCM's biggest scandals, Overdale. Early in the MCM's administration, the government chose to evict tenants of low rent housing in the area to clear the way for a major development project. This was despite recommendations from its own housing committee and the persistent protests of the residents themselves, many of whom were forcibly evicted from their homes and arrested.[1] Four years later, the site is still a parking lot, the result of razing the homes after the evictions. The developers had allowed their construction bond to run out and the future of the site remains in limbo.[2]

Commerce and Industry

A large proportion of those who work in Ville-Marie are employed in white-collar office and service jobs. Of the 225,000 strong labour force employed in the downtown area, almost half work in business services such as finance, communications, insurance and real estate. Most of the remaining jobs are split between consumer services (retail stores, amusement services, restaurants) and government or related institutions (hospitals, universities and CEGEPs, not to mention the three levels of government). Only 9% of those who work in the district are engaged in manufacturing and construction; once the traditional economic base of the inner city, manufacturing and construction has relocated to the suburbs.

Most of the major economic activity is concentrated into compact sections. The area bounded by Drummond, René-Lévèsque, Bleury, and Sherbrooke houses large commercial complexes and office skyscrapers, although Old Montréal was the original commercial centre, and still attracts much development. Streets such as Sherbrooke, de Maisonneuve, Université, René-Lévesque and McGill-College are all major "addresses" for corporate headquarters and real estate developments. The area bounded by St-Laurent, Sherbrooke, Jeanne-Mance, and Ville-Marie is where public sector activity is situated: for example, Place-des-Arts, Complexe Desjardins, the Hydro Québec building, Place Guy-Favreau, the new World Trade Centre and the Palais de Congrès. This public sector area stretches to the southeast as well, with the provincial courthouse and the municipal offices City Hall.

For its part, the City foresees steady expansion of the office function over the next 10-20 years and is working towards creating 1,000,000 square metres of new office space in 10 years. The city is banking on the possibility that the recession will not effect the need or use of commercial space. If this overdevelopment is pursued, we can expect the trappings of the white collar lifestyle (shopping malls, condos) to increase dramatically.

Finally, another important feature of the downtown core is the "underground city." Currently, the space accessible through the metro system stands at 12 square kilometres. This area doubled between 1984 and 1989 but the new master plan aims to stop expansion in favour of a revitalized Ste-Catherine Street above ground.

Transportation and Communications

With all of this activity concentrated in the district, it is no surprise that most transportation networks (and problems that accompany those networks) enter downtown. Three metro lines converge in the core, as well as two autoroutes, two commuter rail lines, and numerous bus routes. Two thirds of commuters to the district use public transit, with the remaining third made up of automobile users and the small number who both live and work downtown. Crowding on public transit remains a major problem, especially during rush hours, although the MUCTC says that by 1993 the two major metro lines will have been renovated to add more capacity. Parking downtown is another huge problem, for those who drive and for those who must endure the pollution and endless landscape of parking lots.

Ville-Marie is made up of a number of important streets and transport arteries. Some of these are used primarily by the car and are not particularly pedestrian- or bicycle-accessible: René-Levesque, Park, Docteur-Penfield, and certain sections of University, des Pins, Sherbrooke, and Côte-des-Neiges. On the other hand, there is considerable pedestrian activity on large numbers of downtown streets. Ste-Catherine (especially between Phillips Square and Peel Street), St-Laurent, St. Denis, St. Jacques, and Sherbrooke are all fairly large streets with significant pedestrian activity, not to mention the large number of smaller streets in areas such as Bishop-Crescent and Old Montréal.

Voter Profile

There are only two voting districts in the central area, and one of them falls partly into Centre-Sud as well. That district (38) covers Montréal's gay village. MCM incumbent Raymond Blain retained the seat he won in 1986 as the first openly homosexual candidate in the country, at any level of politics. In the spring of 1992, Blain died because of AIDS-related complications. His position as vice-chair on the Culture and Community Development standing committee remain open as this book goes to print. The by-election held in November 1992 gave his seat back to Sammy Forcillo, who had held it for two terms before Blain first ran in 1986. The seat was hotly contested, with 12 candidates, including a high number of independents. Two of the independents, Douglas Buckley-Couvrette and Greg Tutko, ran as gay candidates, hoping to reach voters in the gay village who make up 40% of the electorate. Bernard Bourbonnais of Ecology Montréal, who was also gay, ran as a candidate and came in a respectable third place, with 13% of the popular vote.

Peter-McGill district 26 was hotly contested by incumbent Nick Auf der Maur of the MPM and longtime MCM incumbent Arnold

Bennet, moved there from his previous NDG district. Both council-
lors had been active for years, both were originally MCM members.
Auf Der Maur retained his seat, but by 1991, he had switched to the
CPM.

That district also yielded a surprise in the mayoralty race. Both the
CPM and MPM came in second to Doré, but combined, they may well
have beaten him. This is the only district where it is obvious that a split
vote actually changed results.

Concerns

The problems in the downtown core are hard to separate from
some of the larger economic problems of the city as a whole. The
direction the MCM is taking with the area reflects the administration's
strategy for the whole city. Overdevelopment and high tech, high
finance industries are not necessarily reflective of the needs of the
population. Unless the city can make the area attractive for industries
and corporations (which almost automatically means tax breaks that
would shift the tax burden onto the middle and lower classes) there's
no guarantee business will move back from the suburbs, where it is
currently flourishing.

Although the city continues to stress that it wants to attract residents back to the downtown core, most of its priorities concern commercial and tourist needs. The few lots of land it has to develop residentially,
seem geared towards more high rent housing.

The urban plan, having been passed for this district two years ago,
does not seem to have significantly improved problems like office
vacancies or traffic congestion.

Community Advocacy Groups

Canadian Jewish Congress
1950 Docteur Penfield
Montréal, QC
H3W 1M6
931-7531

Centre d'action sida Montréal pour femmes
1168 Ste-Catherine West,
Suite 202
Montréal, QC
H3B 1K1
954-0170

Chez Doris
2196 de Maisonneuve W.
Montréal, QC
H3H 1L1
937-2341
Drop in centre for homeless women.

Chinese Family Services
987 Coté
4th floor
Montréal, QC
H2Z 1L1
861-5244

Comité des chambreurs de Centre-Ville
1199 Bleury #103
Montréal, QC
H3B 3J1
878-0847
Advocacy on behalf of residents of rooming houses

Québec Native Women's Association
1450 City Councillors, suite 440
Montréal, QC
H3A 2A5
844-9618

Community Media

Journal le Droit
1130 Sherbrooke W.,
Montréal, QC
H3A 2M8
845-8922

NOTES

1. Lisa Jenson in Jean-Hugues Roy and Brendan Weston, eds., *Montréal: A Citizen's Guide to Politics*, Black Rose Books Ltd., Montréal, 1990.
2. Herland, Karen, "Overdale rides again," *The Montreal, Mirror*, October 17-October 27, 1991, p. 8.

REFERENCES

Arpin, Claude, "Slums, vacant lots scar downtown zone," *The Gazette*, October 29/1990 p. A6.

Berger, François, "Seringues et condom jonchent les parcs," *La Presse*, October 26, 1990, p. A8.

Bureau des élections, Service du greffe, *Election Montréal 1990*, (election results for councillors and mayor be district) November 6, 1990.

Colpron, Suzanne, "La Centre ville passage oblige d'un demi-million de gens," *La Presse*, October 29, 1990, p. A10.

Herland, Karen, "Overdale rides again," *The Montreal, Mirror*, October 17-October 27, 1991, p. 8.

Roy, Jean-Hugues and Brendan Weston, eds., *Montréal: A Citizen's Guide to Politics*, Black Rose Books Ltd., Montréal, 1990.

Ruddick, Susan, "The Montréal Citizens' Movement: The Realpolitik of the 1990s" in *Fire in the Hearth: The Radical Politics of Place in America*, Davis M. et al eds., London, Verso, 1990.

Ville de Montréal, *Annual Report 1991*,Secrétariat Général, Service de la planification et de la concertation, Bureau des Communications, 2nd Quarter, 1992.

Ville de Montréal, *Master Development Plan for the Central District, Project* Service de l'habitation et du développement urbain, Bureau du plan d'urbanisme, February 1990.

Ville de Montréal, *Plan directeur d'aménagement et de développement de l'arrondissement Ville-Marie*, Service de l'habitation et du développement urbain, October 1990.

Côte-des-Neiges / Notre-Dame-de-Grâce

District VII
Map from Ville de Montréal, Pour mieux vivre Montréal, 1991-1992 4th Quarter,
1991, p. 39.

4.9 CÔTE-DES-NEIGES/NOTRE-DAME-DE-GRÂCE
District VII

Area

The Côte-des-Neiges/Notre-Dame-de-Grâce (CDN/NDG) district covers 22km² in the city's west end. It is a relatively isolated, rather large district, bounded by other, more wealthy municipalities (Montréal Ouest, Hampstead, Côte-St-Luc, Outremont, Ville Mont-Royal, and Westmount) and encompassing what are essentially two distinct communities: Côte-des-Neiges in the northeast, and Notre-Dame-de-Grâce in the southwest. Its population density is lower than other, more central communities (6,808 persons/km²).

The Décarie boulevard runs through the centre of the territory, touching both major parts of the district. Several autoroutes run along the outskirts of the district.

The district's profile is diverse in many ways. Generally, the central part of the territory, nearer to Mont-Royal, enjoys a much higher standard of living than the northern and southwestern edges. CDN suffers from a relative lack of community recreational space.

Topography/Institutions

The district has a large stock of public and semi-public institutions which shape the nature of the district, and contribute to community life. There are several hospitals and medical centres in the district and many of these institutions serve medical needs for the greater Montréal area. There are also a number of educational institutions: L'Université de Montréal, the Loyola campus of Concordia University, Collège Jean-de-Brebeuf, and Collège Notre-Dame.

For the most part, the district is well served by a little over 70 hectares of open public park space. The district is also connected to Mont-Royal Park and to the city's bicycle path network, both of which are important elements of the Green Belt the city is planning to link green space across the city. It is the central part of the district (east NDG and south CDN) that suffers most from a lack of accessible green space. This is also where many of the major institutions in the district can be found. The city is hoping to be able to get some institutional land available for public access.

A number of other public services operate in the area as well, including three public libraries (two in NDG, one in CDN), Maisons de la culture in both areas. Both districts have a fairly healthy network of community groups, in fact, many of the anglophone or ethno-cultural

161

associations which serve the entire city are based here. Space is becoming a problem. In 1991, Multi-Caf, a CDN food bank that serves community lunches was forced to leave the space it had occupied for two years. Directors lobbied for months through their DAC and local councillor before suitable space could be found in a municipal building, almost eight months after notice on their previous offices was given.

Demographics

According to the 1986 census, just over 150,000 people live in the district, a small increase over the 1981 figure. Like most other districts in Montréal, however, CDN/NDG has lost residents steadily over the past 25-30 years (-15% since 1961).

One partial explanation for the decreasing population has been a change in the structure of households in the area. The district is no longer dominated by families the way it was after the Second World War. Average household size is now 2.2 persons; singles, non-family households (people sharing accommodations), and families without children make up the largest proportion of households. One family in five is headed by a single parent (about the same ratio as the city as a whole); however, there are specific areas where there are higher concentrations of single-parent families, such as in NDG below Sherbrooke Street (40%).

The district is unusually diverse ethnically. Only one third of the population defines itself as anglophone or francophone; the remaining inhabitants come from a variety of ethnic backgrounds. Fully 82% of northern CDN's residents do not consider their first language to be English or French.

In terms of income, the district is quite similar to the rest of the city of Montréal; average income in the district is 10-20% higher than that of the city as a whole. This is in part reflected in the high average level of education attained by area residents. Only one sixth of the district's population has less than a grade nine education (compared with one quarter for the city as a whole). In 1986, almost 40% of the district population had some form of university education (nearly double the proportion for the city). This high figure is due in part to the existence of a large student population near both the Université de Montréal and the Loyola campus of Concordia University.

There are large discrepancies, however, average household incomes in central Snowdon can climb up to $60,000 on some streets. Meanwhile, some streets in northern CDN, characterised by low-rent walkups, average revenues are below the poverty line at $19,000.

The district has suffered a little less from the effects of unemployment than the city as a whole; the 1986 census shows a slightly lower average unemployment rate for CDN/NDG, 12.5%, than the municipal average (which in 1986 was about 14%).

Housing

The district has a mix of housing types from high-rise apartments to three storey walkups, to duplexes and rowhouses. CDN/NDG was developed later than other districts of the city; three-quarters of the housing units were constructed after 1946. However, almost four out of every five households are renters (compared three out of five for the city as a whole).

Absentee landlords and an aging or recent immigrant population in northeastern Côte-des-Neiges have led to serious housing problems. Speculation and tenant harassment are rampant in the walk-ups in the area. Local housing organizations work overtime keeping residents informed of their rights.[1] The lift of the ban on condo conversion could adversely affect the area, since this is the type of housing is most susceptible to quick renovations and high turnovers.[2]

Commerce/Industry

The district is served by a number of commercial arteries, offering services to both local residents and consumers from across the Island. There are over 72,000 jobs offered in the district, more than most other districts provide. Nearly 20% of those are offered through the various health and education institutions located in the region.

Most industry is concentrated along Décarie Boulevard or in the industrial parks in the extreme north and south of the district, along Jean-Talon and Saint-Jacques respectively. Both areas benefit from access to rail and road connections; their relative isolation from the rest of the district means that the disturbances resulting from train and truck traffic are not overwhelming. The city is hoping to encourage high tech industry in the northern industrial sector, while manufacturing work is handled in the south.

The main arteries are Décarie Boulevard, Queen Mary Road, Côte-des-Neiges Road, Sherbrooke Street, and Côte-St-Luc Road. The commerce situated along these routes takes a number of forms: local businesses, serving neighbourhood residents; regional commerce and offices, such as restaurants, auto dealerships and garages, and retail, which serve a clientele from beyond the boundaries of CDN/NDG. These arteries form part of the city's larger transportation network and represent access for local residents who drive or use public transportation. However, these roads also bring noise, auto pollution, and safety problems — all of which contribute to a deterioration of the standard of living for local residents.

A CDEC has recently been established to help the local economy. The city is also hoping to establish business centres in the north and south ends of the Décarie expressway — around Jean-Talon and Vendôme metro respectively.

Transportation

There are also a significant number of local streets on which one can find a variety of activities. In CDN, Victoria Street, Van Horne Street, Lacombe Street, and Decelles Street all offer services to local residents; in NDG, Upper Lachine Road, Monkland, Fielding and Somerled Avenues do the same. These streets are often much less congested than the larger arteries; most of them have are services by bus routes, offering feeder service to the transit system.

The district is well-served by no less than ten Métro stops along two lines. In some cases, Métro stations have been integrated into local business centres (such as Snowdon, Côte-des-Neiges, and Plamondon stations), creating significant hubs of activity.

Environment

The Décarie expressway causes problems in terms of noise for local residents.

Perhaps the biggest environmental issue that affects the district concerns Mount-Royal. Two years after a public consultation on the future of the mountain, little has been done. Any plans for the mountain will affect residents, either because of increased traffic through tourism, or loss of green space if the mountain becomes more built up.

Voter Profile

This district houses a large part of the MCM's early foundation. However, many of the initial strong MCM councillors are the ones who bailed out to create the DCM as more reflective of their original goals. Voters in the west-end were forced to chose between party and councillor loyalty. The DCM retained both its seats.

The most serous loss for the DCM occurred in Côte-des-Neiges district 27. There, the DCM lost (with its mayoral candidate) to an incumbent from the MCM. Another interesting twist occurred in Notre-Dame-de-Grâce district 31. Michael Fainstat has represented this district since 1974 for the MCM (in fact, he was the sole MCM Councillor in 1978). He has consistently played a large role in environmental issues, sitting on related committees at both the city and MUC level. The Ecology Montréal candidate fared quite well here, better than anywhere else in the district. The real surprise came during a by-election in 1991 to replace the retired MCM father (and local hero). Yet, DCM candidate, Claudette Demers-Godley, won the district easily in the by-election, nearly doubling the votes of her nearest opponent. By 1992, she had left the party to sit as an independent.

Concerns

The district is marked by growing poverty and the lack of social housing to deal with the problem; this is especially the case with recent immigrants, who are often caught in a bind trying to meet basic needs.The combination of an aging population and deteriorating housing is an important issue. A recent example is the fight over the Benny Farm project located in western NDG. The 200 tenants of the multi-building project are mostly elderly war veterans and the housing is subsidized by the federal CMHC. The federal government wants to relocate residents to a new building that will take far less surface space of the blocks now occupied by the project. The rest of the land will be used to build high-rise condo units.Since 1991, tenants have been fighting to retain their housing, as is. The use of the land is a municipal matter and a consultation process involving the DAC, Executive Committee, and eventually, Council by early 1993 is already underway. Even so, a decision taken in Council in June, 1991, and the master plan, but call for dense development on that site.

The SHDM has bought a lot of the land around the Blue Bonnets race-track and is targeting it for residential, commercial and light industrial development. Its integration into the existing community should be the priority.

Access to public parks is quite haphazard, with some areas having too much, and others too little.

Community facilities (day-cares, seniors centres, youth clubs, cultural facilities) have often failed to keep up with the changing nature of the population, particularly in CDN where community space and recreation facilities are almost nonexistent. The City's plan promises to convert some underused schools into such centres.

The city intends to concentrate commercial activity along Queen Mary and Côte-des-Neiges Roads. This may adversely effect some of the smaller, yet thriving commercial streets scattered throughout the district. They also intend to create business districts around Vendôme Metro and Décarie Boulevard, develop a high-tech industrial park in northern CDN and a business park in NDG.

The City also plans improvements for traffic in the area, including a reserved bus lane along Côte-des-Neiges, extending Royalmount road and improving access to and along Mount Royal. Tensions between MUC police and a large Carribean population in CDN have been mounting steadily over the last few years. Police public relations attempts to deal with the problems have been inadequate to date. Similar problems exist in NDG, where Anthony Griffin, an unarmed 19 year old was shot by an officer in questionable circumstances in 1988. The MCM government's response to these tensions has been to name local parks after Winnie and Nelson Mandela and Mahatma Gandhi.

Community Advocacy Groups

Anti-Poverty Group
6525 Somerled, #2
Montréal, QC
H4V 1S7
489-3548
Welfare rights support group

Association Latino-Américaine de Côte-des-Neiges
5307 Côte-des-Neiges Boul.
Montréal, QC
H3T 1Y4
737-3642

Black Coalition of Québec
5235 Décarie Boul.
Montréal, QC
H3W 3C2
489-3830

CDEC Côte-des Neiges/Notre-Dame-de-Grâce
6000 Côte-des Neiges Road, rm. 590
Montréal, QC
H3S 1Z8
872-8783

Côte-des-Neiges Black Community Council
6999 Côte-des-Neiges, 2nd floor
Montréal, QC
H3S 2B6
737-8321

Côte-des-Neiges/Snowdon Community Council
6655 Côte-des-Neiges, #270
Montréal, QC
H3S 2B4
739-7731
Umbrella group for a variety of local community organizations

Federation of Jewish Community Services
5151 Côte-Sainte-Catherine
Montréal, QC
H3W 1M6
735-3541

Head and Hands
2304 Old Orchard
Montréal, QC
H4A 3P8
481-0277
Health, social, legal services. Youth groups and young mothers' programs

Hellenic Community of Montréal
5777 Wilderton
Montréal, QC
H3S 2K8
340-3580
Greek community association

Jamaica Association of Montréal
4065 Jean-Talon, West
Montréal, QC
H4P 1W6
737-8229

Multi-Caf
5829 Côte-des-Neiges
Montréal, QC
733-0554
Provides food to the area's poor

NDG Black Community Council
2121 Old Orchard
Montréal, QC
H4A 3A7
481-3598

NDG Community Council
6525 Somerled Ave. #1
Montréal, QC
H4V 1S7
484-1471
An umbrella organization also actively operating a food bank

Project Genesis
5940 Victoria
Montréal, QC
H3W 2R8
738-2036
Advocacy in terms of poverty, legal and housing issues

Québec Board of Black Educators
c/o Curtis George
6310 Somerled Ave.
Montréal, QC
H3X 2B8
489-3721

NOTES

1. Herland, Karen, "State of Disrepair," *The Montreal Mirror,* February 13-February 20, 1992, p. 7.
2. Herland, Karen, "Playing House," *The Montreal Mirror,* March 26-April 2, 1992, p. 9

REFERENCES

Bureau des élections, Service du greffe, *Election Montréal 1990,* (election results for councillors and mayor by district) November 6, 1990.
Dossier Urbain Arrondissement Côte-des-Neiges/Notre-Dame-de-Grâce, Service de l'habitation et du développement urbain, Ville de Montréal, July 1989.
Durford, Nancy, "Good signs for tenants," *The Gazette,* March 14, 1991, C1.
Herland, Karen, "Playing House," *The Montreal Mirror,* March 26-April 2, 1992, p. 9.
Herland, Karen, "State of Disrepair," *The Montreal Mirror,* February 13-February 20, 1992, p. 7.

Norris, Alexander, "MCM faces toughest battles in traditional strongholds," *The Gazette*, October 30, 1990, p. A4.

Roslin, Alex, "A prize for developers," *The Montreal Mirror*, August 27-September 3, 1992, p. 8.

Thompson, Elizabeth, "The Master Plan," *The Gazette*, August 29, 1992, p. B2.

Ville de Montréal, *Arrondissement Côte-des-Neiges/Notre-Dame-de-Grâce; Synthèse des enjeux d'aménagement et de développment*, Service de l'habitation et du développement urbaine, Bureau du plan d'urbanisme, 1st Quarter,1990.

Ville de Montréal, *Les Loisirs au coeur de votre quartier*, Fall-Winter, 1990-91.

Ville de Montréal, *Plan directeur de l'Arrondissement Côte-des-Neiges/Notre-Dame-de-Grâce*, Service de l'habitation et du développement urbaine, Bureau du plan d'urbanisme, 2nd Quarter,1992.

Ville de Montréal *Profile Socio-Economique de l'Arrondissement Côte-des-Neiges/Notre-Dame-de-Grâce*, Service de la Planification et de la concertation, Module recherche et planification, March 1989

Sud-Ouest

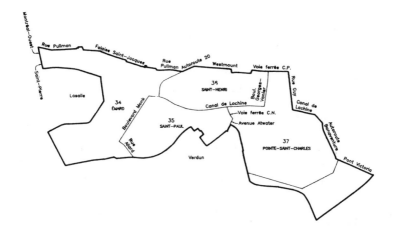

District VIII
Map from Ville de Montréal, Pour mieux vivre Montréal, 1991-1992 4th Quarter,
1991, p. 44.

4.10 SUD-OUEST
District VIII

Area

This district sits at the southwesternmost edge of the city, south of NDG and Westmount and bordered on the east by the downtown core. LaSalle and Verdun determine the boundaries to the west and south of the district.

The area itself is further divided into five planning districts, split in half lengthwise by the Lachine Canal. North of the canal are Saint-Henri and Little Burgundy, and to the south are Ville-Émard, Côte-Saint-Paul and Pointe Saint-Charles.

Saint-Henri and Pointe Saint-Charles are both in transition, moving from an industrial base to an uncertain future. Côte-Saint-Paul and Ville-Émard are more stable, established residential areas with an acceptable economic base. Little Burgundy is quite influenced by its proximity to the downtown core. The area is also highly industrial with large industrial parks situated along parts of the canal, throughout Saint-Henri and along the train tracks that criss-cross the district.

Topography/Institutions

There are 50 parks/public squares in the district, representing 13% of the full territory. They are not evenly divided across the district; there are no real parks in Little Burgundy and those in Pointe Saint-Charles are located mostly on the periphery. In fact, half of the entire district's available green space is Angrignon park, on the western tip of the district.

The district also claims two major sports centres and some indoor pools. Four different libraries exist within the district and one Maison de la culture. There are some primary and secondary schools, and one CEGEP. The number of schools far exceeds the need and some could be redeveloped as community centres or housing.

The area has a fair sprinkling of CLSCs and private health clinics with both the Reddy Memorial and Children's Hospitals nearby. The fierce independence of the district's residents was illustrated in a community-wide fight to keep the Point Saint-Charles community clinic autonomous after a provincial health care reform dictated that it should become part of the CLSC network. Through community organizing, petitions and intense lobbying, the clinic retained its autonomy.[1]

The district is well equipped with social service and community centres, the latter offering adult education, daycare and youth and senior citizen programs. The number of clothing and food donation centres and groups devoted to the defense of unemployment and welfare recipients reflects the low income of many of the district's residents.

Demographics

The district's population currently stands at 68,000 or seven per cent of the city's total. The population has been declining for many years, dropping 45% over the last 30 years compared with just under 15% for the city as a whole. Little Burgundy experienced the biggest decline, 60%, between 1965 and 1974, a period of major gentrification.

Three-quarters of all residents are francophone, although the areas on the east of the district has a much higher percentage of anglophones, about 36%. Little Burgundy also has a higher percentage of people whose first language is neither English nor French than other neighbourhoods.

The district has consistently been overrepresented compared to the city in terms of children under 15 years old. This proportion is beginning to level off, making a number of schools redundant. The number of single parent households in the district is far higher than the city average. Over half of all families in Little Burgundy are single parent and the rates in Pointe Saint-Charles and Saint-Henri are above 40%.

The number of people with less than a grade 9 education is consistently higher throughout all neighbourhoods in the district than the city average. At 40%, Pointe Saint-Charles has nearly twice the city average. The number of university graduates in this district, at over 10%, is less than half the city average. There is nonetheless some indication of an improvement in education levels in the district; even twenty years ago, over 60% of residents in some neighbourhoods had less than a grade 9 education.

Income levels are remarkably low — fully 30% of households have an annual income of under $10,000 and 54% fall under the poverty line. According to an article in La Presse, 20,000 jobs in the area have been lost in the last 30 years.[2]

Again, the two areas most southwest in the district fare much better economically than the other neighbourhoods. Gentrification of Little Burgundy during the seventies created an influx of higher income residents, creating increasing tension between new and established residents.

Almost one-quarter of the district's population relies on welfare for at least part of the year. This proportion is three times the city average. Unemployment is also a major problem; 69% of jobs available in the district are taken by people who live elsewhere. Although official unemployment figures rest at about 16%, a special panel of commercial, community and government representatives (CREESOM) estimated in 1989, that if you factored in welfare recipients and completely discouraged residents who are no longer actively seeking work, the true figure would be closer to 30%.[3]

Housing

There are 28,000 homes in the district. In Little Burgundy alone, 9% of all of the city's HLMs can be found. Fully 40% of Pointe Saint-Charles' housing is some form of social housing.The district's two most southwest neighbourhoods also have the highest proportion of people who own their homes. Although the number of renters overall is not significantly higher than the city average, 30% of renting households spend more than a quarter of their income on rent. In Pointe Saint-Charles and Saint-Henri, the percentage rises to 40. The vacancy rate for the Sud-Ouest (including Verdun) stands at 5.1%.

The vast majority of housing stock is duplex and triplex. Almost 50% of all housing in the area was built before 1946. More recently, schools and warehouses in the northern, Little Burgundy neighbourhood have been converted into condos.

Commerce/Industry

This district was built at the turn of the century around industry situated along the length of the Lachine Canal, which at that time was one of the main transportation routes through the city. In fact, 40% of the district's land is occupied by industry.

Many of the original industries have become obsolete over the years. To help modernize and recoup old industrial sites, the city has set up three PRAIMONTs in the district. Other abandoned factories are being used as artist's studios or have been taken over by light industry, but much more work needs to be done in the district as a whole. The city has decided that the canal is a priority and issued a separate 100 page plan detailing industrial improvements to be made in the area in addition to the standard urban plan for the district.

Commerce in the area is not nearly as well defined. The Atwater market and some antique stores along Notre-Dame Boulevard are the prime commercial sites of interest to people who live outside of the district. Centre and de l'Eglise streets are commercial strips, but they have not satisfactorily kept up with local needs. The most diverse commercial street in the district is Monk in Ville-Émard, which benefits from the only SIDAC program in the district. Overall, it is the eastern part of the district that lacks commercial activity.

Transportation

The industrial parks throughout this district have meant that the area is well planned in terms of accessible roads. Several main streets run throughout the area as well as a few autoroutes. Bus service is well distributed and each of the smaller neighbourhoods has at least one metro stop connecting it to downtown.

Running alongside the Lachine Canal is one of the most popular bicycle paths in the city.

The major problem in terms of traffic circulation is the high volume of truck transport brought to the area by industry. Drivers often rely on residential streets to handle the load. The city has proposed several road extensions and rerouting projects to try to improve the situation.

Environment

Long-term industrial use has had a detrimental effect on the environment. An earlier version of the urban plan released in 1990 "supposed" that soil contamination is a problem in several places. It suggested that adequate clean-up according to provincial standards would be too expensive and all that is necessary is to be careful about what kinds of projects are undertaken in contaminated areas.[4] Yet, SODIM, the industrial paramunicipal bought up much of the land along the Lachine Canal soon after to help re-establish the industrial park. It discovered, after the fact, that soil pollution was so bad that $3 million would be needed to made the land usable.[5]

The Lachine Canal could be an important recreational factor for the district, if it was not so polluted. However, the city's priority is to support industry along the canal, making clean-up less, not more, likely. The city does propose creating green space along the canal, although it would probably be overwhelmed by the industrial activity. Finally, the traffic, noise and air pollution associated with the amount of industry in the district present obvious environmental problems. Especially in many pockets with a mix of both residences and industrial activity.

Voter Profile

All four incumbents won in this district, including independent candidate Germain Prégent in district 36. In that district, the MCM candidate came in a distant second and in all others, the Civic Party candidate placed second.

The Civic Party also consistently ran second behind Jean Doré in all mayoral ballots.

The only change occurred when Marcel Sévigny, of Pointe Saint-Charles district 37 decided to leave the MCM to sit as an independent in 1992. Sévigny had long been a dissident voice within the MCM, often refusing to vote against his conscience, despite party pressure.

Concerns

Major economic renewal is necessary throughout the district. Ville-Émard and Côte-Saint Paul, are far more stable and already on their way to renewal, but there is still room for improvement.

The other parts of the district are far worse off on all counts; Little Burgundy and Saint-Henri both have the added disadvantage of close proximity to downtown, leading to more and more gentrification and a greater state of flux.

The housing stock in most of the area is verging on serious disrepair. Help in terms of renovation is urgently needed, with an eye towards creating more low-cost housing, not condos. The city's only promise in terms of residential development is one project near Atwater Ave. Since the city tries to develop mixed housing projects, only a part of these new units will be subsidized.

Retraining and education programs for local residents are also necessary. The city is considering taking an old, undeveloped landfill site and redefining it as a techno-park dedicated to high tech industries and research. As Eric Shragge points out in *Montréal: A Citizen's Guide to Politics*, "It is doubtful that these types of enterprise will address the needs of the poor. They are capital intensive and require a highly trained labour force." He goes on to suggest that even if the high-tech middle class will be attracted to the new industries in the city, their renewed use of local shops (and the income generated for shop-owners) might not outweigh the gentrification they will bring with them.[6] Unless guarantees and large-scale training programs are included in the plans, local residents will not benefit from the jobs created by the park, and may well lose their homes if the people who get the jobs decide to move into gentrified parts of the area.

The city also needs to provide some guarantees it will deal with the district's environmental problems. The city's report suggests that clean-up costs are prohibitive making remedial measures impossible without the help of other levels of government. The city must not be allowed to pass the buck.

Reducing traffic nuisance caused by trucks travelling to and from factories is necessary. The city has long promised to replace the Wellington Tunnel with a bridge, and that promise is repeated in the master plan. The city also intends to build a road south of the CN yards.

Tensions between residents of Little Burgundy and the MUC police are near the boiling point. Stories of harassment of local residents are rampant and becoming better documented as more people become willing to come forward. Immediate improvements are required to ease the situation.

Community Advocacy Groups

Comité chomage du Sud-Ouest
3400 Delisle
Montréal, QC
H4C 1N1
933-5915

Comité des assistés sociaux de Pointe
Saint-Charles
2408 Centre Rd.
Montréal, QC
H2K 1N3
526-4908

Comité logement Pointe
Saint-Charles
2325 Centre, #106
Montréal, QC
H3K 1J6
932-7742

Ecologie St-Henri
760 Walker Ave.
Montréal, QC
H4C 2H4
933-4571

Le garde manger pour tous
2515 Délisle
Montréal, QC
H3J 1K8
931-8830
Deals with poverty as it relates to malnutrition. Also does public and consumer education.

National Congress of Black Women
2035 Coursol
Montréal, QC
H3J 1C3
932-1107

Negro Community Centre
2035 Coursol
Montréal, QC
H3J 1C3
932-1107

Organisation des assisté-e-s sociaux
2515 Délisle
Montréal, QC
H3J 1K8
932-4045

Projet d'organisation populaire
d'information et de
regroupement-POPIR
4281 Notre-Dame West
H4C 1R7
935-4649
Advocacy group, mostly around housing issues

Relance économique et sociale du
Sud-Ouest
1001 Lenoir, rm. A-230
Montréal, QC
H4C 2Z6
931-5737
Local economic development

Saint Columbus House
2365 Grand Trunk Street
Montréal, QC
H3K 1M8
932-6202
Poverty rights and material aid

Community Media

La Voix Populaire
1735 de l'Église
Montréal, QC
H4E 1G6
768-4777

NOTES

1. Waldie, Paul, "Point's clinic celebrates its victory over Québec," *The Gazette*, June 13, 1992, p. A3.
2. *La Presse*, "20,000 emplois perdus en 30 ans," November 1, 1990, A16.
3. CREESOM, *Sud-Ouest: Organiser notre développement ensemble*, November 1989.
4. Ville de Montréal, *Arrondissement Sud-Ouest; Synthèse des enjeux d'aménagement et de développment*, Service de l'habitation et du développement urbaine, Bureau du plan d'urbanisme, 1st Quarter,1990.
5. Herland, Karen, "The Cost of Employment," *The Montreal Mirror*, October 10-October 17, 1991, p. 8.
6. Eric Shragge in Jean-Hugues Roy and Brendan Weston, eds., *Montréal: A Citizen's Guide to Politics*, Black Rose Books, Montréal, 1990.

REFERENCES

Bureau des élections, Service du greffe, *Election Montréal 1990,*(election results for councillors and mayor by district) November 6, 1990.
CREESOM, *Sud-Ouest: Organiser notre développement ensemble*, November 1989.
Durford, Nancy, "Good signs for tenants," *The Gazette*, March 14, 1991, C1.
Heinrich, Jeff, "Small signs of hope seen in bleak area," *The Gazette*, October 31, 1990, A9.
Herland, Karen, "The Cost of Employment," *The Montreal Mirror*, October 10-October 17, 1991, p. 8.
Hoffmann, André, *Dossier Urbain Arrondissement Sud-Ouest*, Service de l'habitation et du développement urbain, Ville de Montréal, May 1989.
La Presse, "20 000 emplois perdus en 30 ans," November 1, 1990, A16.
Roy, Jean-Hugues and Brendan Weston, eds., *Montréal: A Citizen's Guide to Politics*, Black Rose Books, Montréal, 1990.
Thompson, Elizabeth, "The Master Plan," *The Gazette*, August 29, 1992, p. B3.

Ville de Montréal, *Arrondissement Sud-Ouest; Synthèse des enjeux d'aménagement et de développment*, Service de l'habitation et du développement urbaine, Bureau du plan d'urbanisme, 1st Quarter, 1990.

Ville de Montréal, *Les Loisirs au coeur de votre quartier*, Fall-Winter, 1990-91.

Ville de Montréal, *Plan directeur de l'Arrondissement Sud-Ouest*, Service de l'habitation et du développement urbaine, Bureau du plan d'urbanisme, 2nd Quarter,1992.

Ville de Montréal, *Profile Socio-Economique de l'Arrondissement Sud-Ouest*, Service de la Planification et de la concertation, March, 1989

Ville de Montréal, *Rapport de la Concertation sur les enjeux d'aménagement et de développement Arrondissement Sud-Ouest*, June 1990.

Waldie, Paul, "Point's clinic celebrates its victory over Québec," *The Gazette*, June 13, 1992, p. A3.

Rivière-des-Prairies / Pointe-aux-Trembles

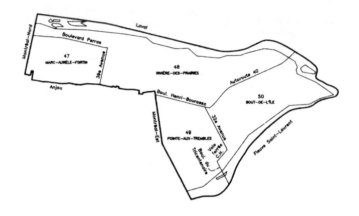

District IX
Map from Ville de Montréal, Pour mieux vivre Montréal, 1991-1992 4th Quarter,
1991, p. 42.

4.11 RIVIÈRE-DES-PRAIRIES/POINTE-AUX-TREMBLES
District IX

Area

This district is the most clearly isolated from the rest of the city. Rivière-des-Prairies was annexed to Montréal in 1963 and Pointe-aux-Trembles joined in 1982. It is bordered on the north, east and south by Rivière-des-Prairies and the Saint-Laurent River. On the west, the district is bounded by Montréal-Nord, Anjou and Montréal-Est. At 41 km², this district covers the largest territory of all of the city's subdivisions.

Henri-Bourassa Boulevard and the 40 autoroute divide Rivière-des-Prairies from Pointe-aux-Trembles. Like Ahuntsic/Cartierville, this district often appears more suburban than urban in terms of population trends and socio-economic factors. The isolation of the district has meant a lack of many kinds of facilities (community, social and institutional development often lags behind residential), and the environment is a major concern for residents.

Institutions/Topography

There are two MUC parks located near the eastern tip of the district along the autoroute. Although they represent a large piece of land, neither is very well planned and both lack facilities for year-round enjoyment. Beyond that, a reasonable amount of green space exists along Rivère-des Prairies and in some of the residential sectors. However, closer inspection reveals that the development and planning of green space has not kept up with residential development.

The installation of community facilities is also suffering the same time lag. Besides one hospital, one college and a couple of other shared institutions, the number of cultural facilities remains quite low. Recently, the province announced its intention to move the downtown Hôtel-Dieu Hospital to Rivière-des-Prairies. Although there is a need for a local hospital, downtown residents are balking at the move. The hospital has, amongst other things, a fairly sophisticated AIDS treatment centre, especially needed downtown. The MCM has balked at the recent announcement to move the institution, but many feel they should have taken a more active role in blocking the move earlier. Discussions around opening an entirely new facility in this district have gone nowhere, despite the probability of its success.

The area counts four libraries, five arenas and a large number of schools. Plans are in the works to create a Maison de la culture in the district.

Demographics

This district represents only 7.5% of all of the inhabitants of Montréal, while the physical area represents fully one-quarter of Montréal's total territory. Even more importantly, this district, and outlying Ahuntsic/Cartierville are the only two that continue to attract new residents. The population nearly doubled between 1931 and 1961 and again in the following 30 years.

The population breakdown by age indicates a preponderance of young couples. In Pointe-aux-Trembles, 20% of the population is in the 25-34 age group. In Rivière-des-Prairies, the highest proportion of residents are under 14 (22%). Within the district, 64% of all residents are married, 13% more than the city average. The percentage of single-parent households is significantly lower than for the city as a whole (about half). There are relatively more older people in Pointe-aux-Trembles but the percentage still falls below the city average.

Pointe-aux-Trembles is 87% francophone. Nearly 40% of Rivière-des-Prairies residents have an Italian background and there is also a growing Haitian community. The percentage of anglophones within the district is less than 3%.

Unemployment figures are among the lowest in the city and compare favourably with the MUC as a whole. Perhaps because of its isolation, the vast majority of residents also work within the district. Some 17,000 jobs are available in the district proper, concentrated in sectors that match residents' education and career choices (community services, manufacturing and commerce, in that order).

Although the percentage of residents with less than a grade 9 education is similar to the city as a whole, the number of residents with a university degree is half that of the city average. Even so, income levels are the same or better than municipal averages, in fact, at $33,613 per household, they're much closer to levels for the greater Montréal area.

Housing

Housing stock tends to be recently built and a trend away from single family dwellings is recent. One third of all housing in the district is single family homes. There are just under 25,000 dwellings in the district, with about 370 hectares of residential territory still to be developed. About 60% of residents own their dwellings. At 18.4 residents/ha, this is also the least densely populated district in the city.

Pointe-aux-Trembles tends to be more densely developed; in each year between 1982 and 1987, 1,000 new homes were constructed. In contrast, Rivière-des-Prairies is still marked by empty lots and much of the housing that exists dates from the sixties and seventies.

The vacancy rate in the district is 5.3%, a figure which includes data for nearby Montréal-Est.

Commerce/Industry

The major shopping centres serving the district are actually located in adjacent MUC municipalities (Galeries d'Anjou, Place Versailles).

There are no major commercial centres within the district. Pointe-aux-Trembles is slightly better off with some commerce located along Sherbrooke Street. Rivière-des-Prairies has bits and pieces of commercial activity dispersed throughout the area. There are plans to build a major shopping mall in the west of the neighbourhood.

Industry is a major force in both neighbourhoods. Small-scale industry exists in Rivière-des-Prairies along the southern CN line. In Pointe-aux-Trembles, medium-sized industry flourishes in the area between the tracks and Sherbrooke street. There are some nine distinct industrial parks, including one Praimont in central Rivière-des-Prairies. Another 340 ha of industrial land has yet to be developed.

Transportation

The shape and placement of the district direct most of the traffic east-west from the rest of Montréal and the MUC. As the area has become more developed, a few north-south routes have been created.

Public transit is weak, with bus routes connecting to only a few nearby metro stations, increasing congestion around these stations.

The district's one bicycle path runs along Gouin Boulevard. Although it is scenic, a lack of planning has meant that some sections of this route are fairly unsafe.

Environment

The preponderance of industry, the presence of at least one landfill site, as well as water treatment plants and snow dumps lead to a host of environmental problems. Pollution from the various industries (and the trucks required by them) needs to be addressed.

The safety of soil in and nearby dumpsites needs to be determined. The Ministry of the Environment has already found some eight contaminated sites within the district. A Hydro-Québec plant located within the district produces PCBs.

The river is heavily polluted and many of the industries continue to dump effluent into the water. An MUC waste water filtration plant has been in the works for several years and is now overdue. Many local plants have built systems dependent on the nonexistent plant and will not bother to create alternative clean-up systems because the new system is expected soon.

A landfill site here is expected to close this year. Although that will help the pollution concerns of local residents, alternate means of waste disposal are now past due.

Voter Profile

Although all four districts elected MCM candidates, there were a few surprises. The Municipal Party came in a respectable second overall. As well, in district 48, the MCM candidate squeaked by the independent incumbent, leaving every other candidate far behind. The independent in that race was an MCM councillor who left the party over a dispute involving discrepancies in the party's membership list.

Although Doré received a firm victory margin, the right-wing parties did fairly well. The other parties had barely two percentage points between them.

Concerns

A lack of public facilities and the environment are the two biggest issues in the region. Fortunately, the area still contains enough un-developed land which could be devoted to public green spaces and community facilities. Local commerce could also use a boost to better serve area residents. Any new residential development in the area must take these issues into account.

This district has received a lot of attention in the city's plan, mostly because there is still so much developable land available. Several different parts of the district, particularly the central area, are the subject of specific plans on the part of the city. Attracting residents to this part of the city, from the suburbs, is clearly a priority. Increased residential density, two Maisons de la culture, controls on new industry and recreational centres are all detailed in the master plan. The City's excitement over being able to plan land from scratch, belies some of the difficulty it might have elsewhere dealing with densely occupied spaces that need priority intervention, like Hochelaga-Maisonneuve, Park Extension, Mile End and parts of Côte-des-Neiges.

Transportation must be replanned to improve access to and from the area (both public and private). Heavy traffic associated with industry needs to be regulated.

Environmental problems must become a priority to ensure the health of current and future residents. The city promises to improve traffic and is enthusiastic about preserving local heritage and green space. Stricter industrial controls will have to be put into place before this district can be considered the idyllic area the city describes.

Community Advocacy Groups

Comité de vigilance des citoyens de Rivière-des-Prairies
8168 boul. Gouin, East,
Montréal, QC
H1E 1B7
494-3842
A wide range of concerns including housing, transportation, pollution and zoning.

Community Media

Hebdo le Point du Montréal-Nord et Rivière-des-Prairies
3737 Monselet,
Montréal-Nord, QC
H1H 1B7
321-8800

REFERENCES

Beliveau, Jules, "La campagne à la ville...pour peu de temps encore," *La Presse,* November 2, 1990, A8.
Bureau des élections, Service du greffe, *Election Montréal 1990* (election results for councillors and mayor by district) November 6, 1990.
Durford, Nancy, "Good signs for tenants," *The Gazette,* March 14, 1991, C1.
SOMER, *Dossier Urbain Arrondissement Bout-de-l'île,* Service de l'habitation et du développement urbain, Ville de Montréal, July 1989.
Roslin, Alex, "The Big Sleaze," *The Montreal Mirror,,* August 6-August 13, 1992, p. 7.
Thompson, Elizabeth, "The Master Plan," *The Gazette,* August 29, 1992, p. B3.
Ville de Montréal, *Arrondissement Rivière-des-Prairies/Pointe-aux-Trembles: Synthèse des enjeux d'aménagement et de développment,* Service de l'habitation et du développement urbaine, Bureau du plan d'urbanisme, 1st Quarter,1990.
Ville de Montréal, *Faites Votre Ville: Rapport de la Concertation sur les enjeux d'aménagement et de développement Arrondissement Rivière-des-Prairies/Pointe-aux-Trembles,* June 1990.
Ville de Montréal, *Les Loisirs au coeur de votre quartier,* Fall-Winter, 1990-91.
Ville de Montréal, *Plan directeur de l'arrondissement Rivière-des-Prairies/Pointe-aux-Trembles,* Service de l'habitation et du développement urbaine, Bureau du plan d'urbanisme, 2nd Quarter,1992.
Ville de Montréal, *Profile Socio-Economique de l'Arrondissement Bout-de-l'île,* Service du Planification et de concertation, March 1989.

Section V

Now What?

SETTING GOALS

You may have picked up this book with a definite issue in mind. You may simply want to know more about how your city works. You may have been looking for information on how to get a seat on a board or Committee that is important to you, or you may want access to resources in case something happens that makes you decide that you're not going to sit back and take it any more. Whichever approach you use, chances are that at some point you're going to want to instigate change.

Every issue is different; in some cases simply befriending someone who has a little power may help you jump over hurdles of red tape. For instance the city's blue collar worker's Environmental Committee sometimes has access to documents before they are released. Good relations with the bureaucrats active in the dossier you're interested in definitely can't hurt. In other cases, a powerful hidden agenda may keep you blocked from the word go. The city has been very careful to include one neighbourhood in each district for its curbside recycling program. If you aren't living in the area being served in your district, you may have to wait until secondary sites are picked in all eight other districts. But, finding out who's responsible for deciding which neighbourhoods are next, and by what criteria, may help you get what you want.

Different strategies to use if you want to take part in a discussion already on the agenda at City Hall, or if you want to introduce a new issue, are outlined briefly. There are already several books available on effective lobbying that go into far more detail on strategizing and preparing than can be offered here. The key point to remember is to do your research, both into the background of the problem and examples of specific ways the city can help you. There is nothing more deflating than finally facing your target in a public forum (say question period at City Hall) only to be dismissed with a vague promise that the problem is under review. These rules apply whether or not you're taking part in discussions at the level of the city's consultation office or simply introducing a small request at the DAC level.

The city's anti-incineration lobby group had its work cut out for it when it took part in public consultations that promoted incineration as the best strategy. If the consultations hadn't been going on, it might have been able to introduce the public to the problems with incineration and influence future planning. Instead, the consultation forced it to take a reactive stance that the Executive Committee may find easier to dismiss as unworkable when it makes its final decisions.

The city's new master urban plan is also going to change the face of lobbying. Demands made to improve traffic circulation, community resources or increase bike paths are probably all going to be dismissed as "already considered" in the plan. Pressure tactics are going to have to be redefined to incorporate demands for specific means and deadlines, otherwise issues will get swept under the rug.

The grass-roots organizing that tried to block the Park Avenue express bus-lane is an example of action stopped by the plan. Local residents concerned about increased traffic on residential sidestreets off of Park Avenue worked with local merchants who were concerned about decreased business due to the restricted parking access the lane would require. Lobbying was intense and organizing meetings were frequent in the neighbourhood in the weeks before the lane was to be introduced. However, the inclusion of the lane in the master plan made blocking it unlikely. Instead, the coalition might have tried to ensure that reserved parking, lower residential traffic speeds and other restrictions would be guaranteed.

Remember to be vigilant; many community groups involved in housing issues were pleased when the MCM announced a freeze on condo conversions, and most thought the battle had been won against gentrification. The MCM lifted that freeze in September 1992, and had been quietly collecting data to build its case for several years. Housing rights groups were, again, forced to react and scramble to meet the city's arsenal of information.

What follows is a general check-list on how to approach issues at City Hall. In-depth discussion of aspects like media-relations and coalition-building are beyond the scope of this project. Far more explicit information on how to handle a press conference or motivate a group can be found in other activist guides or by talking to those who have experience in lobbying.

Starting from Scratch

Since most of the activity at City Hall follows a series of initiatives and priorities determined years ago, redefining what takes place and how is no easy task. Getting involved in a plan that's already underway is much less frustrating, because the rules and procedures are clearly mapped out. Trying to put your issue front and centre is much harder, but it's possible.

One of the first things you need to do to start a campaign is to remember the old feminist slogan "the personal is political." If something has made you mad enough to get out and act, chances are other people will feel the same way. What you need to do is to define the problem in terms of who it concerns, then find a solution and set short and long term goals.

Multi-Caf found itself in that situation last year when the temporary lease on its Côte-des-Neiges space was running out. Having already established a much-needed lunch kitchen and food basket service, finding alternative, accessible space that could accommodate a kitchen and lots of traffic was a priority. The problem was that Côte-des-Neiges lacks community space and there were few such centres available.

The first thing they needed to do was figure out who was going to be affected by the potential loss of the space. Their clientèle would obviously suffer the most. Petitions are an easy way to register the size of the population involved and the scope of the problem. While looking for a new space in existing buildings, they discovered other groups were also concerned about the lack of community space in the area, and who were willing to help them.

At this point you're on the way to building some kind of coalition. Don't be discouraged if the numbers are few, you'll miss the boat entirely if you keep waiting for more help. A handful of committed people with energy and a stake in the issue is all you really need. Once you get a core group together, you have to get down to work. You need to do your research (although it may seem dull). You'll want to know who may be able to help you, and whose toes you may be stepping on. You'll want to find out who's in charge. This is also the time to start checking the media. Is space a problem in other areas? Did a group doing similar work just get space in city property elsewhere? You can also determine which journalists cover these stories, and which ones appear sympathetic. Find out who the city and community spokepersons are on this kind of issue and where they stand. Also find out if there's any way you can connect up with businesspeople or spokespeople from professional associations that might have an interest in your issue and who have voices that carry a lot of weight.

Research also extends to finding out more about what is within the city's power. Go back through this book and find the civil servants, Councillors, etc. who can help. Get maps through the public works department (all sorts of maps of the city detailing traffic, land use, etc. are usually available for under $10).

The city also publishes an internal phone book, available through the Planning and Coordination department. For $10, this is an excellent tool for helping you find your way through the maze of civil servants. Besides listing phone numbers and addresses for different departments, you can get a sense of how these offices are related. The phone book also includes phone numbers of other organizations and the MUC bureaucracy.

Get a copy of the city master plan for your district, to determine if related plans are already underway. If the master plan had been released in 1991, Multi-Caf's directors would have been aware that the creation of community space was to be a priority for the city in the Nôtre-Dame-de-Grace/Côte-des-Neiges district.

The next step would be to see if the plans suit your needs. Are they concrete enough? Are there deadlines? Potential sites? Find out if your local DAC has looked into this issue by going back over minutes of their meetings (available through your Access-Montréal office).

Research the technical aspects of your problem as well. Look into existing policies and precedents. Find out what power the city has, and whether your goals are compatible. Have there been similar situations elsewhere? If so, learn from them. Multi-Caf learned that the city has clear guidelines around providing space to cultural associations, but not community groups. That kind of information may lead you to broaden your campaign altogether, demanding that community groups are granted the same attention as cultural associations.

Whenever you deal with the city in any capacity at all, be aware that it may well take five phone calls to get one answer. Things that may appear to be related may be managed by entirely different departments (in this case, Recreation and Community Development might be responsible for suitable space, Housing and Urban Planning would know if any future plans are being proposed). Existing by-laws and resolutions are monitored through the archives, which also keeps records of all minutes of meetings. Being familiar with them may help guide you to the appropriate department.

When trying to find a path through the bureaucracy, it helps to be as specific as possible. Take note of document titles, which department published them and when, so that you know exactly what you're asking for. If you don't know what exists, go straight to the city library on Sherbrooke Street to find out. There is no central directory for city publications, so unless the person you're talking to has just seen a pertinent document and remembers it, chances are she/he won't know about it. City documents are filed by the service they pertain to, so you'll find all the background documents on urban planning on one shelf. If you don't have the title of the one you need, you'll have to check each one to see if it includes information that can help you.

This is also the time to determine whether your issue is already under consideration, or whether you have to raise the issue yourself. If you find yourself in uncharted territory, you might also consider looking beyond the city itself. Have other local municipalities in the MUC already dealt with your issue? Does Toronto have a workable model of what you'd like to see happen? Knowing how success was achieved elsewhere can help you plan your strategy and other examples will shore up your arguments.

You might look for help from your City Councillor. Write a letter and follow it up with a phone call a week later. Try to get a commitment from her/him to support the issue (pointing out how it will help her/him). If your Councillor is not immediately supportive, try to arrange a face-to-face meeting to argue your case. If a she or he balks at an encounter, point out that your Councillor was elected to represent you, and a refusal won't look good in the media.

Try not to alienate bureaucrats, as well. It may be frustrating getting transferred from office to office but try to keep your cool. You never know which of the voices you run through in a typical round of pass-the-caller may in fact hold the information or influence you need, either now or later. Given the way Councillors jump parties and power shifts from election to election, friends in the civil service may be far more useful in the long-term because of their more constant presence.

You can also concentrate your coalition-building efforts at this point. Contact Councillors who may not be directly involved in your neighbourhood, but who have been helpful in similar situations in the past. Try to get them on your side. Go through the community groups in this guide and find the ones with a local interest or who are concerned by your issue. Do phone arounds to sign petitions or to get people out to events or meetings.

Take this opportunity, not just to look for allies, but for opposition as well, and be prepared for it. Are there other groups vying for the same available space? Find out if you can combine your needs and present a united front.

Bring the issue to a DAC meeting, along with your allies. Present your case, your research and the specifics of your demand. You may also want to invite the media. Hold some kind of event or press conference. Pull out your media list of journalists who deal with related issues and contact them. Having a specific name to send a press release to helps enormously in making sure that it gets read and remembered.

It helps to have a few spokespeople — one who is good at expressing the ideas and emotion of the issue, and someone else who can handle technical questions. Remember that you can't control the media, but that they are too important to alienate. The best you can do is be prepared, accessible, polite and as concise as possible about the importance of your issue. Again, if you've staked out your opposition and can respond to their concerns, you'll come out sounding more polished and professional.

Be there to raise the issue again and keep it in the public eye wherever your Councillor is making an appearance. Try to keep your presentation fresh, incorporating current events and new approaches.

As always, be prepared and stay prepared — don't let your targets get the better of you with information you weren't aware of, or vague promises that can't be pinned down. If the issue is being studied, when is a decision expected?

Existing Channels

Other than issues that you discover on your own, there are many ways in which you can contribute to the dossiers already on the agenda at City Hall. The Executive Committee has the power to determine what issues are being considered, and how (either through study, consultation or legislation). Studies might be accessible through DACs or one of the city's Standing Committee's. Depending on the issue, consultation will also be held at the Standing Committee level, or through the public consultations office. City-wide legislation may get discussed through a Standing Committee that has already done the preliminary consultation work. Usually, by the time an issue gets to the consultation or legislation stage, there's very little room for your input. The most you can expect is a say in the fine-tuning. For instance, when the Culture and Community Development Committee held hearings on the legislation to ban nudity from signs outside of "erotic establishments" in the spring of 1991, it was too late to question the validity of such legislation. The hearings were only useful to help define exactly what would be considered an "erotic establishment."

If you want to have a say in which decisions get made, you have to get in there way before any recommendations reach these bodies. Look for agendas of upcoming meetings in newspaper articles and ads. Although these agendas are not necessarily determined far in advance, The Gazette, La Presse, and occasionally community newspapers run ads with a full agenda, date, time and place about 10 days before each meeting. These ads should run detailed descriptions of what kind of legislation or proposals will be discussed. Full background documentation should be available at local Access-Montréal offices. If you miss an ad, a phone call to the city clerk's office a week before a meeting should tell you everything you need to know.

If you're not sure what's coming up, contact the city clerk's offices, or the archives and get the schedules of all Council, Standing Committee and DAC meetings for the year. These schedules won't be detailed, but they'll help you figure out the timing of more specific announcements. Each Standing Committee also deposits an annual report/prospectus around December at the Office of Commissions and Committees of Council (3770). Although the exact dates of meetings are not always provided, these reports do contain a general outline of what issues will be examined over the year, along with an approximate time frame.

No matter what issues you want to explore, schedules of Council and DAC meetings are helpful just so you know when things might get onto their agendas. For instance, if a report is due out in June, the next Council meeting will have to approve it.

Since decisions made in Council are usually a *fait accompli,* asking questions about items already on an agenda is of minimal use. The question period is at the beginning of Council meetings and you would probably just be told to wait for the discussion (where you have no way of interjecting). Attending these meetings will help you to better understand the process and possibly to get some media attention. Question period does provide an accessible public forum to air your grievances, even if you don't get a satisfactory response. In Multi-Caf's case organizers got a group of people concerned about the same issue to register for question period and ask a series of questions. Stacking question period can be a good publicity tactic. Ensure that your questions are varied enough and that you have enough detailed research and a stack of potential questions. That way, you can keep coming back with more questions if you're not satisfied with the response. The key is to pose the questions differently enough so that Councillors are forced to provide clear answers. If every question sounds the same, you may well get dismissed and the media present will be less interested. If any promises or specifics are provided, make note of them and follow them up.

Prior Intervention: DACs

DACs don't actually make many decisions, and although recent and proposed changes will give them some decision-making power, this is mostly limited to minor expenditures (the acquisition of a park bench or new paint for public facilities). However, DACs are the first public space to discuss certain local decisions and therefore a good place to get things on the agenda.

The current urban plan is a good example. Many of the terms of decisions to be made around whether green space or industry are a priority, or whether certain traffic or facility changes will go through the DACs first. The more prepared and specific you are, the better your chances of actually helping to influence decision-making. The city will be unlikely to change the broad goals of its plans, but priorities, deadlines and other technical decisions can be influenced. Being able to provide facts about the population's changing needs can help you argue your point. Having good, clearly presented ideas will also help you get a hearing in any future consultations on the issue.

Standing Committees

Standing Committees of Council deal predominantly with general legislation (no smoking by-laws or pet control regulations). While they often already have an idea of what legislation they want to see, you can have a say in the wording or the parameters of the legislation in question. Since Standing Committees are more formal than DACs, you'll probably need to have a brief prepared. Call 3770 about two weeks before a public meeting to ensure that your brief will be heard and when and where it must be deposited. A French copy should be provided for the city but you may want to have copies available in both English and French for the actual presentation.

Within the brief, stick to two or three main points, and as usual check your facts and have concrete goals in mind. A request to make public facilities wheelchair accessible will probably get a liberal nod. But it may be interpreted as only applying to buildings under construction, not existing or purchased buildings. Or it may be decided that wheelchair users do not need access to sports facilities and therefore will not be applied to any building that has any recreational use. These are all loopholes that could be plugged. Even if something is obvious to you, don't allow any margin for error.

The same goes for more general demands. A few years ago, Action-Travail des femmes tried to increase the number of women in municipal blue collar jobs. They organized women to apply for jobs when they came up. When they weren't hired, they lobbied the mayor. When that didn't work they took over a Council question period, explaining why they were qualified. The city finally announced a campaign to hire one woman for every four new non-traditional, non-specialized positions. Action-Travail decided that was not enough and filed with the Québec Human Rights Commission to have women get one out of every two positions. They won. However, the truth is that there are not that many new positions being made available. More importantly, the city often argues that women just aren't applying for such jobs. While hiring quotas are part of the answer, more aggressive recruitment is also necessary.

Consultation Office

This is by far the most formal and longest consultation process. Although there are provisions for a shortened version of 10 weeks, public consultations are usually organized for six months.

Each issue for consultation is determined by the Executive Committee. Unlike the more specific topics dealt with through Standing Committees, these consultations are far more global; in the past, issues like the future of the Miron Quarry site or Mount-Royal were addressed. Even though these are open consultations, the Executive Committee retains approval of both the chair and commissioners running the process, so they do maintain some control from the outset.

Once the subject and commissioners are approved, a very detailed process begins. Details on the different kinds of consultations, and the different steps involved, are available through the office. Whenever a consultation is underway, all relevant documentation must be accessible for consultation at Access-Montréal offices and at municipal libraries. The consultation commissioners must prepare their final report no later than six months after the original documents were made available.

Final reports on all consultations are generally available through the office and at municipal libraries. If the prospect of briefs and presentations seems daunting, check through the appendices of previous consultations for the list of participants. Find one with similar concerns and contact her/him for advice on how to go about preparing your own presentation.

After the Show

In all the situations described here, presenting a brief is not enough. Keep track through the Committee office or Access-Montréal of where it goes from there. If there are other public hearings on the issue, attend, chat people up and find out if there are others who share your concerns. Once a report gets submitted to the Executive Committee, find out if your concerns are represented in it and keep on top of how the Committee responds (they are required to do so within 60 days).

It's up to you to remain vigilant. Remember, the Committee or DAC reinterprets everything they hear for the Executive Committee, which then does the same when it presents its response to Council as a whole. At any of these points, your concerns might become buried so try to follow up. Write letters or reframe your demands with individual Councillors throughout the process.

Even losing a battle can become a victory after the fact. Although housing groups lost the battle for Overdale to developers, they managed to have the last laugh. FRAPRU had been very active in the fight. By keeping track of the details of the deal, they had a press release prepared four years later when the developer's option on the land ran out, and the land was still a parking lot. Reporters wouldn't necessarily have known or remembered the deadline. The reminder put the issue back in the public eye and forced the MCM to answer, once again, for its decision.

By being persistent and prepared, you should eventually achieve your goals. Multi-Caf representatives attended several DAC meetings, met with their local Councillor and stacked the question period during a regular Council meeting after a preliminary deadline had passed. They finally got space in a city-run building. Once you have the attention of the media, hold on to it. When it was all over, Multi-Caf opened their new space with a ceremony presenting Mayor Doré with a silver ladle in recognition of the city's help. But Doré won't be able to sit on his ladles for long. By late summer, 1992, the NDG Food Depot found itself in exactly the same predicament Multi-Caf had been in, and the entire process is beginning again since the CDN/NDG district is no better equipped with community space than it was the year before.

Towards Democracy

Once the groundwork is layed, there's no reason to stop. Victories in short-term fights are encouraging, but they may give you a taste for long-term participation. Almost any campaign should end with some kind of evaluation meeting — if for no other reason that to hand out pats on the back or condolences all around. This is also an opportunity to consider moving further. Bureaucrats and Councillors alike are present and working throughout every term, not just when asked to answer for their decisions during elections and audits. As such, there is room to monitor, change, or criticize every step of the way. This is where you can access your power as a citizen and claim your own voice within the municipal structure.

Credibility gained with a win is an easy way to feel motivated and consider building on the momentum. Even a loss can also be used to encourage a group to consolidate efforts, learn from mistakes, and correct them the next time out. Reserve time during your wrap-up meeting to discuss whether or not there are other issues that concern you as a group, or areas you want to be able to influence.

The NDG Food Depot has a clear ally and example in Multi-Caf, as well as a fairly tailor-made list of supporters and strategies. This may be the time to start questioning the city's policy on providing resources and support to community organizations, as well as cultural ones. An alliance would be in a clear position to do so with one victory and a credible voice already established. Moving beyond the district to examine whether other community groups are in a similar situation would be useful. Or the alliance could stay district-focused and lend support to other local battles like the fight to retain the Benny Farm housing project. You may find that you can incorporate these concerns into an existing organization already working in your district. Or, you may want to track down a similar group working elsewhere and try to start a local chapter or encourage them to broaden their base. The key is to keep track of what is going on and always consider how to consolidate your strengths and encourage community-building. The more you build your base and efficiency, the more you'll be equipped to take on City Hall itself.

REFERENCES

Herland, Karen, "Squeezing them out," *The Montreal Mirror*, July 18-July 25, 1992, p. 6.

Kome, Penny, *Play from Strength: A Canadian Woman's Guide to Initiating Political Action* Canadian Advisory Council on the Status of Women, Ottawa, 1983.

Ville de Montréal, Documents sur Le Bureau de consultation de Montréal, Collection of laws, rules, etc. pertaining to the consultation office, unbound document.

APPENDIX A — COUNCILLORS

Given that Councillors don't always stay in the party they were elected to, there are some things worth knowing about them as individuals. This is a list of all the players, the roles they have within government and their record at City Hall. Other valuable details like their community affiliations and previous titles are also provided.

The information here can help you with a number of problems. It obviously comes in handy if you need to find your Councillor or the Councillor elected in the riding of your workplace, community centre, etc. If you need to find a contact at City Hall with an interest in childcare issues to support a project, you may want to target someone who has sat on daycare boards. If you need someone on a particular Committee, you'll find that information here. If there is no indication, 'Committee' refers to a City of Montréal Committee or Council, membership on MUC Committees or other Boards are specified.

Home addresses and phone numbers are listed where available. If only a room number and four digit number are provided, they refer to the Councillor's City Hall office. City Hall's address is 275, rue Notre-Dame East, H2Y 1C6; the general office number is 115 and the general phone number is 872-3134.

Most Councillors spend little time in City Hall itself. Allow a few days, at least, to reach anyone on the Executive Committee, their staff usually screen all calls.

Each Councillor sits on at least one DAC representing her/his riding, and executive position on the DAC is mentioned when relevant. Since the Ville-Marie district only covers territory represented by two Councillors, other Councillors from around the city have been asked to sit on it. Those representatives are also noted. In the interests of space, DACs are referred to by number; their full names are listed here:

Ahuntsic/Cartierville I
Villeray/Saint-Michel/Park Extension II
Rosemont/Petite-Patrie III
Mercier/Hochelaga-Maisonneuve IV
Plateau Mont-Royal/Centre-Sud V
Ville-Marie VI
Côte-des-Neiges/Notre-Dame-de-Grace VII
Sud-Ouest VIII
Rivière-des-Prairies/Pointe-aux-Trembles IX

Information like corporate and property holdings is on record at City Hall in the archives and must be updated annually. Only the highlights of these holdings are listed here. More complete listings are available through archives.

Jean Doré, Mayor — Montréal
1990: Exec Cttee: resp. for intermunicipal and intergovernmental relations, international affairs, communications, personnel, V-C — MUC Council: MUC Exec. Cttee.
1986: same

Councillor since a 1984 by-election.

Former president Université de Montréal students' union (AGEUM); Has worked as press attaché to Réné Lévesque; Director General of the Fed. of ACEFs and had sat on the board of the Ligue des droits de l'homme. Television host on consumer law (Radio-Québec).

He was one of the founding members of the MCM in 1974.

Owns his own residence.

res: 61 St. Norbert H2X 1G5

872-2955 (o)

Alain André, Ahuntsic district 3,CPM, DAC I

1990: Leader of the opposition in Council until defections and by-elections changed the players and left him the lone representative of his party in Council. He decided to merge his party with the CPM in the summer of 1992.

Former political attaché to Yvon Lamarre. Former municipal Court prosecutor. Teaches at John Abbott College.

Owns his residence and another building

res:11010 Verville H3L 2G2

333-6611 (o)

Nick Auf der Maur, Peter-McGill district 26, CPM, DAC VI

1990: V-C Urban Planning and Housing Committee, Official leader of the opposition in Council. On the special Consultative Committee to review the master urban plan.

1986: V-C Urban Planning, Housing and Public Works Committee.

Councillor since 1974. Helped found the MCM, left, and helped found the short-lived Municipal Action Group. By 1985, he retained his seat as an independent. The CPM did not run a candidate against him in 1986, but he did not officially join that party until 1988. He left in 1989 over differences with the leadership and was in the MPM days later. In November 1991, he bolted back to the CPM, effectively ending a merger between the two parties that had been slated to be announced hours before his leap. Yet, by the summer of 1992, the merger had gone ahead, with the two parties retaining the name of the Civic Party.

Former journalist: CBC, *Gazette, Last Post Magazine.*On the board of Nazareth House. Has stock in several corporations including Alcan, Maple Leaf Gardens. Owns his own residence and the house next door.

res: 2134 Tupper H3H 1P2, 933-7939(r), 872-9565 (o)

Diane Barbeau, Hochelaga district 40, MCM, DAC IV

1990: V-C Environment and Public Works Committee, Chair DAC IV. On the special Consultative Committee to review the master urban plan.

1986: Urban Planning, Housing and Public Works Committee.

Chair of Nuclear-free zone Committee in 1986-87.

Councillor since 1986.

Worked to organize several community groups: Toy lending library, Pavillon d'éducation communautaire, a daycare centre. Involved with Resto-Pop.

off: 115, 284-2116

Michel Benoit, Saint-Sulpice district 4, CPM,   DAC I
1990: Urban Planning and Housing Committee, MUC Administration and
    Finance Committee,
V-C DAC I
1986: Administration and Finance Committee. V-C DAC I
MCM Councillor in 1986, and again in 1990. In March 1992 he switched to the
    Civic Party
Has sat on the Board of the Caisse Populaire Lajeunesse and the Ahuntsic
    Business Association. CEGEP professor.
Owns his own residence and two other buildings
res: 9462, de Chateaubriand H2M 1Y1, 381-1758(r), 872-0228 (o)

André Berthelet, Jarry district 12, MCM, DAC II
1990: Chair of City Council, Chair DAC II
1986: Chair of City Council. Chair Special Committee updating Council proce-
    dure. Chair DAC II
Councillor 1974-1978, then again in 1982 until now.
Member of Amnesty International, Ligue des droits et libertés, CEQ. Catholic
    school commission teacher.
Owns his residence.
res: 8066 Henri-Julien, H2R 2B8, 381-5757(r), 872-3607(o)

Fiorino Bianco, Rivières des Prairies district 48, MCMDAC XI
1990: Environment and Public Works Committee
Has been involved with the CSN, Rivière-des-Prairies Chamber of Commerce,
    Founding and executive member of the Italian-Québec Society. President of
    Garderie Educative. Real estate agent.
Councillor in 1990.
Owns his own residence and one other.
off: 8550 Pie IX, H1Z 4E2, 722-2727
res: 7970 Lorenzo Prince RdP., H1E 5Y4, 494-1372

Joseph Biello, Villeray district 10, MCM, DAC II
1990: Executive Committee; resp. for cultural development and intercultural
    relations.
1986: Chair Community Development Committee, and then Chair of the
    Administration and Finance Committee; MUC Advis. Cttee on Intercultural
    & Interracial Relations.
Councillor since 1986.
Member of Amnesty International. Auditor; former civil servant, restaurant
    manager. Owns his own residence.
res: 7233, de Normanville H2R 2T7, 273-3778, 872-29376 (o)

Martine Blanc, Octave Crémazie district 11, MCM, DAC II
1990: Chair Community and Cultural Development Committee. Also sits on
    DAC VI
1986: Chair Cultural Development Committee.
Councillor since 1986.
Has worked organising various public festivals.
off: 115, 872-3134

Ghislaine Boisvert, Pointe-aux-Trembles district 49, MCM, DAC IX
1990: Administration and Quality of Services, MUC Economic Development, V-C DAC IX
1986: Community Development Committee, V-C DAC IX
Councillor since 1986.
Former elected school commissioner. CEGEP administrator.
res: 534, 9e ave. H1B 4C7, 645-1038 (r)

Jacqueline Bordeleau, Bout-de-l'Ile disctrict 50, MCM, DAC IX
1990: Economic Development Committee, MUC Exec. Cttee.
1986: Executive Committee; resp. public works, fire prevention, park planning
Councillor since 1986.
Helped establish a CLSC and Centre d'accueil (sat on both boards.) Social worker.
off: 117, 872-8720

Sam Boskey, Décarie district 33, DCM, DAC VII
1990: DCM member responsible for parliamentary issues.
1986: V-C Cultural Development Committee.
MCM Councillor in 1982. Left the party to help form the DCM along with others who felt the MCM had moved from its leftist roots. Was re-elected in 1990 on the DCM platform. Was briefly official opposition leader in Council in 1991 when shifts between the CPM and MPM gave his party the most opposition seats.
Labour Lawyer, history of involvement in various community groups and former teacher.
res: 2249 Old Orchard, H4A 3A7, 481-6427(r)

Nicole Boudreau, Longue-Pointe district 44, MCM, DAC IV
1990: Community and Cultural Development Committee
1986: Community Development Committee.
Councillor since 1986.
Has worked on school committees, founded and sat on exec. of a local CLSC. Owns her res. and the building next door.
res: 2214, ave de la Bruère H1L 5T1, 355-2869 (h), 872-3134 (o)

Richard Brunelle, Pierre-de-Coubertin district 42, MCM,DAC IV
1990: Montréal Exec. Cttee resp. for environment, waste management, public works and democratization.
1986: Adjunct to Executive Committee (J. Doré) resp. intermunicipal relations; Economic Development Committee; Board of l'Union des municipalités du Québec; Board of the Fédération canadienne des municipalités.
Councillor since 1986.
CSN and health issues. Co-owns residence
res: 5237 Cartier H2H 1X9, 523-8419 (r), 872-2933 (o)

Vittorio Capparelli, François-Perrault district 9, MCM, DAC II
1990: Community and Cultural Development Committee, MUC Environment Committee.
1986: Cultural Development Committee.
Councillor since 1986.

Has been on the board of an Italian-Québec workers group, Community centre and CLSC. Community Organiser; social benefits counsellor.
Owns his building.
res: 7430, rue Chabot, H2E 2L1, 593-5041
off: 1549, Jarry est, H2E 1A7, 721-7373

André Cardinal, Père-Marquette district 15, MCM, DAC III
1990: V-C Economic Development Committee
1986: Adjunct to Executive Committee (J. Bordeleau); Community Development Committee.
1982: Caucus critic on issues of fire prevention
Councillor since 1982.
Journalist, formerly a teacher, CSN strike director, and former *Our Generation* editor.
res: 4376, ave Earnscliffe H4A 3E8, 872-3134(o)

Nicole Caron-Gagnon, Émard district 34, MCM,DAC VIII
1990: Economic Development Committee
1986: Community Development Committee
Councillor since 1986.
Has worked on the board of a youth home and on environmental issues. Sits on the board of l'Alternative communautaire d'habitation de l'Ile de Montréal
res: 5901, rue Mazarin H4E 1E9, 766-9473(r), 872-3134(o)

Jacques Charbonneau, Louis-Riel district 43, MCM, DAC IV
1990: Urban Planning and Housing Committee, MUC Planning Committee
1986: Urban Planning, Housing and Public Works Committee ; MUC Planning.
Councillor since 1986.
Has worked on disabled awareness issues. Owns his own residence.
res: 6390, av. Alexis-Contant H1M 1E9, 251-9483

Réal Charest, Marie-Victorin district 18, MCM, V-C, DAC III
1990: Community and Cultural Development Committee, MUC Economic Development Committee, V-C DAC III
1986: Cultural Development Committee, V-C DAC III
Councillor since 1986.
Has worked on sports clubs, with a research foundation on mental illness and as an administrator for a retirement home. Wine expert. Owns his own residence and another building. Life Insurance Broker.
res: 5600, av. des Plaines H1T 2X1, 255-8091
off: 110, Crémazie Ouest suite 1006 H2P 1B9, 747-0551

Pasquale Compierchio Saint-Michel district 7, CPM, DAC II
1990: Environment and Public Works Committee
Barber.
Owns his own residence.
Only current Civic Party member to have been elected as such in 1990.
res: 9030, 9 av. St-Michel H1Z 3A4, 384-0858 (r), 723-1000 (o) 872-9565(o)

Léa Cousineau, Étienne-Desmarteau district 17, MCM, DAC III
1990: Chair Exec. Cttee, resp. for budget. V-C MUC Public Safety Committee, MUC Exec. Cttee.
1986: Exec. Cttee: resp. for recreation, public health, women's issues, public security and community relations; MUC Exec. Cttee; V-C MUC Public Safety.
Councillor since 1986.
Founding member of MCM, worked within Lise Payette's cabinet around women's issues, has worked on adult education issues and within Centraide. Former teachers' union executive. Co-owns her own residence and the one next door.
res: 10726 Olympia H2C 2W5, 381-5036 (r), 872-2955 (o)

Micheline Daigle, Jean-Rivard district 8, MCM, DAC II
1990: Adjunct to Exec. Cttee (T. Daviau), Community and Cultural Development Committee, V-C DAC II
1986: V-C Community Development Committee.
Councillor since 1986.
Worked with several local community groups (Centre éducatif communautaire Réné-Goupil)
Currently on the board of Caisse Populaire St-Réné-Goupil. Owns her residence as well as 9199.
res: 9197, 24e Avenue H1Z 4A2, 872-8358 (o)

Thérèse Daviau, Plateau-Mont Royal district 22, MCM   DAC V
1990: Montréal Exec. Cttee resp. for recreation and fire prevention. MCM President.
1986: Cultural Development Committee; MUC Exec. Cttee; V-C MUC Public Transport; Chair DAC V
Councillor in 1974-78 and then 1986- now.
Founding member of MCM, has worked within the party since. She actually ran as Mayor Doré's second, gaining her seat since he ran there as a Councillor and also in the mayoral race, ceding the district to her when he was elected Mayor. Lawyer.
off: 115, 872-2966

Claudette Demers-Godley Notre-Dame-de-Grace district 31, Ind., DAC VII
Councillor since 1991.
Elected for the DCM in a 1991 by-election to replace retired MCM legend Michael Fainstat. Fainstat had retained that seat as an MCM stronghold since 1974, in fact, it was the only MCM seat 1978-82. She left the DCM to sit as an independent in June of 1992 following internal disagreements.
Active in lobbying on behalf of the homeless; Chez Doris. YMCA Community worker.
res: 4358, ave. Walkley, H4B 2K5, 484-2422(r)

Giovanni De Michele, Marc-Aurele-Fortin district 47, MCMDAC IX
1990: Urban Planning and Housing Committee, MUC Planning Committee, Chair DAC IX
1986: Planning, Housing and Public Works Committee, Chair DAC IX
Councillor since 1986.

Very involved in amateur sports groups. Runs a truck business.
res: 11876, ave Nicolas-Appert H1E 2R7 648-1742 (r), 872-3134 (o)

Jean Durivage, Saint-Paul district 35, MCM, DAC VIII
1990: Chair Administration and Quality of Services Committee. Chair DAC
VIII. Member of the Metropolitan Council of Public Transit.
1986: V-C Administration and Finance Committee. Chair DAC VIII
Councillor since 1986.
Has worked on the boards of youth homes, Urgence Sud-Ouest, Caisse
Populaire, other local groups, Optimist Club. Owns his own residence and
another building. Accountant.
res: 6960, av. Lamont, H4E 2T9, 767-7209

Sammy Forcillo, St-Jacques district 38, CPM, DAC, VI
Elected in the 1992 by-election
Had been a Councillor under Drapeau form 1978-1986.
Accountant. Has been a member of the Civic Party for 40 years.
res. 2154 de la Visitation, H2L 3C7, 598-5070

Manon Forget, De Lormier district 21, MCM, DAC V
1990: Adjunct to Exec. Cttee (J. Biello), Community and Cultural Development
Committee, Chair DAC V
Committee. Chair MUC Research Committee, on the board of the MUC Arts
Council. On the special Consultative Committee to review the master
urban plan. Member of the Metropolitan Council of Public Transit.
1986: Adjunct to Executive Committee (K. Verdon) resp. for cultural issues;
Cultural Development
Councillor since 1986
Board of Montréal Museum of Contemporary Art, involved with some union
and women's groups. Radio-Québec Production Ass't
off: 120, 872-2439

Pierre Gagnier, Cartierville district 1, CPMDAC I
Councillor since 1990.
Elected in 1990 with the Municipal Party. Switched to independent status in
January 1992 and then joined the Civic Party within three months.
President of an industrial equipment firm.
Shares in CAE Electronics, Noranda, CP Ltd. and others
res: 11850, rue des Meulles H4J 2E6, 331-5105(r), 872-9565 (o)

John Gardiner, Mile End district 24, MCM, DAC V
1990: V-C of the Exec. Cttee resp. for economic development, tourism and
housing. Leader of MCM parliamentary caucus.
1986: Exec. Cttee: housing, urban planning, heritage and traffic routes; Leader
of the majority in City Hall.
1982: Critic on housing issues.
Councillor from 1974-78 and again from 1982 to now.
Has worked as a teacher & school commissioner, helped create Milton-Parc
co-ops.
off: 215, 872-3108
39% turnout, 67%, 41% margin —Ville-Marie district 40

Konstantinos Georgoulis Park Extension district 13, MCM, DAC II
1990: Chair Environment and Public Works Committee
1986: Cultural Development Committee; MUC Public Safety ; MUC Advis.
Cttee on Intercultural & Interracial Relations.
1982: cultural communities critic.
Councillor since 1982.
Worked in several community groups, Pres. of the Greek Workers' Association,
helped to organize unions. Social worker,
res: 5925, rue Hutchison H2V 4B7, 276-6272

Pierre Goyer, St-Edouard district 14, Ind., DAC III
1986: Urban Planning, Housing and Public Works Committee; MUC Planning
Cttee. On the special Consultative Committee to review the master urban plan.
Elected with the MCM in 1986. One of the founding members of the DCM over
that term, elected as such in 1990. By June 1992, had left the party to sit as an
independent.
Councillor since 1986.
Co-operative housing administrator. Graduate studies in urban planning.
off: 115, 872-3134

Pierre Lachapelle, Fleury district 5, MCM, DAC I
1990: Chair Planning and Housing Committee. On the special Consultative
Committee to review the master urban plan.
1986: Planning, Housing and Public Works Committee; MUC Public Transit.
Councillor since 1986.
Worked in the civil service at the federal ministry of energy, mines and natural
resources, member of several professional biologist organizations. Active in
Transport 2000, churchwarden.
res: 10720, du Sacré-Coeur H2C 2T3, 381-5511

Serge Lajeunesse, Sainte-Marie district 39, MCM, DAC V
1990: V-C DAC V
1986: Cultural Development Committee, V-C DAC V
Councillor since 1986.
Member of the Optimist Club and the Knights of Columbus. Helped set up a
child safety programme and works as a volunteer at a recreational centre.
Also on the board of a Caisse Populaire.
res: 2420, rue Parthenais H2K 3T5, 523-3966

Sylvie Lantier, Sault-au-Récollet district 6, MCM, DAC I
1990: V-C Administration and Finance Committee.
Has worked with women's issues and organized sessions on family violence.
On the board of a shelter for immigrant women. Social worker.
Former member MCM Party Executive.
res: 10 225, Jeanne-Mance H3L 3B7, 389-4820(r), 872-3134(o)

André Lavallée, Bourbonnière district 19, MCM, DAC III
1990: Exec. Cttee. resp. for urban planning, urban and community development (inc. welfare dept.) and traffic. On the special Consultative Committee
to review the master urban plan. Also sits on DAC VI

1986: Chair Urban Planning, Housing and Public Works Committee (Chaired Ville Marie DAC VI)
Councillor since 1986.
Was coordinator of Comité logement Rosemont and has been involved in several community groups. Board of the Rosemount CLSC.
off: 115, 872-6473

Gérard Legault, L'Acadie district 2, MCM, DAC 1
1990: Urban Planning and Housing Committee, MUC Economic Development Committee, Chair DAC I
1986: Community Development Committee; MUC Valuation, Finance and Econ. Dev't; Chair DAC I
Has worked as Director of professional services in several hospitals. Board of the Québec March of Dimes. Doctor.
Owns some buildings. Shares in Alcan, Télémedia and other companies.
Councillor since 1986.
res: 225, rue Mesplet, H3M 1T5, 331-3020 poste 237(o)

Michel Lemay, Rosemont district 20, MCM, DAC III
1990: Adjunct to Exec. Cttee (L. Cousineau), Administration and Quality of Services Committee,Chair MUC Administration and Finance Committee, MUC Exec. Cttee. On board of SOTAN.
1986: MUC Exec. Cttee; Chair MUC Valuation, Finance and Economic Dev't Cttee.Chair DAC III
Has helped establish several community groups (housing, daycare, retired people). He also does consulting for small businesses.
Councillor since 1986.
res: 4740 St. Zotique est H1Y 2G8, 721-9127, 872-2371(o),

Sharon Leslie, Loyola district 32, MCM, DAC VII
1990: Adjunct to the Exec. Cttee (R. Brunelle), Environment and Public Works Committee, V-C DAC VII
1986: Chair Community Development Committee, V-C DAC VII
Councillor since 1986.
Worked in many community groups, NDG Community Council. Coordinated the Montréal Womens' Network.
res: 3503, boulevard Décarie, H4A 3J4, 483-2991 (r), 872-2439(o)

Ginette L'Heureux, de Maisonneuve district 41, MCM, DAC IV
1990: Adjunct to the Exec. Cttee. (J. Doré) international affairs, Administration and Quality of Services Committee. MUCTC board. Member of the Metropolitan Council of Public Transit.
1986: Adjunct to the Exec. Cttee. (J. Doré) international affairs, Administration and Finance, MUCTC board.
Councillor since 1986.
Was political attaché to Louise Harel, has worked with a variety of groups from recreational to economic summit, etc.
off: 104, 872-3104

Abe Limonchik, Côte-des-Neiges district 27, MCM, DAC VII
1990: Chair Economic Development Committee; Chair DAC VII, V-C MUC Economic Development Committee, MUCTC board, Chair DAC VII, Member of the Metropolitan Council of Public Transit.
1986: Chair Economic Development Committee, MUCTC board, Chair DAC VII
1982: Critic on issues of public transportation.
Councillor since 1982.
Worked for Domtar for 34 years. Scientific researcher. Founding member and former president of the MCM. Currently sits on the Canadian Federation of Municipalities.
res: 4968, av. Victoria, H3W 2N3, 737-7437(r), 872-2233(o)

Diane Martin, Louis-Hébert district 16, MCM, DAC III
1990: Adjunct to Exec. Cttee (J. Gardiner), Economic Development Committee, MUC Administration and Finance Committee, Chair DAC III, also sits on DAC VI. On the special Consultative Committee to review the master urban plan.
1986: Economic Development Committee. V-C DAC III
Councillor since 1986.
Has worked with QFL unions and womens' groups. Economist.
off: 115 872-8358

Scott McKay, Honoré-Beaugrand district 45, MCM,DAC IV
1990: Environment and Public Works Committee, MUC Environment Committee.
1986: Administration and Finance Committee; MUC Environment Quality.
Councillor since 1986.
Has worked for Environment Canada and has worked and taught on several aspects of water treatment. Worked on an ecological magazine, with STOP and the Coop d'Information et de recherche Ecologiste du QC. Graduate studies in environment. Teacher.
res: 2950, rue Honoré-Beaugrand H1L 5Y6,
872-3134 (o)

Nicole Milhomme, Tétraultville district 46,MCM, DAC IV
1990: Economic Development Committee, V-C DAC IV
1986: Economic Development Committee. Was on the first Nuclear-free zone Committee, V-C DAC IV.
Councillor since 1986.
Has been active in FTQ affairs and is the president of her union local.
off: 115 872-3134(o)353-3211

Robert Perrault, Laurier district 23, MCM, DAC V
1990: Adjunct to J. Doré resp. for regional harmony, Chair of the Board of the STCUM. Member of the Metropolitan Council of Public Transit.
1986: V-C Executive Committee; economic development, accessibility of information and services, public consultations and decentralising of transportation. Chair of the Board STCUM.
1982: Opposition critic for economic issues.
Councillor since 1982.

Worked on youth, recreation and festival-type projects. Former director of federation of provincial recreation organisations. Boards of the Société de promotion des aéroports de Montréal, Centre d'initiative technologique de Montréal.
off: 360, Saint-Jacques ouest, #701 H2Y 1P5, 280-5531(o), 873-2439(o)

Germain Prégent, Saint-Henri district 36, Ind., DAC VIII
1986: Community Development Committee
Councillor since 1986
Elected with the Civic Party in 1986. Left the party in 1988 soon after Auf der Maur joined. Has remained solidly independent since then.
On the boards of the Caisse-Populaire Saint-Henri, Centre de Santé Saint-Henri. Owns his residence. Runs a hat shop.
off: 4831 Nôtre-Dame ouest H4C 1S9, 932-4905, 932-6456

Michel Prescott, Jeanne-Mance district 25, Ind., DAC V
1990: MUC Administration and Finance Committee.
1986: Adjunct to the Exec. Cttee. (M. Fainstat); Economic Development Committee.
Councillor since 1982. Left to sit as an independent in September 1992 because of growing dissatisfaction with Mayor Doré's leadership and the direction the party was taking.
Active in Ligue des droits et libertés. Director for Africa of Canada World Youth and has worked with Theatre and Theatre Director organizations. Lawyer.
off: 115, 872-3134, 845-8044(o)
1986: 43% turnout, 79%, 62% margin
1990: 30% turnout, 34.4%, 11.4% over EM (Civic and Municipal both within 3% behind this).

Marvin Rotrand, Snowdon district 30, DCM, DAC VII
1990: DCM member responsible for MUC-wide issues.
1986: Community Development Committee; MUC Public Safety,
1982: Critic on public safety issues.
Elected with the MCM in 1982. A founder of the DCM in 1989.
Founder/editor of *Ptarmigan Magazine*. Taught Cree in Northern Québec. Teacher. Runs his own business.
res: 4355, av. Rosedale H4B 2G8, 731-1313

Marcel Sévigny, Pointe Saint-Charles district 37, Ind., DAC VIII
1990: Urban Planning and Housing Committee, V-C DAC VIII
1986: Urban Planning, Housing and Public Works Committee, V-C DAC VIII
Elected with the MCM 1986. Was a dissident within the party more frequently in the nineties, often challenging party discipline. Resigned to sit as an independent in February 1992.
Was a cop for nine years, worked on housing issues, coops and founding president of FECHIM, sat for one year on CIDEM-habitation. Member of the Ligue des droits et libertés.
res: 507, rue Fortune app. 31, H3K 2R7, 872-0920(o)

Hubert Simard, Darlington district 28, MCM, DAC VII
1990: Adjunct to Exec. Cttee. (A. Lavallée); Urban Planning and Housing
Committee, Chair MUC Planning Committee, MUC Exec. Cttee, Chair DAC
VI
1986: Adjunct to the Exec. Cttee. (J. Gardiner); Urban Planning, Housing and
Public Works
Committee; MUC Exec. Cttee; Chair MUC Planning Committee: Responsible
for the preservation and improvement of natural spaces and shores of
Montréal.
1982: Critic on issues of urban planning.
Councillor since 1982.
Sat on the planning committee for the mountain, and was president of the
Building Heritage Preservation Committee of Montréal. Active in day-care.
Urban Planner.
off: 117, 872-2233

Saulie Zajdel, Victoria district 29, MCM, DAC VII
1990: Administration and Quality of Services Committee until 1991, MUC
Public Security Committee. Also sits on DAC VI
1986: Economic Development Committee; MUC Valuation, Finance and Econ.
Dev't
Councillor since 1986.
Member of the community relations committee of the Canadian Jewish Con-
gress and on the Board of a shelter for battered Jewish women.
Businessman.
res: 6925, rue Lemieux H3W 2V6, 738-3396

APPENDIX B - ELECTION RESULTS

Mayor	Turnout	MCM	CPM	MPM	DCM	EM	Ind.	Comments
Mayor	35%	J. Doré 59%	20%	10%	5%			2nd term
District	Turnout	MCM	CPM	MPM	DCM	EM	Ind.	Comments
Cartierville 1	35%	33 %	16%	P. Gagnier 48%	3%	—	—	CPM 01/92
Acadie 2	37%	G. Legault 51%	34%	13%	3%	—	—	2nd term
Ahuntsic 3	45%	28%	25%	A. André 38%	—	8%	—	CPM 06/92
Saint-Sulpice 4	40%	M. Benoit 56%	27.0%	15%	2%	—	—	CPM 03/92
Fleury 5	42%	P. Lachapelle 55%	30%	9%	—	7%	—	2nd term
Sault-au-Recollet 6	38%	S. Lantier 37%	33%	26%	—	3%	3%	1st term
Saint-Michel 7	40%	33%	P. Compierchio 40%	21%	1%	—	—	1st term
Jean-Rivard 8	31%	M. Daigle 49%	30%	18%	—	3%	—	2nd term
François-Perrault 9	37%	V. Capparelli 44%	28%	28%	—	—	—	2nd term
Villeray 10	40%	J. Biello 60%	16%	17%	—	5%	—	2nd term
Octave-Crémazie 11	40%	M. Blanc 57%	31%	9%	3%	—	—	2nd term
Jarry 12	32%	A. Berthelet 70%	18%	3%	—	7%	—	4th term
Parc-Extension 13	58%	K. Georgoulis 36%	30%	32%	1%	—	—	3rd term
Saint-Edouard 14	37%	33%	10%	20%	P. Goyer 37%	—	—	Ind. 03/92
Pere-Marquette 15	34%	A. Cardinal 55%	31%	5%	—	6%	—	3rd term
Louis-Hebert 16	32%	D. Martin 59%	27%	6%	—	9%	—	2nd term
Etienne-Desmarteau 17	36%	L. Cousineau 55%	31%	15%	—	—	—	2nd term
Marie-Victorin 18	43%	R. Charest 50%	32%	13%	4%	5%	—	2nd term
Bourbonnière 19	36%	A. Lavallée 68%	18%	11%	2%	—	—	2nd term
Rosemont 20	38%	M. Lemay 45%	13%	38%	—	—	—	2nd term
Lorimier 21	30%	M. Forget 73%	14%	5%	—	6%	—	2nd term
Plateau Mont-Royal 22	33%	T. Daviau 63%	17%	—	3%	10%	—	Mayor's 2nd
Laurier 23	32%	R. Perrault 59%	14%	12%	—	9%	2%	3rd term
Mile End 24	32%	J. Gardiner 49%	12%	14%	10%	16%	—	4th term
Jeanne-Mance 25	30%	M. Prescott 34%	19%	18%	—	23%	3%	Ind. 09/92
Peter-McGill 26	28%	38%	9%	N. Auf der Maur 48%	—	—	4%	CPM 11/92
Côte-des-Neiges 27	29%	A. Limonchik 38%	8%	23%	29%	—	—	3rd term
Darlington 28	26%	H. Simard 54%	20%	10%	11%	—	5%	3rd term
Victoria 29	32%	S. Zajdel 73%	6%	5%	11%	—	5%	2nd term

District							Comments	Term
Snowdon 30	38%	14%	8%	10%	M. Rotrand 68%	—		3rd term
Notre-Dame-de-Grâce 31	45%	15%	22%	17%	C. Demers-Godley 41%	2%	—*	2nd term
Loyola 32	35%	S. Leslie 32%	13%	30%	25%	—		3rd term
Décarie 33	30%	20%	12%	21%	S. Boskey 47%	—		2nd term
Émard 34	33%	N. Caron-Gagnon 61%	28%	4%	8%	—		2nd term
Saint-Paul 35	33%	J. Durivage 69%	23%	5%	—	—		2nd term
Saint-Henri 36	33%	15%	8%	3%	3%	G. Prégent 68%	7%	2nd term
Pointe Saint-Charles 37	30%	M. Sévigny 65%	24%	11%	—	—		Ind. 02/92
Saint-Jacques 38	30%	16%	S. Forcillo 54%	—	13%			92 by-election
Sainte-Marie 39	27%	S. Lajeunesse 62%	22%	8%	5%			2nd term
Hochelaga 40	32%	D. Barbeau 56%	20%	22%	—			2nd term
Maisonneuve 41	31%	G. L'Heureux 51%	27%	15%	4%			2nd term
Pierre-de-Coubertin 42	?%	R. Brunelle 60%	29%	6%	5%			2nd term
Louis-Riel 43	36%	J. Charbonneau 66%	18%	17%	—			2nd term
Longue-Pointe 44	35%	N. Boudreau 66%	20%	11%	4%			2nd term
Honoré-Beaugrand 45	38%	S. McKay 55%	15%	29%	2%			2nd term
Tetreaultville 46	30%	N. Milhomme 62%	24%	11%	3%			2nd term
Marc-Aurèle-Fortin 47	37%	G. de Michele 47%	15%	31%	—	4%	4% 2nd term	*
Rivière-des-Prairies 48	42%	F. Bianco 43%	8%	5%	3%	—	39%	2nd term
Pointe-aux-Trembles 49	40%	G. Boisvert 49%	6%	37%	1%	1%	7%	2nd term
Bout-de-l'île 50	40%	J. Bordeleau 66%	6%	27%	1%	—		2nd term

— : indicates no candidate or a vote of less than 1%.
Parties and dates listed under comments indicate where and when the Councillor switched parties during her/his term.

*District 31: November 1991 by-election, Demers-Godley won with the DCM, became independent in 06/92. Independent category includes three candidates, combined vote under 2%.
District 38: By election results after November 1.
District 48: Two independent candidates. Only incumbent G. Berthiaume recorded here.

All election results from City Archives, Elections Office division of the City Clerk's Office.
All percentages are rounded off to the nearest whole number. Only the winners' names are listed.
Results for the White Elephant Party are not included in this table. Originally conceived as a joke several years ago, the party has gained a certain credibility for its ability to accurately mock some of the contradictions and excesses of electoral politics. Still, none of the 16 candidates it ran around the city managed to attract even 5% of the vote in any district.

APPENDIX C — MUC MEMBERS

Yves Ryan
Mayor — Montréal-North Chair
MUC Council ; MUC Exec. Cttee
4242, place Hôtel de Ville
Montréal-Nord, QC
H1H 1S5
328-4000

Michel Hamelin
Chair — Executive Committee —
MUC; STCUM
2, Complexe Desjardins
C.P. 129, Bureau 2117
Montréal, QC
H5B 1E6
280-3500

Irving L. Adessky
Mayor — Hampstead
MUC Public Safety
5569, chemin de la Reine — Marie
Hampstead, QC
H3X 1W5
487-1441

Ovide T. Baciu
Mayor-Roxboro
MUC Administration and Finance
13, rue Centre Commercial
Roxboro, QC
H8Y2N9
684-0555

Yvon Boyer
Mayor — Saint-Pierre
69, 5e Avenue
Saint-Pierre, QC
H8R 1P1
364-5153

Peter C. Briant
Mayor — île de Dorval
P.O. Box 2266
L'île Dorval, QC
H9S 5J4
481-0701

Jacques Cardinal
Mayor — Sainte-Geneviève
MUC Planning
13, rue Chauret
Ste-Geneviève, QC
H9H 2X2
626-2535

Ovila Crevier
Mayor — Senneville
Administration and Finance
35, chemin Senneville
Senneville, QC
H9X 1B8
457-6020

Vera Danyluk
Mayor — Mont-Royal
MUC Planning
90, ave. Roosevelt
Mont-Royal, QC
H3R 1Z5
340-2900

Jacques Denis
Mayor — Saint-Raphaël-de-l'Ile-Bizard
MUC Environment
350, rue de l'Eglise
St-Raphael-de-l'Ile-Bizard, QC
H9C 1G9
620-6331

Guy Dicaire
Mayor — Lachine
MUC Exec. Cttee
1800, boul. Saint-Joseph
Lachine, QC
H8S 2N4
634-3471

Nunzio Discepola
Mayor — Kirkland
Chair MUC Administration & Finance
17 200 boul. Hymus
Kirkland, QC
H9J 3Y8
630-2712

Edward Janiszewski
Mayor — Dollard-des-Ormeaux
12 001 boul. de Salaberry
Dollard-des-Ormeaux, QC
H9B 2A7
684-1010

Roy Kemp
Mayor — Beaconsfield
303, boul. Beaconsfield
Beaconsfield, QC
H9W 4A7
697-4660

Malcolm Knox
Mayor — Pointe-Claire
STCUM
451, boul. Saint-Jean
Pointe-Claire, QC
H9R 3J3
630-1200

Yvon Labrosse
Mayor — Montréal-est
Conseil des Arts, MUCTC Board
11 370, rue Notre Dame est
Montréal-Est, QC
H1B 2W6
645-7431

Bernard Lang
Mayor — Côte-Saint-Luc
MUC Exec. Cttee; V-C MUC Ad-
ministration and Finances
5801, boul. Cavendish
Côte-Saint-Luc, QC
H4W 3C3
485-6800

Michel Leduc
Mayor — LaSalle
V-C MUCTC Board, Chair MUC En-
vironment
55, ave. Dupras
LaSalle, QC
H8R 4A8
367-1000

René Martin
Mayor — Sainte-Anne-de-Bellevue
MUC Environment

109, rue. Sainte-Anne
Ste-Anne-de-Bellevue, QC
H9X 1M2
457-5531

Marcel Morin
Mayor — Pierrefonds
MUC Public Safety
13 665, boul. Pierrefonds
Pierrefonds, QC
H9A 2Z4
620-5111

Anne Myles
Mayor — Baie d'Urfé
MUC Economic Development
20 410, chemin Lakeshore
Baie-D'Urfé, QC
H9X 1P7
457-5324

Bernard Paquet
Mayor — Ville Saint-Laurent
MUC Economic Development
777, boul. Laurentien
Saint-Laurent, QC
H4M 2M7
744-7300

Richard Quiron
Mayor-Ville D'Anjou
V-C MUC Planning
7701, boul. Louis-H-Lafontaine
Anjou, QC
H1K 4B9
352-4440

Raymond Savard
Mayor — Verdun
4555, ave. Verdun
Verdun, QC
H4G 1M4
765-7000

John Simms
Mayor — Montréal West
50 Westminster Ave. South
Montréal West, QC
H4X 1Y7
489-8201

Peter F. Trent
Mayor — Westmount
MUC Environment
4333 Sherbrooke West
Westmount, QC
H3Z 1E2
935-8531

Peter B. Yeomans
Mayor — Dorval
MUC. Exec. Cttee; Chair MUC
Public Safety
60, ave. Martin
Dorval, QC
H9S 3R4
633-4040

Frank Zampino
Mayor — Saint-Léonard
MUC Planning
8400, boul. Lacordaire
Saint-Léonard, QC
H1R 3B1
328-8411

APPENDIX D — ACRONYMS

All acronyms are listed by common reference. In cases where an acronym stands for a French title, the English is also provided.

ACEF   Association Coopératives d'économie familiale
Family consumer protection group originally established through the labour movement.

AMARC   Association Montréalaise d'action récréative et culturelle.
Paramunicipal corporation.

BAM   Bureau Accès-Montréal, Access-Montréal Office.
Established by the MCM throughout the city to provide access to municipal services.

BCM   Bureau Consultation Montréal, Office of Public Consultations.
Established by the MCM to handle city-wide consultations on major policy issues.

BIM   Bureau Interculturel de Montréal
Established by the MCM to ensure that City employees are sensitive to the needs of various cultural communities and to ensure that services are available in various languages.

CEDC   Community Economic Development Corporations also **CDEC**
Corporations de développement économique communautaires.
Centres financed jointly through three levels of government but administered by the city to help encourage small/local economic ventures.

CHJM   Corporation d'habitations Jeanne-Mance.
Paramunicipal corporation.

CIDEC   Commission d'initiative et de développement culturels.
City service working on cultural development.

CIDEM   Commission d'initiative et de développement économiques de Montréal.
City service working on economic development.

CLSC   Centres locaux de services communautaires.
Neighbourhood health centres under the provincial government.

CMHC   Canadian Mortgage and Housing Corporation
Federal program to fund housing programs.

CN   Canadian National
Rail line

CP   Canadian Pacific

CPM   Rail line
Civic Party of Montréal.
Right-wing ruling Montréal party under Jean Drapeau from the mid-fifties to the mid-eighties, now the official opposition with only four members.

CREEEM *Comité de relance de l'économie et de l'emploi de l'est de Montréal.*
Round-table committee of community, business and government interests that produced a report on economic issues and strategies for the Hochelaga-Maisonneuve area in the mid-eighties.

CREESOM *Comité de relance de l'économie et de l'emploi du Sud-ouest de Montréal.* Round-table committee of community, business and government interests that produced a report on economic issues and strategies for the Sud-ouest area in the mid-eighties.

CTED   *Centre de tri et d'élimination des déchets.*
Waste sorting centre at the site of the Miron Quarry.

DAC   *District Advisory Council , also CCA: Comité Conseil d'Arrondissement.*
Established by the MCM as mini-councils to handle local administrative issues.

DCM   *Democratic Coalition of Montréal*
Municipal party established in 1989 by disgruntled ex-MCM councillors.

EM   *Ecology Montréal.*
Municipal "green" party established just before the 1990 elections.

FRAP   *Front d'action politique*
Populist municipal political movement, precursor to the MCM.

FRAPRU *Front d'action populaire en réaménagement urbain*
Very active housing and tenant's rights group.

GIUM   *Groupe d'intervention urbaine de Montréal*
Independent urban planning consultants.

HLM   *Habitation à loyer modique. Low-income housing*
Refers to subsidized housing produced by specific programs.

MCM   *Montréal Citizens' Movement also RCM: Rassemblement des citoyen-nes a Montréal.*
Ruling municipal party.

MPM   *Municipal Party of Montréal*
Right-wing municipal party.

MUC   *Montréal Urban Community, also CUM: Communauté urbaine de Montré(*
Administration representing the island's 29 municipalities, one of which is the city of Montréal.

MUCTC   *Montréal Urban Community Transport Committee, also* **STCUM:** *Société de transport de la Communauté urbaine de Montréal.*
Greater Montréal public transit system.

OMHM   *Office municipal d'habitation de Montréal.*
Paramuncipal corporation.

OSBL   *Organisme sans but lucratif, Non-profit organisations.*
Non-profit housing associations, similar to co-ops, but differently financed and administered.

PRAIMONT *Program de rénovation des aires industrielles de Montréal.*
SODIM program to help the city acquire and renovate outmoded industrial properties.

PROCIM *Program de coopération industrielles de Montréal.* S
ODIM program to help owners improve their industrial properties.

SHDM   *Société de l'habitation et de développement de Montréal.*
Paramunicipal corporation.

SIDAC   *Société d'initiative et de développement d'artères commerciales.*
Established to "revitalize" commercial streets.

SIMPA   *Société immobilière du patrimoine architectural de Montréal.*
Paramunicipal corporation.

SODEMONT *Société de développement de Montréal.*
Precursor to SHDM.

SODIM   *Société de développement industriel de Montréal.*
Paramunicipal corporation.

SOMHAM   Société municipal d'habitation de Montréal
Precursor to SHDM.

SOPAC   Société du Palais de la civilisation.
Paramunicipal corporation.

SOTAN   Société des terrains Angus.
Paramunicipal corporation.

SRRR   Stationnement sur rues réservé aux résidents
Program of reserved parking for residents on neighbourhood streets.

INDEX

MONTRÉAL

A Citizen's Guide to City Politics

edited by Jean-Hugues Roy and Brendan Weston

This citizen's guide attempts to critically inform the reader of what has happened to Montréal since the demise of the Jean Drapeau era. Some of the city's best known journalists, community activists, urbanists, politicians and academics guide the reader through the maze of local politics. Montréal is scrutinized from every angel: housing and urban planning, ecology, public transportation, public health, its governing institutions and democracy, economic development, relations between ethnic groups, and crime. What emerges is a clear picture of the policies and actions that influence the development of Montréal, with a vision of what the future could be like given the will and the imagination.

…[this] work should be interesting to a wider readership than the citizens of Montreal, for all our urban centres suffer from many of the same problems. We can all learn from Montreal's problems and intended solutions…we should be thankful to the editors.
Canadian Book Review Annual

Montréal is more than worthwhile…the writing is high calibre…visible minorities speak for themselves, just as women, tenants and even the MCM were permitted to do.
McGill Daily

250 pages
Paperback ISBN: 0-921689-70-5
Hardcover ISBN: 0-921689-71-3

DISSIDENCE
Essays Against the Mainstream
Dimitrios Roussopoulos

While the forces that make history work themselves out, the dissenting minority is employed at keeping alive the vista of the possible which stretches before us, a sometimes modest thoughtfulness which, without pretending to solve everything at once, constantly strives to give human meaning to everyday life.

Dissidence reflects a range of essays, bold and acute that are fundamentally related to the most urgent and least understood problems and solutions that confront our society. This collection, written over twenty years, drives towards the building of the community way of life, a participatory democracy even in the jaws of Leviathan. It reflects conscientious objection, not just to war, but to the whole fabric of a dehumanized society. It stands for civil disobedience, not just of individuals, but, hopefully, by large numbers of alienated people. Most important, this definition of dissent is not intended as a moral gesture only, but as a determined attempt to transform society by abolishing the concentrations of power.

Dissidence is a collection of writings by Dimitrios Roussopoulos from the journal he founded—*Our Generation*. Part of the Montréal Left, which stood at the crossroads of the European and North American left, these writings reflect the unique politico-cultural cauldron this city created from the sixties to the eighties. The best of the Montréal Left always stood apart from that of the Canadian and North American Left. The contribution of Dimitrios Roussopoulos is often that of a dissenter, not only from mainstream society, but also from within the Left. To dissent means to live simply, speak truth to power, and keep the people upper most in mind. This is not a part-time, but a full-time vocation, standing and working outside the mainstream and its dominant institutions. The motive is always the same, over the years, stir intelligent people to thought, to controversy, and to action.

Dimitrios Roussopoulos is an editor, writer and economist. He has written widely on international politics, democracy, social change and ecology.

250 pages, index
Paperback ISBN: 1-895431-40-9
Hardcover ISBN: 1-895431-41-7

GREEN POLITICS
Agenda For a Free Society
Dimitrios Roussopoulos

It isn't easy to present the truth about the destruction of the earth without falling into the trap of apocalyptic despair, nor is it easy to challenge current assumptions about progress and what the future holds. This book courageously confronts these issues to suggest that we *can* create a new society that is ecologically sustainable, economically viable and socially just.

Widespread patterns of alienation are obliging us to reconsider both the neglected issues of community and of the individual. *Green Politics* is rooted in the conviction that there is a set of principles from which new and innovative solutions, based on a clear appreciation of our interdependent relationship with the environment, may emerge.

An international survey of various Green political parties is presented, featuring their programmes and progress. The result is a stimulating book that challenges accepted ideas about how the world should be organized and suggests the possibility of a safe and more satisfying future for all of us.

Dimitrios Roussopoulos is an editor, writer and economist. He has written widely on international politics (*The Coming of World War Three*), democracy (*The Case For Participatory Democracy*, with C. George Benello) and social change.

200 pages, index
Paperback ISBN: 0-921689-74-8
Hardcover ISBN: 0-921689-75-6

CULTURE AND SOCIAL CHANGE

Social Movements in Québec and Ontario

edited by Colin Leys And Marguerite Mendell

The renovation of society is not only necessary but is, in fact, emerging in the activities and ideas of both the new and the old social movements. In contrast with the current tendency to see 'culture' only as an increasingly commodified instrument of social control in the hands of a power elite, the work collected in this volume reveals cultural transformations occurring in the older social movements, such as the labour movement and the churches, and creative new energies being released in the culture of the new social movements such as the women's movement, the ecology movement and community organizations.

The distinguished contributors to *Culture and Social Change*, through a convergence of practical experience and theoretical analysis, have produced a clear, well-written work that is sure to become the authority on the development of broader social projects. The list of contributors includes Laurie Adkin, Gregory Baum, John Clark, Micheline De Sève, Jean-Pierre Deslauriers, Louis Favreau, Mona Josée Gagnon, Henri Lustiger-Thaler, Michael McConkey, Joe Mihevc, Gregor Murray, Serge Quenneville, and Rosemary Warskett.

Marguerite Mendell holds a Ph.D. in economics from McGill University and is principal at the School of Community and Public Affairs, Concordia University, Montréal, where she also teaches political economy. Colin Leys has an M.A. in philosophy, politics and economics from Oxford University, and teaches political studies at Queens University, Kingston.

230 pages
Paperback ISBN: 1-895431-28-X
Hardcover ISBN: 1-895431-29-8

POLITICAL ARRANGEMENTS

Power and the City

edited by Henri Lustiger-Thaler

Municipalities have clearly become invisible phantoms in the current constitutional debate. Yet, once we look at the tangled history of cities and regions in Canada, we soon realize that urban centres contain the deepest and most profound contradictions of the federal and provincial welfare State, and their declining quality of politics. Cities, though left politically impotent by the machinations of senior levels of government, remain unpredictable actors in the fine-tuning of Canada Ltd.

In *Political Arrangements: Power and the City* urban sociologist Henri Lustiger-Thaler presents a timely collection of writings which puncture, once and for all, the curious Canadian myth that meaningful politics somehow only occurs on the provincial and federal levels of the State.

This book examines the age-old question of democracy in light of the specificity of the Canadian urban experience. It soberly assesses the failure of the mainstream 'democratic' imagination by developing much needed linkages within the current round of nation-State building to the activities of social movements, the growing and contradictory terrain of contemporary urban politics, aboriginal self-government and Canadian cities, women and municipalities, the relationship between global concerns and local politics, and the movement to entrench municipalities in provincial and federal charters. The contributors are: Jane Jacobs, Kent Gerecke, Barton Reid, Caroline Andrew, Mike McConkey, Engin Isin, Pierre Hamel, Annick Germain, Warren Magnusson, Pierre Filion, Massimo Bergamini, Evelyn Rupert, and Ron George.

Henri Lustiger-Thaler holds a Ph.D. from the Université de Montréal. He has taught and researched at the University of Cambridge, and is currently teaching urban sociology and social theory at Concordia University in Montréal.

232 pages
Paperback ISBN: 1-895431-54-9
Hardcover ISBN: 1-895431-55-7

CITIES WITHOUT CITIZENS
Modernity of the City as a Corporation
Engin F. Isin

In Canadian history, the development of the modern city as a corporation spans the period between the 1780s and 1850s, but its lineage can be traced to the twelfth century in English and European history where the city originally evolved as an autonomous association of citizens entitled to the rights and privileges of freemen. After the fifteenth century, however, the citizen became a subject of the emerging European States, and in the nineteenth century, a subject of a national State. By the time British North America was settled, the city as a corporation emerged as a city without citizens: its inhabitants did not possess any specific status.

How cities evolved from autonomous entities with citizens to modern corporations without citizens is the subject of this book. By studying political and legal discourse, Isin unfolds a broad history of the origins of the modern city, providing an indispensable resource.

This research is a very important work which shows that local democracy has never really had a chance in Canada...The evidence presented in these chapters is invaluable. I know of nowhere else that such a discussion exists. Isin adds a whole new understanding to the reality of local government in Canada.
Professor Kent Gerecke, Urban Planning, University of Manitoba, editor of *City Magazine*, and *The Canadian City*

Engin Isin holds a Ph. D. from the University of Toronto. He currently teaches history and urban studies at York University, and is associated with the Canadian Urban Institute.

256 pages, index, appendices
Paperback ISBN: 1-895431-26-3
Hardcover ISBN: 1-895431-27-1

FROM THE GROUND UP

Essays on Grassroots and Workplace Democracy

C. George Benello

edited by Len Krimerman, Frank Lindenfeld, Carol Korty and Julian Benello

Foreword by Dimitrios Roussopoulos

Should today's activists aim for more than reformist changes in the policies and personnel of giant corporations and the government? In this collection of classic essays, C. George Benello persuasively argues that modern social movements need to rise to the challenge of spearheading a radical reorganization of society based on the principles of decentralization, community control, and participatory democracy. Integrating some of the best of New Left thought with more contemporary populist and Green perspectives, Benello's essays and the commentaries of Harry Boyte, Steve Chase, Walda Katz-Fishman, Jane Mansbridge and Chuck Turner offer important insights for today's new generation of practical utopians.

Surveying all of it, George's life, work, and thought exhibit an unusual and comprehensive consistency. He was a philosopher, educator, and activist who wrote about and practically promoted the implementation of his concerns for peace, social justice, local self-reliance, and economic democracy. He served as an inspiration to many organizers active in the social movements which have emerged in North America and elsewhere over the last thirty years...Arguably, George focused his most creative energies on developing a practical strategy for building models and precursors of the new society in the here and now.
—from the introduction

Where the utopian confronts the practical, Benello is perhaps most creative...From the Ground Up...is a valuable contribution to creating a new politics.
Z Magazine

C. George Benello, active in the movement for grassroots and workplace democracy from the early 1960s until his death in 1987, founded the Federation for Economic Democracy, the Industrial Cooperative Association, and the journal *Changing Work*.

251 pages, index
Paperback ISBN: 1-895431-32-8
Hardcover ISBN: 1-895431-33-6